ARCHITECTS
OF VICTORY

ARCHITECTS
OF VICTORY
Six Heroes of the Cold War

Joseph Shattan

Published in the United States by
The Heritage Foundation
214 Massachusetts Avenue, N.E.
Washington, D.C. 20002
1-202-546-4400
www.heritage.org

Jacket design by Alexander Hunter

ISBN 0-89195-082-6 (cloth)
ISBN 0-89195-084-2 (paper)

To my parents
Irene and William Shattan

Table of Contents

Introduction

The confrontation between the United States and the Soviet Union known as the Cold War was the most prolonged conflict in our nation's history. When it exploded into battle, as in Korea and Vietnam, it cost tens of thousands of American lives.

But even during its non-lethal phases, the Cold War dominated not only our foreign and defense policies, but our very existence. We knew in our bones that in some profound way, our country, our culture, and our very way of life were being tested. We knew that a great deal depended on how we met this test. And we knew that if worst came to absolute worst, we and all we held dear would be incinerated in a nuclear holocaust.

As things turned out, the United States won the Cold War as totally and decisively as any conflict has ever been won. Our adversary, the Soviet Union, no longer exists; the Communist ideology in whose name it waged its war against us is totally discredited; and our democratic capitalist way of life stands vindicated. The Evil Empire that brought ruin and terror to so many millions is well and truly dead, and America killed it.

When the Berlin Wall fell in 1989 and it was clear that the United States had won the Cold War, I was serving in the White House as Vice President Dan Quayle's speechwriter. What amazed me back then was how the Bush Administration downplayed our victory. I understood why we were so reticent: President Bush wanted to avoid doing anything that might embarrass or undermine the Soviet Union's Mikhail Gorbachev. Yet I also thought that in passing over our victory as lightly as it did, the Bush Administration had left a huge debt unpaid—a debt of gratitude to the heroic figures who made our victory possible. Not paying this debt struck me as an act of gross impiety; hence this book.

Determining who the architects of America's victory actually were was no easy task, however, since it required, in the first place, an explanation of how the Cold War was fought and won. Many such explanations have been advanced, but let me just mention two of the most prominent. The first is that the Cold War was started by Harry Truman, exacerbated by Ronald Reagan, and finally ended by Mikhail Gorbachev. This is the viewpoint that informs CNN's 24-part 1998 documentary, *Cold War*. Elsewhere, I have offered detailed—and heated—objections to it.[1] Suffice it to say that anti-Americanism, not a desire to get at the truth of things, is the animating passion behind *Cold War*.

Another frequently offered explanation for the end of the Cold War— usually made in response to the contention that the policies of the Reagan Administration may have had something to do with the Soviet Union's demise—is that nobody really defeated the Soviet Union; rather, it collapsed of its own accord, the victim of its insurmountable inner contradictions. There is certainly some truth in this contention: A system that was at once so inefficient and oppressive as the Soviet Union's was bound, sooner or later, to expire out of sheer unnaturalness. But what proponents of this viewpoint overlook is that by the late 1970s, the West was not in such great shape either. On the contrary, the spirit of doing anything to secure a dubious peace was in the ascendant—witness the strength of the nuclear freeze movement in Western Europe and even the United States.

Leo Labedz, the late editor of the British Soviet affairs journal *Survey*, often said that the Soviet Union and the West were engaged in a process of "competitive decadence," and that what would have collapsed first absent the Reagan administration—the Soviet Union or the West's will to resist the Soviet Union—was an open question. Fortunately, the Reagan Administration's policies ensured that this question could be counted among the "what ifs."

As I see it, the Cold War can be divided into three phases. In the first phase (1945–1970), the United States and its allies came to recognize that the Soviet Union had replaced Nazi Germany as their principal adversary, and devised a strategy—containment—to deal with it. In the second phase (1970–1980), containment was discredited by the war in Vietnam, and the United States was casting about uneasily for a new strategy. In the final phase (1980–1991), the United States adopted a new approach to the Cold War and launched an all-out attack—ideological, economic, technological, and military—in order to undermine the Soviet *system*. This approach proved successful, making any more phases unnecessary.

The thesis of this book is that six great figures shaped the West's response to the Soviet challenge over the course of the Cold War and are principally responsible for America's victory: Harry Truman, Winston Churchill, Konrad Adenauer, Alexander Solzhenitsyn, Pope John Paul II, and Ronald Reagan.

Truman and Adenauer belong to the first phase of the struggle, and both deserve credit for saving Western Europe from Soviet domination. In Harry Truman's case, the reasons are obvious: the Greek–Turkish aid package, the Marshall Plan, the Berlin Airlift, and NATO. Adenauer, however, seems largely forgotten in the United States today (when I asked an intern at The Heritage Foundation, a very bright and capable college student, to search the Web for information on Adenauer, he confessed that he had never heard of the fellow); yet by aligning West Germany clearly and unequivocally with the Free World, Adenauer had almost as much to do with America's eventual victory as Truman did.

Alexander Solzhenitsyn's great contribution to America's victory came during the second phase of the struggle. It was largely thanks to him that American anti-Communists on both the left (the AFL–CIO) and the right (the Reagan Republicans)—who were disoriented and demoralized by America's defeat in Vietnam and the subsequent policy of détente—returned to their earlier conviction that the Cold War was at bottom a titanic moral struggle between good and evil, freedom and tyranny. At the time, "realists" such as former Secretary of State Henry Kissinger were dismayed by this "moralistic" approach; but in retrospect, it is clear—even to Dr. Kissinger—that for the United States to summon the energy to prevail, the Cold War had to be viewed in a moral perspective.[2]

The two great figures of the third phase of the struggle are Pope John Paul II and Ronald Reagan, and in my view neither would have succeeded without the other. The Pope is one of the architects of victory because it is impossible to conceive of what occurred either in 1989 or 1991 without the rise of Solidarity in Poland in 1981, and it is impossible to imagine the rise of Solidarity absent the Pope. Though it called itself a free trade union, Solidarity was really a nonviolent revolutionary movement aimed at toppling Soviet tyranny in Poland, and the Polish Pope was its principal inspirer, advocate, and protector. Acting through their Polish surrogate, General Wojciech Jaruzelski, the Soviets managed to suppress Solidarity—but, again thanks to the Pope (along with timely assistance from William Casey's CIA and Lane Kirkland's AFL–CIO), it was never destroyed. And when, under Mikhail Gorbachev, the Soviet Union released its grip on Poland, Solidarity was able to step into the power vacuum and inspire other anti-Soviet movements in Eastern and Central Europe—and then in the Soviet Union itself. In other words, the rise and success of Solidarity finally vindicated the much-criticized domino theory.

But why was Gorbachev's Soviet Union willing to release its grip on Poland in the first place? Here we come to Ronald Reagan's great contribution. When he came into office, Reagan believed that the Soviet Union, for all its outward signs of vigor, was faced with insoluble economic and social problems at home. If the United States exploited these problems, it could bring about a process of internal reform leading to what the key foreign policy document of the Reagan era, National Security Decision Directive 75, called "a more pluralistic political and economic system in which the power of the privileged ruling elite is greatly reduced."[3]

This was not Harry Truman's containment policy; it was rollback—eroding the *nomenklatura's* internal power.

Following the detailed game plan laid out in NSDD 75, Reagan proceeded to hit the Soviet Union very hard. Soviet leaders indignantly accused Reagan of trying to reverse the gains of détente, and they were absolutely right. The Reagan Doctrine, the Strategic Defense Initiative, the Democracy Initiative, the military buildup, the covert assistance to Solidarity, and the various economic sanctions against Moscow were all meant to force an already shaky system to embark on a course of radical reform.

And when a Soviet reformer named Mikhail Gorbachev came along halfway through Reagan's presidency, the veteran Hollywood actor (much to the chagrin of many of his conservative allies) embraced him with all his warmth and charm—*but never once let up on the pressure*. The result was that Gorbachev was forced to adopt ever more far-reaching reforms until the system over which he presided, and which he had sought to save, finally collapsed—just as Ronald Reagan hoped it would. As Stephen Sestanovich strikingly put it, what Reagan did "was hand [Gorbachev] a gun and suggest that he do the honorable thing."[4]

My final great hero of the Cold War, Winston Churchill, surely would not have considered himself an architect of victory, for the simple reason that the policies he advocated were never adopted during his lifetime. This is a great pity, for had the West followed his strategy in 1919 and strangled the Bolshevik regime in its infancy, the United States would not have had to fight the Cold War in the first place. More important, millions upon millions of ordinary people—Ukrainian peasants and Afghan children, Polish officers and Hungarian freedom-fighters, Russian priests and American GIs—all would have been able to live out their lives in peace. Churchill once called World War II the "unnecessary war" because it could have been so easily prevented. The Cold War was even less necessary—if only the West had taken Churchill's advice!

But Churchill's contribution to the anti-Communist cause did not end in 1919. On March 5, 1946, in his famous "Iron Curtain" speech in Fulton, Missouri, he called for a showdown with Moscow to achieve a lasting "settlement," and while he did not enter into the details of such a final settlement (other than to say that it should result in "the establishment of conditions of freedom and democracy as rapidly as possible in all countries"), it was clear from subsequent remarks that he envisaged using America's overwhelming nuclear superiority to force Stalin to disgorge his newly acquired empire in Central and Eastern Europe.

In other words, well before Reagan, Churchill advocated a rollback strategy in place of containment. In 1946, his advice was not heeded by the Truman Administration; in 1981, his basic approach became America's as well. Indeed, there is something very Churchillian about Ronald Reagan's determination to win, rather than merely manage, the Cold War.

I wrote this book both because I thought it very much needed writing and because I felt I could do it right. I knew it would be a difficult task, as indeed it was; I also knew it would be an essentially hopeless undertaking, since explaining what makes another person tick is impossible (which is why there are no such things as definitive biographies, only better or worse approximations), and it was that, too; but I had not expected to find the entire experience so moving. Yet how could anyone not be deeply moved after prolonged exposure to each of these great men?

I have not the slightest doubt that we are morally obliged to study the lives of the evil geniuses of history, if only to remind ourselves that in every generation evil exists and must be resisted and destroyed. But were I tasked with preparing a portrait of a Hitler, say, or a Stalin, I think I would feel sullied and depressed. By contrast, being in the presence of a Solzhenitsyn or a Wojtyla, a Churchill or an Adenauer, or America's two great Cold War Presidents, Harry Truman and Ronald Reagan, leaves one feeling morally and intellectually invigorated.

It also made me realize that the most basic explanation for America's victory in the Cold War is that we could draw upon the immensely rich intellectual, moral, and spiritual resources of Western civilization as embodied not only in great Americans, but also in great Europeans. Konrad Adenauer used to say that he considered himself, in equal measure, both a German and a European. I consider myself both an American and a Westerner, and feel proud and blessed to belong to these two great and thriving human communities.

I would like to thank my friend Adam Meyerson, Vice President of The Heritage Foundation, for his patience, forbearance, encouragement, criticism, and unwavering support. Without him, this book never would have seen the light of day.

I also want to thank Michael Joyce, President of the Lynde and Harry Bradley Foundation, and Edwin Feulner, President of The Heritage Foundation, for their generous financial assistance.

I am grateful as well for the help I received from Brian Gross, Robert Hessen, Charles Lichenstein, Norman Bailey, John Lenczowski, Wladyslaw Pleszczynski, John Corry, Robert H. Ferrell, Richard V. Allen, George Weigel, Richard Pipes, Herbert Meyer, Ronald Radosh, John Dunlop, Alexander Leyfell, Neal Kozodoy, Lee Edwards, Jeane Wacker, Jim Jatras, Gus Weiss, Spencer Warren, Charles Fairbanks, Matthew Spalding, Jeff Wright, Peter Redpath, John McConnell, Eli Lehrer, Joseph Kopecky, Walter A. McDougall, Andrei Vandoros, and William Shattan, in addition to the following members of the Heritage Publishing Services staff who were responsible for preparing the manuscript of this book for publication: Ann Klucsarits, Director of Publishing Services; William T. Poole, Copy Editor; and Michelle Smith, Senior Design and Layout Specialist.

Finally, a very special word of thanks to my wife Jaine, both for her many substantive contributions and her calming influence, and to my two sons, Lewis and Phillip, without whose constant interruptions this book might well have been finished sooner, but under far less pleasant circumstances.

I — Harry S. Truman

Setting the Course

Harry S. Truman:
Setting the Course

On January 5, 1950, after a dinner aboard the presidential yacht *Williamsburg*, Winston Churchill admitted that his first impression of Harry Truman at the Potsdam Conference in 1945 had not been favorable. "I must confess, sir," Churchill told Truman, "I held you in very low regard then. I loathed your taking the place of Franklin Roosevelt." Churchill paused for what seemed a long time. "I misjudged you badly," he continued. "Since then, you, more than any other man, have saved Western Civilization."[1]

To be sure, Truman's policies did not succeed in saving *all* of Western civilization. In the wake of Nazi Germany's defeat in World War II, the Soviet Union occupied Eastern Europe and—in violation of its pledges at the 1945 Yalta Conference to hold free elections—proceeded to establish Communist police states throughout the region, brutally suppressing anti-Communist forces. But it was thanks to Harry Truman that Soviet expansionism was contained. The historic initiatives taken during his presidency—Greek–Turkish aid, the European Recovery Program (better known as the Marshall Plan), the Berlin Airlift, and the creation of both NATO and the Federal Republic of Germany—enabled Western Europe to escape Soviet domination and laid the groundwork for the liberation of the occupied parts of Western civilization in that *annus mirabilis*, 1989.

Underlying Truman's policies was the conviction that Soviet totalitarianism was no different from Nazi totalitarianism. Both the Communists and the Nazis violated the rights of man at home and sought to expand abroad. To secure a world in which democratic values might flourish, Truman believed, the U.S. had no choice but to contain Soviet expansionism—through economic and military aid if possible, through force of arms if necessary. Over the long run, a successful policy of containment would cause Soviet leaders to lose their faith in the inevitability of a global Communist triumph. Only then could negotiations with Moscow contribute to a safer, more peaceful world.

Because the Truman Administration's policy of containment set the course for U.S. foreign policy over the next 35 years, it seems in retrospect to have been a natural, even inevitable response to Soviet aggressiveness. At the time, however, it was seen as nothing of the sort. Truman's predecessor as President, Franklin Delano Roosevelt, had pursued a very different policy toward Moscow—an approach aimed at cementing an enduring Soviet–American friendship—and when Truman succeeded FDR, he was determined to follow in his footsteps, even if doing so meant going against his own instincts. How Harry Truman gradually worked his way out from under FDR's long shadow, placed his own stamp on U.S. foreign policy, and secured the survival of Western civilization is one of the great sagas of American history.

Early Years in Missouri

Harry Truman was born in Lamar, Missouri, in 1884. His father, John Truman, was a feisty, hardworking, moderately successful farmer and livestock trader. His mother, Martha Ellen Young, "had the iron will and sense of duty that went with her Baptist faith."[2] Both sets of grandparents were pioneers, having migrated to the Missouri country from Kentucky in the 1840s.

When Harry was six years old, the family moved to Independence, Missouri, once the jumping-off point for the Oregon trail, a town "scarcely removed from frontier days," without paved streets, electric lighting, or a water system. "Adult men still commonly carried knives or guns; fistfights were commonplace. Harry Truman learned about the behavior expected of males in a setting that prized the manly virtues and the inner-directed personality."[3]

But Harry was different. Because he had weak eyes (a doctor diagnosed "malformed eyeballs"[4]) young Harry was forced to wear thick, expensive, easily damaged glasses, which prevented him from engaging in the usual rough-and-tumble childhood activities. Instead, Harry took up the piano. "He displayed remarkable aptitude," writes biographer Alonzo Hamby, and in his early teens "seriously aspired to a career as a concert pianist, rising every day at 5:00 A.M. for two hours of practice on the family's Kimball upright before going off to school."[5]

Harry's high school provided him with an education that was "old-fashioned, solid, and not terribly different from the education that Franklin D. Roosevelt was receiving at Groton at about the same time.... As a teenager, Harry read Cicero, Plutarch, Caesar and Marcus Aurelius, learning and never forgetting the vices and virtues of the ancients." Add to that his love of reading—especially American history—and his immersion since early childhood in the rhythms, cadences, and teachings of the Bible, and it is difficult *not* to conclude that Truman was "a truly educated man, short on vocational skills, perhaps, but well-grounded in the liberal arts."[6]

After graduating from high school, Harry had hoped to attend West Point but was barred from doing so by his poor eyesight. John Truman's unexpected financial reverses prevented Harry from attending college, and after four years in Kansas City, the young man abandoned his promising career as a bank clerk and, acceding to his father's wish, returned home to help run the family farm. Although Truman did not enjoy his eight years of backbreaking farm labor, he never complained, and the experience eventually proved quite useful to the future politician. "A man who had sown a 160-acre wheatfield in Missouri with four mules, and who 'could plow a straight furrow,' had a powerful appeal for a nation which had only recently become industrial."[7]

In his free time, Truman began to court Elizabeth (Bess) Wallace, whom he had known since Sunday school days. Bess came from one of the wealthiest families in Independence, and her widowed mother looked down on the Trumans. Harry and Bess were married in 1919 after a nine-year courtship.

Gaining a "Sense of Command"

Shortly after his father's death in the fall of 1914, Harry left the family farm and set out to make his fortune as a small businessman. He invested all the capital he could raise in a lead and zinc mine, but the mine failed and Harry lost $5,000. Next, he invested in an oil and gas exploration partnership and barely broke even. By this time, the United States had shed its neutrality and was fighting alongside England, Russia, and France in World War I. Despite being past the draft age, Harry volunteered for service.

Between September and November 1918, Battery D of the 129th Field Artillery Regiment, commanded by Captain Truman, saw frequent combat in the Vosges mountains and Meuse–Argonne offensive. Truman became "a first-rate artillery officer, who figured shell trajectories, risked death, and above all led men under battlefield conditions." The experience "obliterated forever the gnawing sense of physical inadequacy that he had carried over from childhood" and "gave him a sense of command.... 'My whole political career,' he was to say many years later, 'is based upon my war service and war associates.'"[8] (Shortly before America's entry into World War II, Truman, by now both a colonel in the Army reserves and a U.S. Senator, tried to enlist; he was turned down.)

In 1921, one of those war associates, Jim Pendergast, introduced Truman to his father Michael, whose brother, Thomas J. Pendergast, was the "big boss" of Kansas City's notoriously corrupt political machine. Truman's haberdashery business had failed in the postwar recession, and he was about $6,000 in debt. Nonetheless, in the 38-year-old Truman, with his pioneer roots and distinguished war record, the Pendergasts saw a potentially effective vote getter. Approached by Michael Pendergast to run for the eastern judgeship of Jackson County—an administrative rather than a legal position—as a Pendergast ally, Truman readily agreed. On the brink of middle age, he had stumbled on his true vocation: professional politics.

Although Truman turned to politics only after his business ventures had collapsed, he discovered, as biographer Robert Ferrell has written, that "properly undertaken, [politics] was a noble career—every bit as important as the work of any doctor, lawyer or teacher. He threw all his enormous energies into it, every waking hour.... And considering his extraordinary talents, the result was something to watch."[9]

The paradox at the heart of Truman's political career was that, although personally honest and conscientious, he made his way, first as a county judge and then, after 1934, as junior Senator from Missouri, "thanks to a corrupt party machine whose parochiality would have made Jane Austen seem cosmopolitan."[10] Truman's association with the Pendergast machine proved especially embarrassing after he arrived in the Senate. Widely regarded, in the words of the *St. Louis Post-Dispatch*, as "Ambassador in Washington of the defunct principality of Pendergastia,"[11] he was regularly snubbed by the White House even though he campaigned for the 1934 Democratic Senate nomination by claiming to be "heart and soul for Roosevelt" and, once in office, loyally toed the Democratic Party line. He did, however, strike up a friendship with Senator Burton K. Wheeler of Montana. "The liberal Wheeler, who had run on the Progressive ticket with 'Fighting Bob' LaFollette in 1924, had a profound influence on Truman, maturing and crystallizing the Missourian's instinctive but somewhat fuzzy liberalism."[12]

Wheeler's friendship and the support of organized labor proved critically important to Truman in 1940, when he had to fend off a challenge to his Senate seat from Missouri governor Lloyd Stark. By this time, the Pendergast machine that had elected Truman to the Senate in 1934 was in ruins, and Truman lacked the funds to finance an effective political campaign. Widely expected to lose his reelection bid, Truman instead won a stunning upset victory (to be repeated in the 1948 presidential race) which finally established him as a political power in his own right and paved the way for an extremely successful second Senate term.

World War II made Harry Truman. As chairman of the Senate Committee to Investigate the National Defense Program, Truman attracted national attention through a series of hard-hitting reports documenting the wasteful way in which war contracts were being awarded. By his own estimate, Truman saved the government $15 billion. No longer the "Senator from Pendergast," Truman was a respected figure. In 1943, he made the cover of *Time* magazine.

The favorable reputation Truman gained during World War II led FDR to choose him as his running mate in 1944. But FDR was amazingly inconsiderate in the way he did it. "The president never extended Truman the courtesy of a personal invitation to join the ticket," writes historian William E. Leuchtenburg.

Informed that Truman was balking at running for vice-president, he replied, in a telephone conversation designed for Truman to overhear, "Well, you tell him if he wants to break up the Democratic party in the middle of a war, that's his responsibility," then slammed down the phone. Shaken by this unceremonious invitation, Truman, though recognizing that he had no option save to say yes, asked, "Why the hell didn't he tell me in the first place?"[13]

"Harry, the President Is Dead"

In January 1945, at the start of Franklin Roosevelt's fourth term, the President's doctors, alarmed by the seriousness of his heart condition, concluded that he would live only if he avoided tension. "Given the pressures of the presidency," writes Henry Kissinger, "that assessment was tantamount to a death sentence."[14] Yet despite his precarious health, Roosevelt made no effort to prepare his new Vice President for the duties he almost certainly would inherit. As Truman later told his daughter, "He never did talk to me confidentially about the war, or about foreign affairs or what he had in mind for the peace after the war."[15]

Given his almost total lack of contact with the President, it is hardly surprising that when Eleanor Roosevelt told him, on April 12, 1945, "Harry, the President is dead," a deeply shaken Truman felt "like the moon, the stars, and all the planets had fallen on me."[16] It is equally unsurprising that the new President immediately vowed to serve, in effect, as executor of Roosevelt's political estate, pointing frequently to FDR's portrait and saying, "I'm trying to do what he would like."[17]

In domestic affairs, FDR's legacy was clear, and doing what Roosevelt would have liked was not difficult. In foreign affairs, though, carrying out the President's wishes was more problematic, inasmuch as FDR had confided his long-term foreign policy objectives to virtually no one. As

British historian Hugh Thomas has written, "Truman was in fact anxious to carry out Roosevelt's policy in international subjects, providing, that is, that he could discover exactly what it was."[18]

In a different administration, the Secretary of State would have provided the new President with detailed briefings on his predecessor's views and goals. In the Roosevelt Administration, however, both of FDR's Secretaries of State, Edward Stettinius and Cordell Hull, were almost as much in the dark as Truman was. Roosevelt undercut his own State Department because he believed it was intellectually and bureaucratically ossified. "You should go through the experience of trying to get any changes in the thinking, policy and action of the career diplomats," he explained to Federal Reserve Board Chairman Marriner Eccles, "and then you'd know what a real problem was."[19] Roosevelt especially distrusted the State Department's Soviet specialists, since most of them were strongly anti-Soviet, whereas he was trying to establish a new, amicable relationship with Joseph Stalin, the Soviet dictator.

In FDR's view of the postwar world, Soviet–American cooperation was crucial. Along with Great Britain and China, the Soviet Union and the United States would be responsible for maintaining global law and order. In Henry Kissinger's words, "Roosevelt envisioned a postwar order in which the three victors, along with China, would act as a board of directors of the world, enforcing the peace against any potential miscreant, which he thought would most likely be Germany—a vision that became known as the 'Four Policemen.'"[20]

Roosevelt recognized that profound ideological disagreements divided the United States and the Soviet Union, but refused to believe that these differences would prevent the Soviet Union and the United States from maintaining their "Grand Alliance" once the Second World War ended. He thought that if only he and Stalin met, he could win the dictator's friendship and secure Soviet cooperation into the postwar era. In the words of George Kennan:

> Until the final days of his life, Franklin Roosevelt seems
> to have clung to a concept of Stalin's personality, and
> of the ways in which the latter might be influenced,

that was far below the general quality of the president's statesmanship and reflected poorly on the information he had been receiving about Soviet affairs. He seems to have seen in Stalin a man whose difficult qualities—his aloofness, suspiciousness, wariness, and disinclination for collaboration with others—were consequences of the way he had been personally treated by the leaders of the great European powers. FDR concluded that if Stalin could only be exposed to the warmth and persuasiveness of the president's personality, if, in other words, Stalin could be made to feel that he had been "admitted to the club" (as the phrase then went)—admitted, that is, to the respectable company of the leaders of the other countries allied against Germany—his edginess and suspiciousness could be overcome, and he could be induced to take a collaborative part in the creation of a new postwar Europe.[21]

But Roosevelt's personal charm, however great, could not possibly have persuaded Stalin to set aside his deeply held anti-Western beliefs and cooperate with the United States. "Stalin's thinking about democratic capitalists remained rooted to the spot," writes John Lewis Gaddis. "He always suspected their motives...."[22]

Toward the very end of his life, Roosevelt may have begun to suspect that he had badly misjudged Stalin. On March 23, 1945, after learning from his ambassador in Moscow, Averell Harriman, that Stalin had violated his Yalta pledge to hold democratic elections in Poland, he became quite angry, banged his fists on the arms of his wheelchair, and said, "Averell is right. We can't do business with Stalin. He has broken every one of the promises he made at Yalta."[23] (At the February 1945 Yalta Conference, the United States, Great Britain, and the Soviet Union reached an agreement on Poland, pledging that "the three governments will jointly" act to assure "free elections of governments responsive to the will of the people." Stalin also signed the "Declaration on Liberated

Europe" at Yalta, committing the Soviet Union to respect "the right of all people to choose the form of government under which they will live.")

Whatever the nature of the calculations and reappraisals that took place in the mind of "one of America's subtlest and most devious presidents"[24] during his final days, Harry Truman was privy to none of them. As far as the new President could tell, "doing what FDR would like" in foreign affairs meant winning the war against Germany and Japan, supporting the United Nations, and working closely with the Soviet Union and Great Britain. Four days after assuming office, President Truman declared that "Nothing is more essential to the future peace of the world than continued cooperation of the nations which had to muster the force necessary to defeat the conspiracy of the Axis powers to dominate the world."[25] It would take Harry Truman nearly two years to change his mind.

"I Gave It to Him Straight"

Harry Truman was far more skeptical of the Soviet Union than FDR had been, viewing it as a totalitarian police state that had much in common with its Nazi foe. When Hitler invaded the Soviet Union in 1941, Senator Truman told a reporter: "If we see that Germany is winning, we should help Russia and if Russia is winning we ought to help Germany and that way let them kill as many as possible, although I don't want to see Hitler victorious under any circumstances."[26] A month after becoming President, Truman wrote a memo to himself underscoring his continued distrust of the Soviets:

> I've no faith in any totalitarian state, be it Russian, German, Spanish, Argentinian, Dago, or Japanese. They all start with a wrong premise—that lies are justified and that the old, disproven Jesuit formula, the end justifies the means, is right and necessary to maintain the power of government. I don't agree, nor do I believe that either formula can help humanity to the

long hoped for millennium. Honest Communism, as
set out in the "Acts of the Apostles," would work. But
Russian Godless Pervert Systems won't work.[27]

Truman's distrust of the Soviet Union was reinforced by his Secretary
of State, Edward Stettinius, who on April 13, in his first conversation
with the new President, informed him that the Soviets were "consis-
tently sabotaging" the Yalta accords.[28] These accords called for the establishment of a "Provisional Government of National Unity" in Poland, to be made up of both Communists and non-Communists and to
be followed by free elections. Yet instead of promoting national unity,
the Soviets—who now occupied Poland—were systematically hunting
down anti-Communists while helping their Communist followers con-
solidate their power. Stettinius's anti-Soviet views were seconded by the
U.S. ambassador to Moscow, Averell Harriman, who told Truman on
April 20 that what the Soviets were doing in Poland and the other newly
occupied nations of Central and Eastern Europe amounted to "a bar-
barian invasion of Europe."[29]

Truman shared these views. At a meeting of his principal foreign policy
advisers on April 23, he declared that so far, Roosevelt's agreements with
the Soviets "had been a one-way street." If the Russians refused to cooperate, "they could go to hell." Later that day, he told Soviet Foreign
Minister Vyacheslav Molotov (who paid a courtesy call on Truman while
en route to San Francisco to attend the founding meeting of the United
Nations) that the United States was tired of waiting for the Soviet Union
to carry out the agreements it had entered into freely at Yalta. When
Molotov indignantly exclaimed, "I have never been talked to like that in
my life," Truman curtly replied, "Carry out your agreements, and you
won't get talked to like that." Charles Bohlen, a State Department Soviet specialist who served as Truman's translator, later said that Truman's
remarks to Molotov "were probably the first sharp words uttered during
the war by an American President to a high Soviet official."[30]

In the two weeks following his April 23 meeting with Molotov, writes
Thomas, "Truman seemed convinced that a 'tough method'...was the
right one with Russia."[31] Recounting his exchange with Molotov to his

good friend Joseph E. Davies, Truman bragged, "I gave it to him straight. I let him have it. It was the straight one-two to the jaw.... The Soviets only understand the 'tough method.'"[32]

But instead of making the Soviets more tractable, the tough method seemed only to provoke them further. "After Truman's blunt talk with Molotov," writes Deborah Welch Larson, "relations with the Soviets deteriorated rapidly. The [April 28–June 23, 1945] San Francisco UN Conference, representing the world's hopes for an enduring peace, was disrupted by noisy, acrimonious squabbles between the United States and the Soviet Union."[33] On June 11, *Time* reported that "last week the possibility of World War III was more and more in the horrified world's public eye. That there were those who looked upon war between the democratic, capitalist United States and authoritarian, Communist Russia as 'inevitable' was no longer news."[34]

President Truman was shocked by the apparent deterioration in Soviet–American relations. So too were other influential voices in the Truman Administration and the Democratic Party, including Secretary of War Henry Stimson, Secretary of Commerce Henry Wallace, and Mrs. Roosevelt. In his distress, Truman turned to Davies—"the self-deceiving but underestimated lawyer"[35]—who told him that "I have found that, when approached with generosity and friendliness, the Soviets respond with even greater generosity. The 'tough' approach induces a quick and sharp rejoinder that 'out-toughs' anyone they consider hostile."[36]

Drawing on his presumably vast experience as U.S. ambassador to Moscow from 1936–1938, during the height of the Great Terror (in reality, Davies was appallingly ignorant of Soviet conditions, and his memoir, *Mission to Moscow*, was so abject an apology for Stalin and all his works that Soviet specialists at the State Department dubbed it *Submission to Moscow*), Davies proceeded to let an ill-informed and insecure Truman in on the "inside story" of Soviet–American relations. "In recounting the history of the Grand Alliance, Davies tried to show how the Soviets could have received the impression that Britain and the United States were in collusion to 'bleed Russia white.'" At the 1943 Teheran

Conference, FDR had managed to allay Soviet suspicions, but now, Davies claimed, "recent U.S. actions in San Francisco" had rekindled them.[37]

The new President paid close attention to the ex-ambassador's presentation. "What can be done?" he inquired anxiously. Davies suggested a meeting between Truman and Stalin in Moscow. "What if Stalin won't come?" asked Truman. "It is no wonder that I am concerned over the matter. It is a terrible responsibility and I am the last man fitted to handle it.... But I shall do my best." The President wound up repudiating his initial tough line:

> On May 16, Truman conceded to Roosevelt's daughter that the "get tough" policy had been a mistake. He excused himself by claiming that all his advisers had urged him to "get tough" with Russia. Two days later, Truman told Wallace that he had no confidence in the State Department whatsoever, and planned to get new leadership as soon as possible.[38]

At the close of the San Francisco Conference, Stettinius was replaced as Secretary of State by FDR's "assistant president," the wily James F. Byrnes.

Truman now dispatched two outspoken friends of the Soviet Union— Joseph E. Davies and FDR's closest aide, Harry Hopkins—to London and Moscow, respectively. Believing, with Davies, that the Soviets were being uncooperative because they thought the United States and Britain were "ganging up" on them, he assigned Davies the unenviable task of persuading Churchill to step aside and give Truman and Stalin the opportunity to meet alone before the forthcoming Anglo–American– Soviet summit. Meanwhile, the ailing Hopkins was told to inform Stalin that for the sake of peace (as Truman put it in a note to himself), "Poland, Rumania, Bulgaria, Czechoslovakia, Austria, Yugo-Slavia, Latvia, Lithuania, Estonia, et al [*sic*] make no difference to U.S. interests"— and that a free election in Poland could be as free as Boss Hague or Tom Pendergast might stage it.[39] For his part, Truman assured the American Society of Newspaper Editors that he harbored no anti-Communist sentiments. "I don't give a damn what kind of government the Russians have if they are satisfied," he declared, "and they seem to be, or some 30 million...wouldn't have died for them."[40]

Davies proved unable to win Churchill's acquiescence to a separate Soviet–American meeting, but Hopkins' meetings with Stalin were more successful. They quickly resolved the thorny Polish problem through American concessions that undermined the London-based Polish government-in-exile, thereby clearing the way for Stalin's agreement to meet with Truman and Churchill in Potsdam, just outside Berlin, in mid-July. News of this deal elated Truman. "I just put across all by myself the most wonderful thing without any help from Stettinius," he crowed to Secretary of the Treasury Henry Morgenthau. "I just finished talking with Harry Hopkins, and I am the happiest man in the world over what I have been able to accomplish."[41]

Truman believed he had learned a valuable lesson from his diplomatic triumph: "If you could sit down with Stalin and get him to focus on the problem, Stalin would take a reasonable attitude, whereas if the problem never got around to Stalin...it might be handled by the Molotov clique."[42] In fact, there was no such thing as a "Molotov clique." The Soviet foreign minister was never anything more than Stalin's obedient tool, but to deceive gullible Westerners, Stalin and Molotov occasionally resorted to the diplomatic equivalent of "good cop, bad cop." Remarkably, this charade often proved effective.

"I'm not afraid of Russia," Truman confided to his diary on June 7. "They've always been our friends and I can't see any reason why they shouldn't always be."[43] He would soon abandon this rather desperate faith in the constancy of Soviet friendship; but when he set out for Potsdam in the summer of 1945, Truman had convinced himself that Stalin wanted a friendly Soviet–American relationship just as earnestly as he did.

"I Can Deal With Stalin"

When Truman arrived at Potsdam on the evening of July 15, 1945, the war in Europe was over, but the conflict in the Pacific was expected to rage on for another year and a half. It seemed vital, therefore, to confirm that Stalin's Yalta promise to enter the war against Japan within three months of Germany's defeat (in exchange for major territorial concessions in China) still held good. Beyond that, Truman, like Roosevelt, longed to establish a personal relationship with Stalin. And, of course, the broad principles, if not the details, of peace treaties with Germany and her European allies had to be worked out.

Gaining Stalin's promise to enter the war against Japan proved easy, since Stalin was quite eager to lay claim to a share of Japan's war booty— and then some. Gaining overall Allied agreement on the general outlines of a postwar settlement in Europe proved impossible, since the Americans and British sought to salvage at least the possibility of a return to democratic rule in Russian-occupied nations such as Poland, while Stalin attempted to entrench these nations ever more firmly in the Soviet bloc. But although it is clear in retrospect that "Roosevelt's dream of the Four Policemen came to an end at the Potsdam Conference,"[44] at the time it merely seemed that problems which the three leaders had failed to resolve would be worked out eventually by their foreign ministers.

Truman's initial impression of Stalin was quite positive. On July 17, Truman looked up from his desk and saw Stalin standing in the doorway. "I got to my feet and advanced to meet him," Truman wrote in his diary.

> He put out his hand and smiled. I did the same, we shook, I greeted Molotov and the interpreter, and we sat down. After the usual polite remarks we got down to business. I told Stalin that I am no diplomat but usually said yes and no to questions after hearing all the arguments. It pleased him…. I can deal with Stalin. He is honest—but smart as hell.[45]

Truman especially appreciated Stalin's low-key manner. (George Kennan also has commented on Stalin's "unassuming, quiet facade, as innocently disarming as the first move of the grand master at chess…."[46]) Indeed, "the Russian's brevity and engaging appearance of modesty struck Truman as a relief from the flattering Churchill,"[47] whom Truman had met only the day before and whose ardent praise of the United States led a skeptical Truman to write, "I am sure we can get along if he doesn't try to give me too much soft soap."[48]

Unlike so many of Stalin's other Western admirers, Truman did not allow his personal liking for the dictator to blind him to Soviet expansionism. He was particularly outraged by Stalin's decision, in violation of Yalta understandings, to hand over about a quarter of Germany to Poland without consulting either the U.S. or Britain. "Just a unilateral arrangement without so much as a 'by your leave,'" Truman fumed in his diary. "I don't like it."[49] Nevertheless, he remained "captivated"[50] by Stalin's personality:

> "I like Stalin," he wrote to Bess on July 29 [1945].... "He is straightforward. Knows what he wants and will compromise when he can't get it. His foreign minister isn't so forthright." He left Potsdam hoping that Stalin's health would allow him to hold on as Soviet dictator and fearing that he might be overthrown by a less accommodating military clique. The impression would stick. Four years later, Truman would tell Jonathan Daniels, "Stalin is as near like Tom Pendergast as any man I know."[51]

For Truman to equate Stalin with his earliest political sponsor, Kansas City machine boss Pendergast, was a high compliment. Truman thought that Stalin, like Pendergast, was a shrewd, tough bargainer—perhaps inclined to cut some corners here and there, but a man of his word nonetheless. To avoid alienating such a straightforward personality, Truman decided that Stalin would have to be told that on July 16, the very eve of the Potsdam Conference, the United States had detonated an atomic device in the New Mexico desert.

After discussing with Churchill how best to break the news, Truman approached the Soviet despot on July 24. "I saw the President go up to Stalin," Churchill recalled in his memoirs,

and the two conversed alone with only their interpret-
ers…. I knew what the President was going to do. What
was vital to measure was its effect on Stalin. I can see it
all as if it were yesterday. He seemed to be delighted. A
new bomb! Of extraordinary power! Probably decisive
on the whole Japanese war! What a bit of luck! This
was my impression at the moment, and I am sure that
he had no idea of the significance of what he was being
told….[52]

For once, however, Churchill was wrong: Stalin had learned about
the Anglo–American effort to build a bomb long before Truman had.
"Espionage appears to have been of greater assistance to the Soviet bomb
development project than we had once thought," writes John Lewis
Gaddis.

As early as March 1943, Igor V. Kurchatov, [American
atomic physicist J. Robert] Oppenheimer's Russian
counterpart, was assessing the information it yielded
as having "huge, inestimable significance for our state
and science."… "It was a very good intelligence operation by our Chekists," Molotov recalled years afterwards. "They neatly stole just what we needed."[53]

Stalin's seeming lack of interest in Truman's revelation was actually a
ruse. ("Stalin's greatness as a dissimulator," writes Kennan, "was an integral part of his greatness as a statesman."[54]) In reality, he was terribly
worried and immediately contacted Lavrentiy Beria. "Truman is trying
to exert pressure, to dominate," he told his State Security Chief.

But a policy of blackmail and intimidation is unacceptable to us. We therefore gave no grounds for thinking that anything could intimidate us. Lavrentiy, we
should not allow any other country to have a decisive
superiority over us. Tell Comrade Kurchatov that he
has to hurry with his parcel. And ask him what our
scientists need to accelerate work.[55]

What is remarkable about this exchange is not that Stalin interpreted Truman's candor as an attempt at intimidation—most national leaders, upon learning that another power had acquired a weapon of unprecedented lethality, would have reacted similarly—but that his suspicions were totally unfounded. "Within weeks of Hiroshima," writes Gaddis, "American officials had abandoned the idea that an atomic monopoly could become a usable instrument of diplomacy, shifting instead to an immediate search for international control."[56] It was Churchill, not Truman, who recognized that the bomb was a "usable instrument of diplomacy," and over the next five years, he urged the Americans to use it.[57] But Truman, while eventually coming to accept the bomb's utility in *containing* Soviet power, never regarded it as a legitimate means of coercion.

"I'm Tired of Babying the Soviets!"

Truman left Potsdam with sharply contradictory attitudes toward the Soviet Union. On the one hand, his personal exposure to Soviet highhandedness during the negotiations over Poland's western borders reinforced all of his democratic, anti-Communist convictions and left him more convinced than ever that the Soviets were bent on expansion. On the other hand, his meetings with Stalin reassured him that an amicable Soviet–American relationship was possible. These conflicting perceptions left "his mind...divided, one side wanting to stand on principle and assert American power and ideals, the other wanting to work out a compromise with the Soviet Union."[58]

How to advance American ideals while remaining on friendly terms with a state bent on subverting those ideals would have taxed the time, patience, and skills of the most experienced diplomatist; but for the new President, Soviet–American relations was only one of many vexing problems demanding his immediate attention. Not surprisingly, therefore,

> Truman, increasingly preoccupied with domestic reconversion, appears to have paid only limited attention to diplomacy after Potsdam.... For the time being, he was willing to leave specifics to [James F.] Byrnes,

who quickly and rashly assumed the same attitude that he exercised as unofficial "assistant president" under Roosevelt.[59]

James F. Byrnes, who was appointed Secretary of State by Truman because he was present at the Yalta Conference and enjoyed a (wrongful) reputation for foreign policy expertise, believed that the principal obstacle to improved Soviet–American relations was Washington's refusal to recognize Soviet-installed puppet regimes in Hungary, Bulgaria, and Romania. He therefore saw it as his main task to devise diplomatic compromises that would enable Washington to recognize these governments. His negotiating style was described acidly by George Kennan, who saw him in action in Moscow:

> He plays his negotiations by ear, going into them with no clear or fixed plan, with no definite set objectives or limitations. He relies entirely on his own agility and presence of mind and hopes to take advantage of tactical openings…. [H]is main purpose is to achieve some sort of agreement, he doesn't much care what. The realities behind this agreement, since they concern only such people as Koreans, Rumanians, and Iranians, about whom he knows nothing, do not concern him.[60]

Byrnes's negotiating tactics were denounced as "appeasement" by conservative Republicans, who argued that instead of trying to devise ingenious ways to recognize Soviet puppet governments, the United States ought to demand that Moscow strictly carry out its Yalta commitments and hold free elections in Eastern Europe. The American mission in Bucharest likewise regarded Byrnes's agreement to extend diplomatic recognition to the Romanian Communist regime in exchange for the addition of two non-Communist cabinet members as a "sellout," and considered resigning en masse.[61] Truman, meanwhile, was increasingly disturbed by Byrnes's failure to consult with him in advance and began to suspect his own Secretary of State of deliberately snubbing him. Moreover, Truman came to feel that Byrnes's critics were right. "I'm tired of babying the Soviets!" he declared on January 5, 1946, in a letter to Byrnes.[62]

But if Truman did not wish to "baby" the Soviets, he also did not wish to confront them. "Neither Truman nor Roosevelt had the slightest idea of sending troops to secure any goal in the East of Europe, nor did they organize any combination of economic leverage, propaganda, intimidation, cajolery on a considered basis, to pursue those goals."[63] Even when Stalin began ratcheting up the pressure on Turkey and Iran, Truman, though outraged, told his Cabinet that "we were not going to let the public know the extent to which the Russians tried our patience but that we were going to find some way to get along with the Russians."[64]

Thus, when Washington political columnists Joseph and Stewart Alsop complained, in an early January 1946 column sharply critical of Truman, that the President had no coherent policy for Russia, they were exactly right. Instead, Truman simultaneously entertained a jumble of contradictory ideas about the Soviet Union:

- A belief that the Soviets were implacably expansionist;
- A conviction that somehow Stalin did not share this aggressive orientation;
- A suspicion that Molotov or some other, equally sinister figure was really behind recent Soviet moves;
- A determination to continue FDR's policy and try to get along with the Soviets no matter what;
- An unwillingness either to accept or challenge the communization of Eastern Europe;
- A general sense of helplessness because, as Truman put it in a letter to a Member of Congress on November 16, 1945, "at the rate we are demobilizing troops, in a very short time we will have no means with which to enforce our demands—a just and fair peace—and unless we have that means we are heading directly for a third world war;"[65] and
- A recognition that, as Truman candidly told his aides, he simply did not know what to do.

Truman's doubts and anxieties were heightened by a speech delivered by Stalin on February 9, 1946. "It would be wrong to believe that World War II broke out accidentally," Stalin maintained. "In reality, the war broke out as an inevitable result of the development of world economic and political forces on the basis of modern capitalism." Since "modern capitalism" continued to exist after Nazi Germany's defeat, some members of the Truman Administration, such as Secretary of the Navy James Forrestal, took Stalin's speech to mean "that there was no way in which Democracy and Communism could live together." Other Administration officials believed that the United States was at fault: "It was obvious," said the pro-Soviet Henry Wallace, who would have become President of the United States had Truman not replaced him as Roosevelt's running mate in 1944, and who now served as Truman's Secretary of Commerce, "[that] our military was getting ready for war with Russia.... We are challenging [Stalin], and his speech was taking up the challenge."[66]

To help clarify matters, Secretary Byrnes asked George Kennan, a young Foreign Service Officer who was near the end of his tour of duty as Minister-Counselor in Moscow, to comment on Stalin's February speech. This was the opportunity Kennan had been waiting for:

> For eighteen long months I had done little else but pluck people's sleeves, trying to make them understand the nature of the phenomenon with which we in the Moscow embassy were daily confronted and which our government and people had to learn to understand if they were to have any chance of coping successfully with the problems of the postwar world. So far as official Washington was concerned, it had been to all intents and purposes like talking to a stone. The Russian desk in the State Department had understood; but it had generally been as helpless as we were, and beyond it all had been an unechoing silence. Now, suddenly, my opinion was being asked.... Now, by God, they would have it.[67]

Kennan's 8,000-word "Long Telegram," sent from Moscow on February 22, 1946, "was probably the most important, and influential, message ever sent to Washington by an American diplomat."[68] It "helped reshape Washington's view of the world."[69] Essentially, Kennan "postulated a complete reversal of the Roosevelt foreign policy of seeking compromise, understanding and cooperation with the Soviet Union. He did not couch his dispatch in those terms, of course, but the message of the Long Telegram was 'Wake up—this is what is *really* happening.'"[70]

In Kennan's view, growing Soviet–American friction was not the product of misunderstanding, poor communication, or the ascendancy of some mysterious hard-liner in the Kremlin; rather, "it was inherent in the Soviet Union's perception of the world."[71] As he put it succinctly in a lesser-known March 20 telegram, "Nothing short of complete disarmament, delivery of our air and naval forces to Russia and resigning of power of government to American communists" would alleviate Stalin's distrust; even then, Stalin would probably "smell a trap, and continue to harbor the most baleful misgivings."[72]

The impact of the Long Telegram on official Washington, wrote Kennan in his 1967 memoir, "was nothing less than sensational.... The President, I believe, read it. The Secretary of the Navy, Mr. James Forrestal, had it reproduced and evidently made it required reading for hundreds, if not thousands, of higher officers in the armed services.... My reputation was made. My voice carried."[73] In 1974, however, Kennan

> said wistfully that he was not sure Truman had known who he was, even though he briefed the president. "I met with [Truman] once or twice during this period.... I suspect he was vaguely aware that there was a young fellow over in the State Department who had written a good piece on the Russians—I doubt whether Truman ever really read anything I wrote, though. Certainly, I don't think he grasped my position."[74]

Whether Truman actually read the Long Telegram is unclear. Ferrell asserts that "the president does not seem to have read the Long Telegram, nor perhaps ever heard of it."[75] Hamby, on the other hand, claims that "Truman read it and almost certainly was influenced."[76] David McCullough also believes that Truman read it, but writes that, "on Truman, in particular, it does not appear to have had any profound or immediate effect...."[77]

As for its impact on other senior White House officials, although Byrnes informed Kennan that he read the telegram with the "greatest interest" and thanked him for his "splendid analysis," it seems to have affected him very little, and its basic message—that Soviet–American differences could not be resolved through diplomacy—was most unwelcome. Truman's Under Secretary of State, Dean Acheson, also paid little attention to the Long Telegram. Years later, he admitted that "we responded to [Kennan's recommendations] too slowly."[78]

But the Long Telegram did lead to one important Administration initiative. On February 28, with Kennan's telegram in mind, Navy Secretary Forrestal asked President Truman to dispatch a naval task force to the East Mediterranean to hearten the governments of Greece and Turkey, both of which were threatened by Communism. The President agreed, but assembling the proposed task force proved impossible, and eventually only the battleship *Missouri* was sent to Turkey carrying the remains of the deceased Turkish ambassador to Washington. Nevertheless, this marked "a new departure: a sign that the United States would be prepared to supplement the traditional role of Britain in the Mediterranean."[79]

The Iron Curtain

Nor was Kennan the only experienced observer offering advice to an obviously floundering Truman Administration. On March 5, 1946, two weeks after Kennan cabled his Long Telegram, Winston Churchill delivered what would come to be known as his "Iron Curtain" address in Fulton, Missouri. "From Stettin in the Baltic to Trieste in the Adriatic," Churchill informed the students and faculty of Westminster College, "an iron curtain has descended across the Continent." Soviet Russia, he continued, does not desire war. "What they desire is the fruits of war and the indefinite expansion of their power and doctrines.... I am convinced that there is nothing they admire so much as strength, and there is nothing for which they have less respect than for weakness, especially military weakness." To bring Russian aggression to a halt, Churchill called for a new Anglo–American alliance.

Churchill's speech was sharply attacked on both sides of the Atlantic, and from both ends of the political spectrum. On the left, Nobel laureate Pearl Buck called it a "catastrophe," and George Bernard Shaw said it was "nothing short of a declaration of war on Russia." On the right, Senator Robert Taft of Ohio endorsed Churchill's criticisms of the Soviet Union but warned that "it would be very unfortunate for the U.S. to enter into any military alliance with England, Russia, or any other country in time of peace," while Senator George Aiken of Vermont declared, "I'm not ready to enter a military alliance with anyone."[80]

Truman also distanced himself from the speech. "On the one hand," writes Truman's counsel, Clark Clifford,

> he recognized the power and insight of Churchill's speech and Kennan's Long Telegram; on the other, he still harbored the hope that some sort of agreement with Stalin would be possible. It was for this reason that President Truman told reporters on the train leaving Fulton that he had not read the speech in advance [even though he had]. President Truman did not feel he could take the same position as a former Prime Minister, who could speak unconstrained by the limitations of office. Much to our relief, Churchill, understanding perfectly the President's situation and deeply grateful for the gesture that the President had made in introducing him, did not contradict him.[81]

To disassociate his administration even further from Churchill's address, Truman instructed Under Secretary of State Dean Acheson not to attend a reception for Churchill the following week in New York. "The President even sent Stalin a message emphasizing that he still held out hope for better relations," recalls Clifford. "He issued an invitation to him to make a similar speech in Missouri, 'for exactly the same kind of reception,' and said he would introduce Stalin personally as he had Churchill."[82]

Far from being placated, however, Stalin, in a March 13 *Pravda* interview, compared Churchill to Hitler and angrily denounced his speech as a "call to war."[83] Nonetheless, on March 26, the Soviet government suddenly announced that it was withdrawing all its troops from Iran. "Throughout the rest of the year," writes historian Adam Ulam,

> the Soviets watched passively while the Iranian government liquidated the separatist regimes and executed their leaders.... The presumption is overwhelming that it was Churchill's speech that did the trick. With all the debate going on about that speech, the Russians were loath to present additional evidence that its main thesis was sound.[84]

Meanwhile, Truman renewed his efforts to reach an accommodation with Stalin. On March 19, 1946, he informed his new ambassador to Moscow, General Walter Bedell Smith (who had replaced Averell Harriman), to deliver a letter to Stalin that contained an invitation to visit the United States. He also explained his Soviet policy, the essence of which was strict reciprocity:

> [The President] told me to make it very clear to Stalin, and through him to the men who control the Kremlin [once again, shades of the Molotov clique!] that the United States had made agreements in Yalta and Potsdam in good faith. But he also wished me to make it very clear to the Kremlin that our continued adherence to these agreements would be made impossible by continued Soviet disregard of their own obligations.

"It was obvious," Smith concluded, "that one of the President's major preoccupations was to set things right with the Soviet Union, but without sacrificing further the position and interests of the United States and its Western allies."[85]

On April 4, during a late night meeting with Stalin in the Kremlin, Smith duly delivered Truman's invitation, which Stalin declined for reasons of health. Then, after assuring the Soviet dictator that "the American people were willing and anxious to meet the Soviet Union halfway, because they were convinced that if our two nations understood and cooperated with each other the peace of the world would be assured," Smith bluntly came to the point. "How far is Russia going to go?" he asked.

> Looking directly at me, Stalin replied "We're not go-ing much further."
>
> "You say 'not much further'," I observed, "but does that 'much' have any reference to Turkey?"
>
> "I have answered President Truman and have stated publicly that the Soviet Union has no intention of at-tacking Turkey, nor does this intention exist."[86]

"We Might as Well Find Out"

Despite Stalin's pledge, on August 7, 1946, the Soviets called for the joint Soviet–Turkish defense of the Dardanelles—a demand which American officials interpreted as a pretext for Soviet naval bases in the Turkish straits.

Stalin's demands backfired. On August 15, an alarmed Dean Acheson, who served as Acting Secretary of State during Byrnes's frequent travels abroad (Byrnes was out of the country for 241 of his 546 days as Secre-tary of State), and whose view of the Soviets had hardened considerably, presented the President with a joint State–War–Navy memorandum on Turkey and the Soviet Union. According to one authoritative account,

> The memorandum saw the Soviet Union's primary objective as obtaining control of Turkey through the ostensible purpose of enforcing joint control of the Straits. Since such control would facilitate Soviet con-trol of the Near East, it was in the vital interests of the United States that the Soviet Union not succeed (whether through force or the threat of force) in its unilateral plan with regard to the Straits.... An appeal to reason was insufficient. The only thing which would deter the Russians would be the conviction that the United States was prepared, if necessary, to meet ag-gression with force of arms.[87]

In the subsequent discussion, which included Navy Secretary Forrestal and top military aides, Acheson urged that the United States send a firm note to the Russians rejecting their demands, along with a naval task force to the region. If the Russians refused to back down, Acheson emphasized, the situation could lead to war. Truman accepted all of Acheson's recommendations. "We might as well find out," he said, "whether the Russian were bent on world conquest now as in five or ten years."[88] Thus, he was prepared to pursue the suggested policy "to the end."[89]

"One of the generals," write Walter Isaacson and Evan Thomas, "whispered a critical question to Acheson. Had he made it sufficiently clear that the policy might lead to war?" Upon hearing the question, Truman removed a large map of the Near East from his desk drawer and began lecturing the group about the strategic significance of the eastern Mediterranean. "When he finished," Acheson later recalled, "none of us doubted he understood fully all the implications of our recommendations."[90] In 1949, Acheson told Turkish Foreign Minister Necmeddin Sadak that Truman "considered this the most important decision he had made subsequent to the bombing of Hiroshima."[91]

Fortunately, the Soviets did back down,[92] and nothing was heard of their Turkish Straits proposal again. But Truman's show of resolve thoroughly alarmed his dovish Secretary of Commerce, Henry Wallace. On September 12, at a left-wing rally in New York's Madison Square Garden, Wallace gave a speech that was widely interpreted as a sharp attack on the Administration's Soviet policy. Secretary Byrnes—then engaged, at a 21-nation Foreign Ministers' Conference in Paris, in a futile effort to conclude a German peace treaty with Moscow—demanded Wallace's resignation.

Truman reluctantly complied, and with Wallace's departure, the last advocate of Roosevelt's foreign policy was gone from Truman's inner circle. Increasingly, Truman would be influenced by

> aides and advisers who had staked out no previous turf on foreign policy, people who like Truman were fundamentally centrists.... Gradually, they came to the conclusion that the Soviet leaders possessed a very different view of the world, that therefore no tolerable

compromises were likely with them, and that Stalin was more than just a tough political boss. Truman's own conceptual journey appears to have been very similar to theirs.[93]

The Clifford–Elsey Report

Of these aides, none was more influential than Clark Clifford. Born in Kansas in 1906, Clifford received a law degree from Washington University and practiced with a St. Louis firm until entering the Navy in 1944. Selected as a White House naval aide in 1945, he supplemented his duties by assisting Judge Samuel I. Rosenman, Truman's (and FDR's) general counsel. When Rosenman left the Administration in 1946, the gifted naval aide succeeded him as counsel.

At a Cabinet meeting on July 16, Truman expressed his growing frustration with the Soviets. "The Russians are trying to chisel away a little here, a little there," he said. "If the Paris Conference busts up, I want to be ready to reveal to the whole world the full truth about the Russian failure to honor agreements."[94] He assigned Clark Clifford the task of producing a full report of Soviet violations.

Clifford turned to his assistant, a young Harvard-trained historian and intelligence officer named George Elsey, who suggested that the project be expanded into a broad overview of Soviet foreign policy. After the President approved the new idea, Clifford and Elsey drew up a list of the senior officials whose views they would consult: Admiral William D. Leahy, who spoke for the Joint Chiefs of Staff; James Byrnes and Dean Acheson at the State Department; Secretary of War Robert Patterson; Secretary of the Navy James Forrestal; Attorney General Tom Clark; and Sidney Souers, Director of the Central Intelligence Group, predecessor of today's CIA. Also consulted were George Kennan, who had returned recently from Moscow, and his fellow Sovietologist, Charles Bohlen. "I did not realize it at the time," Clifford later recalled, "but I had received permission to begin what turned out to be the first peacetime interagency foreign policy review of American–Soviet relations."[95]

Entitled "American Relations with the Soviet Union," the Clifford–Elsey report finally answered the question that had obsessed Truman ever since he became President: What explains Soviet behavior? The report asserted flatly that

> The key to an understanding of current Soviet foreign policy is the realization that Soviet leaders adhere to the Marxian theory of ultimate destruction of capitalist states by communist states, while at the same time they strive to postpone the inevitable conflict in order to strengthen and prepare the Soviet Union for its clash with the western democracies.... So long as these men adhere to these beliefs, it is highly dangerous to conclude that hope of international peace lies only in "accord," "mutual understanding" or "solidarity" with the Soviet Union.[96]

The report also anticipated the argument Kennan would advance almost 10 months later in his famous "X" article in *Foreign Affairs* advocating the "containment" of the Soviet Union.[97] Clifford and Elsey called on the United States to "maintain military forces powerful enough to restrain the Soviet Union and to confine Soviet influence to its present area." (Later, Clifford wrote, "Elsey and I amused ourselves imagining that, had our report been circulated, future historians might have referred to the policy of 'restrainment' instead of 'containment.'"[98]) If this policy proved successful, the report concluded, "it is our hope that [the Soviet leaders] will change their minds and work out with us a fair and equitable settlement...."[99]

The Clifford–Elsey report provided President Truman with the theoretical framework he desperately needed both to understand Soviet foreign policy and to conduct American foreign policy. Yet far from welcoming it, the President was left more agitated than ever. As Clifford recalls in his memoirs, on the morning of September 25, the day after submitting his report, he received a phone call from the President:

> "I stayed up very late last night reading your report," he began. "Powerful stuff."

"Thank you, Mr. President."

"Clark, how many copies of this memorandum do you have?"

"Twenty," I replied.

"Have any been distributed yet?"

"No sir. They are all in my safe at the office."

"Well, please come down to your office now, and get all twenty copies. I want them delivered to me at once." The President offered no explanation for his surprising instructions, but I set out for the White House immediately, got all twenty copies out of my safe and took them to the Oval Office. "I read your report with care last night," the President said. "It is very valuable to me—but if it leaked it would blow the roof off the White House, it would blow the roof off the Kremlin. We'd have the most serious situation on our hands that has yet occurred in my Administration." Then the President took the reports from me, and neither I, nor Elsey, nor anyone else, ever saw them again.[100]

Even though the Clifford–Elsey report represented the considered views of his senior foreign policy advisers, Truman probably buried it because he feared that if word of its unflinchingly harsh assessments (including a recommendation that "the United States must be prepared to wage atomic and biological warfare"[101] against the Soviet Union) ever reached the public, it would unleash a "jingoistic crusade"[102] that would prevent any accommodation with Stalin. As Alonzo Hamby writes, Truman "had not yet fully given up on a general accord with the Soviet Union, especially if he could deal on a man-to-man basis with Stalin.... As late as September 1946, his personal attitudes toward the USSR remained mixed and allowed room for hope about the future."[103]

Despite being buried by the President, however, there is no doubt that the Clifford–Elsey report (unlike Kennan's Long Telegram) influenced Truman significantly. "For one thing," writes Clifford, "he completely dropped the idea of a long-term low-rate loan to the Soviets comparable to the British loan extended earlier in the year—which, as recently as September 18, he had favored. After he read our report, he never mentioned such a loan again."[104] Moreover, although the President did not accept the report's recommendation that "the American people should be fully informed about the difficulties of getting along with the Soviet Union,"[105] and even though he continued to insist in his public statements that "we must not permit differences in economic and social systems to stand in the way of peace, either now or in the future,"[106] five months later, when events finally forced his hand and compelled him to alert the American people to Moscow's aggressive designs, key ideas in the Clifford–Elsey report found expression in what became known as the Truman Doctrine.

A Call to Arms: The Truman Doctrine

The Truman Doctrine, which Alonzo Hamby has rightly called "the decisive step in what soon would be called the Cold War,"[107] came about because Great Britain, exhausted by the Second World War, could no longer maintain the burdens of world power and because the Truman Administration, in assuming some of those burdens, felt compelled to justify such a momentous step to the American people. On February 21, 1947, the British government informed the Truman Administration that its aid to Greece and Turkey would end on March 31. As recounted by Clifford,

> The British expressed the hope that the U.S. would assume the burden in both countries, which they estimated would be between $240 million and $280 million for Greece, and about $150 million for Turkey. These sums, still substantial today, were staggering in 1947 dollars, totaling about 1 percent of a federal budget of only $41 billion.[108]

The United States had received informal notification of British intentions in the final months of 1946, and State Department officials already were planning to step into the breach when the British note arrived.

In Turkey, the situation seemed clear enough: A sovereign nation, determined to resist Soviet pressure, required American assistance to remain financially solvent and politically independent. In war-ravaged Greece, matters were more complicated. There, a Communist-dominated guerrilla movement sought to overthrow a government that many Americans regarded as reactionary, if not fascist. Yet American policymakers correctly believed that the Greek guerrillas were supplied by Communist regimes in Bulgaria, Albania, and Yugoslavia, and that such support would not be forthcoming without Stalin's approval. (When Yugoslavia's Communist boss, Josip Broz Tito, cut off military assistance to the guerrillas in the wake of his 1948 split with Stalin, their rebellion quickly collapsed.) Through his Communist satellites, Stalin was intervening in the Greek civil war, and if the United States did not act quickly, his intervention would prove decisive.

Whatever hopes Truman had entertained about reaching an understanding with Stalin were now, finally and irrevocably, cast aside. When State Department officials presented him with a proposal for $250 million in aid to Greece and another $150 million for Turkey, he quickly approved it. All that remained was to secure Congress's approval. To that end, on February 27, 1947, President Truman, Secretary of State George C. Marshall (who had replaced Byrnes in January), and Under Secretary of State Acheson met with congressional leaders and bluntly warned them that if Greece and Turkey fell to the Soviet Union, Soviet domination might extend to Europe, the Middle East, and Asia. Deeply impressed, the legislators promised to support the Administration's request if the President would publicize the arguments they had just heard.

Truman was happy to comply. "Watching President Truman tackle this challenge," Clark Clifford later wrote,

> I felt he had come a long way since the messy Wallace
> affair and the loss of Congress to the Republicans barely
> three months earlier.... Now he seemed ready for what
> Senator [Arthur S.] Vandenberg [a former Republican
> isolationist from Michigan and now the chairman of
> the Senate Committee on Foreign Relations and his
> party's leading foreign policy spokesman] told him was

his "date with destiny." He was willing, he told me, to "lay it on the line" with the American people. He did not spend time, as most Presidents would have, studying "option papers." He simply wanted to see a speech draft before making a final decision.[109]

The speech that Truman delivered on March 12, 1947, to a joint session of Congress was the product of many hands, including Acheson, Clifford, Elsey, and Truman himself. It began by describing the plight of Greece—"threatened by the terrorist activities of several thousand armed men, led by communists"—and Turkey. It then argued that the difficulties in which Greece and Turkey found themselves were not confined to those two nations:

> At the present moment in world history, nearly every nation must choose between alternative ways of life. The choice is too often not a free one. One way of life is based upon the will of the majority, and is distinguished by free institutions, representative government, free elections, guarantees of individual liberty, freedom of speech and religion, and freedom from political oppression. The second way of life is based upon the will of a minority forcibly imposed upon the majority. It relies upon terror and oppression, a controlled press and radio, fixed elections, and the suppression of personal freedoms.

Having in effect divided the world rhetorically into a democratic zone of freedom and a Communist zone of tyranny (without, however, mentioning the Soviet Union by name), the President unequivocally identified the United States with the zone of freedom:

> I believe it must be the policy of the United States to support free peoples who are resisting attempted subjugation by armed minorities or by outside pressures. I believe that we must assist free peoples to work out their own destinies in their own way. I believe that our help should be primarily through economic and finan-

cial aid, which is essential to economic stability and
orderly political processes.... The seeds of totalitarian
regimes are nurtured by misery and want. They spread
and grow in the evil soil of poverty and strife. They
reach their full growth when the hope of a people for a
better life has died. We must keep that hope alive.

He then swung back to the plight of Greece and Turkey: "Should we
fail to aid Greece and Turkey, the effect will be far-reaching to the West
as well as to the East.... I therefore ask the Congress to provide authority for assistance to Greece and Turkey in the amount of $400 million
for the period ending June 30, 1948."

Truman concluded his address by arguing that only the United States
could do the job:

> The free peoples of the world look to us for support in
> maintaining their freedoms. If we falter in our leader-
> ship, we may endanger the peace of the world—and
> we shall surely endanger the welfare of this Nation.
> Great responsibilities have been placed on us by the
> swift movement of events. I am confident that the
> Congress will face these responsibilities squarely.[110]

The historic character of Truman's address was recognized immediately, and it was widely understood that, as Truman told his Cabinet on
March 7, the decision to request money from Congress for Greece and
Turkey "is only the beginning. It means [the] U.S. going into European
politics."[111] For its part,

> The *New York Times* called the speech "a radical change
> [in American foreign policy] in the space of 21 min-
> utes," and described Congress as "bewildered" and
> "much shaken" as it faced "one of the toughest dead-
> lines in modern history." James Reston said the speech
> was "comparable in importance" to the Monroe Doc-
> trine. Senator Vandenberg issued a strong statement
> of support, which had been worked out in advance
> with Dean Acheson.[112]

The Senate approved Truman's aid package by a vote of 67 to 23; the House, by a voice vote.

In one sense, Harry Truman's decision to address Congress over Greek–Turkish aid showed that he had "internalized" the theory of restrainment/containment, as well as the views of his senior foreign policy advisers, as laid out in the Clifford–Elsey report. But in another, more profound sense, it simply meant that Truman had finally resolved to be Truman—a political leader with views and ideas of his own—and not merely FDR's successor and stand-in. During his first two years in office, Truman had tried dutifully to continue FDR's legacy of friendship with Stalin, even though it went against his own deepest foreign policy instincts. By 1947, he at last felt free to give voice to his bedrock conviction that Nazism and Communism were both mortal enemies of freedom and that the United States was morally obliged to help build a world in which liberty and the rule of law reigned supreme. As Truman put it in a letter to his daughter several weeks after his historic address:

> The attempt of Lenin, Trotsky, Stalin, et. al., to fool the world and the American Crackpots Association, represented by Jos. Davies, Henry Wallace, Claude Pepper and the actors and artists in immoral Greenwich Village, is just like Hitler's and Mussolini's so-called socialist states. Your pop had to tell the world just that in polite language.[113]

Revitalizing Europe: The Marshall Plan

If the Truman Doctrine was America's call to arms in the Cold War, the European Recovery Program—popularly known as the Marshall Plan—was the Truman Administration's boldest and most original Cold War initiative. Fearful that Western Europe's prolonged postwar economic slump threatened to bring Communist parties to power, first in France and Italy and then throughout the rest of the continent, Secretary of State George Marshall, in a commencement address at Harvard University on June 5, 1947, warned that "Europe's requirements for the next three or four years of foreign food and other essential products—principally from America—are so much greater than her present ability to pay that she must have substantial additional help or face economic, social, and political deterioration of a very grave character." The United States was willing to provide the necessary assistance, but "the initiative, I think, must come from Europe. The role of this country should consist of friendly aid in the drafting of a European program and of later support of such a program so far as it may be practical for us to do so."

Despite believing that unless "substantial" U.S. aid were soon forthcoming, Western Europe would soon fall under Moscow's sway, Marshall also did not want the U.S. to be blamed for the division of Europe that would result inevitably from an American refusal to invite the participation of the Soviet Union and its satellites in a European Recovery Program. Consequently, he was careful not to present the plan as an anti-Communist initiative. "Our policy," he declared, "is directed not against any party or doctrine but against hunger, poverty, desperation and chaos…. Any government that is willing to assist in the task of recovery will find full cooperation, I am sure, on the part of the United States government."[114]

Nevertheless, American policymakers privately anticipated (and devoutly hoped) that the Soviet Union would refuse to participate. At first, Stalin's decision to send Foreign Minister Molotov and a large delegation of Soviet experts to the Paris conference called to devise a European response to Marshall's offer of assistance suggested that the Americans had miscalculated. But when it became apparent in Paris that participation in the Marshall Plan would require the Soviet Union to submit detailed disclosures of its economic needs, Stalin ordered his representatives to walk out. "The Soviet Union," Molotov explained on July 2, saw the Marshall Plan "as a bid to interfere in the internal affairs of European countries, thus making the economies of these countries dependent on U.S. interests."[115] In lieu of the Marshall Plan, the Soviet Union offered its satellites the "Molotov Plan," which simply consolidated Moscow's hold over the economies of Eastern Europe.

Had Stalin not refused to participate in the Marshall Plan, it is difficult to see how the $17 billion European Recovery Program submitted to Congress by Truman on December 19, 1947, could have been passed. As it was, the proposal encountered significant opposition; but thanks to what Truman called "the brilliant, intelligent leadership" of internationalist Republicans like Senator Vandenberg and Representative Charles Eaton on the one hand, and the brutal Communist coup in Czechoslovakia in February 1948 on the other, the Senate and the House passed the Marshall Plan by votes of 69 to 17 and 318 to 75, respectively.[116] The European Recovery Program eventually transferred about $13 billion in U.S. assistance to Western Europe and was especially instrumental in reviving the economies of France, Germany, and Italy. Paul Johnson has rightly called it "the most successful scheme of its kind in history."[117]

With passage of the Marshall Plan, Western Europe's economic revival was assured, but her security remained in doubt—a point that Britain's Foreign Secretary, Ernest Bevin, emphasized to Secretary Marshall during the latter's visit to London early in 1948. Bevin told Marshall that, despite the onset of Europe's economic recovery, both the presence of massive Soviet forces in Eastern Germany and the general intransigence of the Soviets had left the countries of Western Europe very uneasy about the future. Could the U.S. do anything to help offset Soviet military power? Marshall suggested that the Europeans first try to establish their own defense arrangements and then turn to the U.S. for additional support.

Bevin thereupon became the moving force behind the Pact of Brussels—a mutual defense pact concluded in April 1948 by Britain, France, Belgium, the Netherlands, and Luxembourg. Over the course of the next year, secret negotiations to broaden the pact took place with the U.S., Canada, and other European nations. Finally, on April 4, 1949, the North Atlantic Treaty was signed in Washington by the U.S., Belgium, Canada, Denmark, France, Great Britain, Iceland, Italy, Luxembourg, the Netherlands, Norway, and Portugal (Greece and Turkey joined in 1952, and West Germany joined in 1955). This treaty, which stipulated that an attack on one member would be considered an attack on all, was America's first permanent peacetime alliance. On July 21, 1949, the Senate consented to the North Atlantic Treaty by a vote of 82 to 13. "Thus," writes Henry Kissinger, "the North Atlantic Treaty Organization came into being as a way of tying America to the defense of Western Europe. NATO provided for an unprecedented departure in American foreign policy: American, along with Canadian, forces joined Western European armies under an international NATO command."[118]

Just as important as the creation of NATO was the merger—largely at the Truman Administration's insistence—of the British, French, and American zones of occupied Germany into a new structure: the Federal Republic of Germany. In June 1948, in an effort to derail this process, Stalin initiated a full-scale blockade of West Berlin, which was located deep within the Soviet occupation zone.[119] Truman's response to Stalin's challenge was firm. As he put it in his diary on July 19, "We'll stay in Berlin—come what may.... I don't pass the buck nor do I alibi out of any decision I make."[120] Truman rejected a proposal by the U.S. Zone Commander, General Lucius Clay, to break the blockade by using armed convoys. Instead, the U.S. mounted a massive airlift which succeeded in supplying the besieged city with all its needs. On May 12, 1949, recognizing defeat, Stalin called off the blockade.

"For Some Great Purpose"

The Marshall Plan, NATO, the Berlin airlift, and the creation of the Federal Republic of Germany were remarkable initiatives that secured Western Europe's freedom and prosperity in the Cold War, as well as Harry Truman's place in history. But Truman did not intend to confine the policy of containment to Western Europe. Believing that "God has created us and brought us to our present position for some great purpose,"[121] he was prepared to use American power to contain Communist aggression anywhere in the world.

Thus, when Communist North Korea invaded South Korea on June 25, 1950, Truman quickly decided to come to the South's defense. "Communism," he said, "was acting in Korea just as Hitler, Mussolini, and the Japanese had acted ten, fifteen, and twenty years earlier. If this was allowed to go unchallenged it would mean a third world war."[122] Truman did not allow North Korea's aggression to go unchallenged, and according to the polls, the American public supported his "police action" by a margin of 10 to 1.

Truman's willingness to use American force to defend the cause of freedom around the world was a major departure in American history. The more traditional approach had been formulated by Secretary of State John Quincy Adams in 1821. "America does not go abroad in search of monsters to destroy," declared Adams in a Fourth of July oration. "She is the well-wisher of the freedom and independence of all. She is the champion only of her own."[123] Yet, while the Truman Administration did not intervene reflexively in every case when Communists threatened to seize power (during the Chinese civil war, for example, it gave only lukewarm support to the Nationalists, believing, as Truman said in 1947, that the anti-Communist leader, Chiang Kai-shek, presided over "the most corrupt government in the history of the world"[124]) it is fair to say that, beginning with Truman's presidency, America *did* become the champion of all nations threatened by Soviet imperialism.

President Truman's adoption of containment undoubtedly saved both Western Europe and South Korea from the horrors of Soviet domination, and this achievement, as Alonzo Hamby has written, "was Churchillian in its significance."[125] But containment also forced the American people to make countless sacrifices for the sake of other peoples' freedom, and in the wake of the war in Vietnam, Americans grew weary of this endless, thankless task.

Thus, in the 1980s, the United States adopted a new approach to the Soviet Union: Instead of trying to change Soviet minds by demonstrating that aggression would never succeed, the purpose of American policy became to change the Soviet system. The author of this new policy was Ronald Reagan, but its inspirer was Winston Churchill.

2 Winston Churchill
Seizing the Initiative

Winston Churchill: Seizing the Initiative

Winston Churchill titled the last volume of his wartime memoirs *Triumph and Tragedy*. The triumph was plain enough: After five and a half years of war, Hitler's Germany had finally been beaten. The tragedy was not yet apparent to Churchill's contemporaries—and certainly not to the Americans—but was all too clear to him: The Soviet Union now dominated Central and Eastern Europe, and was poised to threaten Western Europe as well.

Churchill had seen it coming and had "warned" and "pleaded" with Roosevelt and then Truman to block the Soviet advance—but to no avail. Now, with victory in sight, "I moved amid cheering crowds, or sat at a table adorned with congratulations and blessings from every part of the Grand Alliance, with an aching heart and a mind oppressed by forebodings." When he addressed his people after receiving Germany's unconditional surrender, Churchill gave voice to his fears. "On the continent of Europe," he declared,

> we have yet to make sure that the simple and honorable purposes for which we entered the war are not brushed aside or overlooked in the months following our success, and that the words "freedom," "democracy" and "liberation" are not distorted from their true meaning as we have understood them. There would be little use in punishing the Hitlerites for their crimes if law and justice did not rule, and if totalitarian or police governments were to take the place of the German invaders.[1]

Nor was Churchill's futile attempt to awaken the Americans to the Soviet danger his only such effort to go unheeded. Time and again, throughout his long career, the anti-Soviet policies that Churchill advocated were rebuffed. After the October 1917 Russian Revolution, Churchill's desperate attempt to overthrow the newly installed Bolshevik regime was derailed by Britain's Prime Minister, David Lloyd George; during World War II, his warnings about growing Soviet power were ignored by Franklin Roosevelt; and after World War II, his call for an immediate showdown with Stalin was rejected by Harry Truman. At the close of his career, the history of Western policy toward Moscow must have struck Churchill as little more than a series of wasted opportunities—lapses in statecraft made all the more tragic because he had advanced wiser alternatives. Fifteen years after his death, however, an American President named Ronald Reagan finally adopted an approach to Soviet–American relations that was, to a considerable degree, Churchillian. The result was victory.

Warp and Woof

Winston Churchill was born in 1874, was elected to Parliament in 1900, retired from office in 1955, and died in 1965. His son, Randolph, best summarized him. In 1950, Randolph professed to be astonished that anyone could find "inconsistencies" in a character "so strongly woven" as his father's:

> The warp is the warp of Old England, of Crécy, of Agincourt, of Sir Francis Drake, of John, Duke of Marlborough, and all that is linked with the fortune, glory and romance of England and her Empire. The woof is that of the great Liberal tradition of Gladstone, of John Morley, of Herbert Asquith and of David Lloyd George.[2]

Both of these elements of Churchill's character—the English warp and the Liberal woof—contributed to the formation of Churchill's Soviet policies. His Liberal belief in the enduring value of parliamentary democracy naturally disposed him to oppose the Bolsheviks, whose avowed goal was the replacement of freely elected governments with a "dictatorship of the proletariat;" but his equally powerful English commitment to the balance of power led him to seek common cause with the Bolsheviks when Nazi Germany sought to conquer Europe, thereby menacing Britain herself.

"This Awful Tyranny and Peril"

When the Bolsheviks seized power in 1917, Churchill had just been named Minister of Munitions by Lloyd George. Charged with producing the maximum number of tanks, planes, and machine guns, he had little to do with Britain's decision, taken in the spring of 1918, to dispatch troops to Archangel and the Caucasus in order to safeguard the huge stock of military supplies Britain had shipped to Russia and prevent the oil fields of Baku from falling into German hands. He did, however, strongly support the intervention.

Indeed, he favored even sterner measures. When he learned that Soviet troops, in the summer of 1918, had broken into the British embassy in Petrograd and killed the British naval attaché, he urged the government "to mark down the personalities of the Bolshevik Government as the objects upon whom justice will be executed, however long it takes…. The exertions which a nation is prepared to make to protect its individual representatives is one of the truest measures of its greatness as an organized State."[3]

By the time Churchill was appointed Minister of War in January 1919, Germany had surrendered and thousands of British soldiers found themselves stranded in the midst of a brutal Russian civil war, their exact mission unclear. Lloyd George assigned his new War Minister the task of bringing these men home safely—but Churchill had other ideas. Employing an "active defensive" strategy, he actually increased the number of troops in Soviet Russia in order—so he argued—to secure their safe withdrawal. With the rest of the British Cabinet preoccupied with other pressing postwar issues, Churchill single-mindedly sought to overthrow the Bolshevik regime by lending support and encouragement to a succession of White Russian generals—Kolchak, Denikin, Wrangel, Yudenich—and even considered going to Russia himself "to help mold the new Russian Constitution."[4]

Churchill's determination to uproot Bolshevism from Russia sprang from an extraordinary gift of insight: the ability to cut through the tangle of events and concentrate on what was truly decisive. In 1933, Churchill was among the first Western statesmen to recognize that Hitler's Germany posed a fundamental threat to Western civilization; in 1919, he was the first to identify Lenin's Russia as the primary threat. "Theirs is a war against civilized society that can never end," he wrote of Lenin and Trotsky.

> They seek as the first condition of their being the over-throw and destruction of all existing institutions and of every State and Government now standing in the world. They too aim at a worldwide and international league, but a league of the failures, the criminals, the unfit, the mutinous, the morbid, the deranged and the distraught in every land; and between them and such order of civilization as we have been able to build up since the dawn of history there can, as Lenin rightly proclaims, be neither truce nor pact.[5]

The barrage of invective unloosed by Churchill against the Bolshe-viks was unparalleled in modern British political history. "Criminality and animalism," "fungus," "cancer," "a plague bacillus," "a deadly and paralyzing sect," "a barbarism...devoured by vermin, racked by pesti-lence," "avowed enemies of...civilization," "criminals," "deranged and distraught," and "subhuman" were among his choicer epithets.[6] The Bolsheviks, he informed the British Cabinet in 1920, have "committed, and are committing unspeakable atrocities, and are maintaining them-selves in power by a terrorism on an unprecedented scale, and by the denial of the most elementary rights of citizenship and freedom."[7]

Churchill's indictment of Bolshevism, although quite accurate in ret-rospect, seemed wildly excessive to Lloyd George, who found Churchill "so obsessed by Russia" that he was spending "hundreds of millions" on a vain effort to topple the Communists.[8] Though forced to abandon his anti-Bolshevik crusade, Churchill presciently warned Parliament that the Great Powers "would learn to regret the fact that they had not been able to take a more decided and more united action to crush the Bolshevik peril at its heart and center before it had grown too strong." For now, however, "We must trust for better or worse to peaceful influences to bring about the disappearance of this awful tyranny and peril."[9]

"Kill the Bolshie, Kiss the Hun"

The Russian Revolution profoundly affected Churchill's view of the world. The Soviet Union, it now seemed to him, had replaced Imperial Germany as the main threat to British security. Establishing a powerful counterweight to Soviet power and influence in Europe became the primary object of his statecraft. Germany obviously had a potentially crucial role to play in containing the Bolsheviks. It followed that a defeated Germany should not be humiliated by the Allies, that her legitimate grievances should be addressed, and that Germany, Great Britain, and France should cooperate in the postwar era against the Bolshevik menace.

On November 10, 1918, a day before the armistice that ended World War I, Churchill informed the War Cabinet that "We might have to build up the German Army, as it was important to get Germany on her legs again, for fear of the spread of Bolshevism."[10] Given the vast amounts of blood and treasure Britain had expended to defeat the German army, as well as the general conviction that in fighting the "Hun," the Allies were defending civilization itself, Churchill's willingness even to contemplate any buildup of Germany's military might must rank as one of the purest expressions of balance-of-power reasoning ever penned.

In the immediate postwar years, exploiting Germany's anti-Bolshevik potential became one of Churchill's principal themes. "In my view," he wrote in 1920, "the objective we should pursue at the present time is the building up of a strong but peaceful Germany which will not attack our French allies, but which will at the same time act as a moral bulwark against Bolshevism in Russia." Churchill summarized this approach in a pithy formula: "Kill the Bolshie, Kiss the Hun."[11]

Envisioning a postwar partnership between Britain and Germany to contain Bolshevism, Churchill informed the War Cabinet in February 1919 that he wished "to see Germany treated humanely and adequately fed, and her industries restarted."[12] He opposed a vindictive peace settlement not only out of compassion—although compassion for a fallen foe was an important facet of Churchill's character—but also because he feared that such a settlement would drive Germany into the Soviet camp. This was Churchill's nightmare scenario: a vengeful, embittered Germany allying herself with a Bolshevized Russia to challenge Great Britain.

Besides affecting his foreign policy views, Churchill's fervent anti-Communism also had a major impact on his domestic political fortunes. Because his career is so closely bound up with the great issues of war and peace, it is sometimes forgotten that Churchill first made his political mark in domestic affairs. Elected to Parliament in 1900 as a Conservative, he broke with the Right in 1904 and joined the Liberals. The immediate cause of the breach was Conservative abandonment of free trade, but the deeper cause was Churchill's growing commitment to social reform.

Churchill's interest in social issues came about as a result of a 1901 dinner at the Athenaeum club, during which Liberal statesman John Morley handed him a copy of a newly published book on living conditions in York. As Churchill wrote to a Birmingham Conservative leader 12 days later,

> I have lately been reading a book by Mr. Rowntree called *Poverty*, which has impressed me very much, and which I strongly recommend you to read. It is quite evident from the figures which he adduces that the American laborer is a stronger, larger, healthier, better fed and consequently more efficient animal than a large proportion of our population, and that is surely a fact which our unbridled Imperialists, who have no thought but to pile up armaments, taxation and territory, should not lose sight of. For my own part, I see little glory in an Empire which can rule the waves and is unable to flush its sewers.[13]

Because most of his fellow Tories did not share his view that "honest effort in a wealthy community should involve certain minimum rights" and that poverty at home "makes world wide power a mockery and defaces the image of God upon earth," Churchill was a dissident Tory even before the free trade controversy forced an open break. His efforts as a Liberal to alleviate the lot of the poor brought him to the attention of the leader of the Fabian Socialists, the formidable Beatrice Webb. "The big thing that has happened in the last two years," she noted in her diary in 1910, "is that Lloyd George and Winston Churchill have practically taken the *limelight*, not merely from their own colleagues, but from the Labor Party. They stand out as the most advanced politicians." She even foresaw the possibility of some younger members of the Fabian Society "enrolling themselves behind these two radical leaders."[14]

Given the "advanced" social agenda championed by Churchill during the first two decades of the 20th century, it is surprising that members of the Labor Party should have regarded him as their chief enemy in the third. But in the 1920s, British Labor Party leaders (as well as pro-Labor intellectuals like Sidney and Beatrice Webb) were decidedly pro-Soviet and were outraged by what they called "Mr. Churchill's Private War" against the young "Workers' State."

For his part, Churchill came to regard the Labor Party as the "advanced guard" of Bolshevism in Britain. A Labor government, he wrote in a letter to *The Times* on January 18, 1924, would cast "a dark and blighting shadow on every form of national life."[15] Thus, when the Liberal Party joined with Labor three days later to defeat the Conservatives and make Labor leader Ramsay MacDonald the new Prime Minister, Churchill rejoined the Tories. Only the Conservative Party, he now declared, offered a strong enough base "for the successful defeat of socialism."[16]

"The Only Hope of Checking the Nazi Onrush"

If Churchill's anti-Bolshevism drove him to the right domestically, his growing alarm about Germany after Hitler came to power in 1933 drove him to the left internationally. Churchill believed that the only way to maintain peace in Europe was by "weaving together a combination of countries strong enough" to deter Hitler's bid for continental hegemony. As part of that combination, Churchill now included the Soviet Union. In his view, it was the Nazis, not the Bolsheviks, who were now the principal menace.

To contain Hitler, the former archenemy of the Bolsheviks advocated a Franco–British–Russian alliance "as the only hope of checking the Nazi onrush."[17] With remarkable frankness, Churchill laid out the reasoning behind this amazing turnaround in a friendly meeting with the Soviet ambassador to Britain, Ivan Maisky, in 1938:

> Twenty years ago I strove with all the energy in my power against Communism, because at that time I considered Communism, with its idea of world revolution, the greatest danger to the British Empire. Now Communism does not present such a danger to the Empire. On the contrary, nowadays German Nazism, with its idea of the world hegemony of Berlin, constitutes the greatest danger for the British Empire. Therefore, at the present time I strive against Hitler with all the energy in my power…. [W]e and you share the same path. This is the reason why I am in favor of close co-operation between England, France and the USSR.[18]

Churchill's words deeply impressed the Soviet emissary. In a cable to Moscow, Maisky wrote that "Churchill is a major and forceful figure, whereas the other members of the cabinet are colorless mediocrities, fearful of letting the wolf into the sheepfold; Churchill can crush all of them especially in the event of some kind of crisis." He then predicted that "Churchill will come to power when the critical moment in England's fortunes arrives."[19]

And that is exactly how it came to pass. In the spring of 1940, at the age of 65, Winston Churchill became Britain's Prime Minister and Minister of Defense, presiding over a war with Germany that he had done everything in his power to prevent. The fall of France the following month, leaving Britain the only nation fighting Nazi Germany, was indeed "the critical moment in England's fortunes."

Isolated in her island fortress, her Atlantic lifeline nearly severed by German submarines, Britain seemed to be in a hopeless position, and Churchill, even after becoming Prime Minister, had to fend off determined efforts by appeasement-minded members of his Cabinet to reach an agreement with Hitler. Nonetheless, Churchill found reasons for optimism. First, he did not think that the 1939 Nazi–Soviet Pact would long endure: It was an "unnatural act."[20] Second, he believed that America's eventual entry into the war would guarantee Hitler's defeat. He proved right on both counts.

Hitler Attacks the Soviet Union

Hitler attacked the Soviet Union on June 22, 1941. The previous evening, Churchill told his private secretary, John Colville, that a German attack on Russia was certain and that Britain would go all-out to help the Russians. When Colville remarked that helping the Russians was a betrayal of everything "the arch anti-Communist" Churchill had stood for, Churchill replied "that he had one single purpose—the destruction of Hitler—and his life was much simplified thereby. If Hitler invaded Hell he would at least make a favorable reference to the Devil."[21]

Churchill knew that a German attack on Russia was imminent because British intelligence had cracked Germany's ultra-secret Enigma code and was able to read encrypted German radio messages detailing forthcoming air, land, and sea operations. In an effort to establish a personal relationship with Stalin and drive a wedge in the Nazi–Soviet alliance, Churchill passed on the information contained in these Ultra intercepts to Stalin. But the Soviet dictator refused to believe that Hitler would start a war without first presenting the Soviet Union with an ultimatum setting forth Germany's political, economic, and territorial demands. Stalin was fully prepared to meet these demands and dismissed Churchill's revelations as a thinly disguised attempt by "the British and their American friends…to push him into a war with Germany."[22]

The news of Hitler's invasion, Colville noted, "produced a smile of satisfaction" on Churchill's face.[23] A number of Churchill's colleagues predicted that Russia could not last six weeks against the German onslaught, but Churchill disagreed: "I will bet you a Monkey to a Mousetrap that the Russians are still fighting, and fighting victoriously, two years from now."[24] On the evening of June 22, without consulting any of his Cabinet members in advance, Churchill offered British economic and military aid to Russia in a broadcast over the BBC:

> The Nazi regime is indistinguishable from the worst features of Communism. It is devoid of all theme and principle except appetite and racial domination. It excels all forms of human wickedness in the efficiency of its cruelty and ferocious aggression. No one has been a more consistent opponent of Communism than I have for the last twenty-five years. I will unsay no word that I have spoken about it. But all this fades away before the spectacle which is now unfolding. The past with its crimes, its follies and its tragedies, flashes away....[25]

In 1942, Churchill's balance-of-power policy culminated in an Anglo–Soviet treaty. But while recognizing that he had to support the lesser enemy (the Soviets) in order to defeat the more menacing aggressor (the Germans), Churchill never mistook this marriage of convenience for a genuine love affair, and neither did the Soviets. In his memoirs, Churchill describes the security arrangements Soviet Foreign Minister Molotov insisted upon when he arrived in England in the spring of 1942 to sign the accord—a startling revelation of Soviet paranoia:

> Extraordinary precautions were taken for Molotov's personal safety. His room [at Chequers, the Prime Minister's country residence] had been thoroughly searched by his police officers, every cupboard and piece of furniture and the walls and floors being meticulously examined by practiced eyes. The bed was the object of particular attention; the mattresses were all prodded in case of infernal machines, and the sheets and blankets were rearranged by the Russians so as to leave an opening in the middle of the bed out of which the occupant could spring at a moment's notice, instead of being tucked in. At night a revolver was laid out beside his dressing gown and his dispatch case.[26]

"A Wonderful Old Tory"

By forcing Hitler to divert the bulk of his military resources to the Russian front, Germany's invasion of the Soviet Union brought desperately needed relief to Britain. But Churchill believed that, in order to win the war and maintain its influence in the postwar world, Britain would have to establish the closest possible association with the United States. To build such a "special relationship," Churchill set out to win the trust of the American President. As he confessed to Colville in 1948, "No lover ever studied every whim of his mistress as I did those of President Roosevelt."[27]

Perhaps one reason why Churchill courted Roosevelt so ardently—frequently referring to himself as Roosevelt's "lieutenant"; quipping famously that "the Prime Minister of Great Britain has nothing to conceal from the President of the United States" when Roosevelt inadvertently entered Churchill's room while the naked Englishman was emerging from his bath; allowing Roosevelt's key aide and alter ego, Harry Hopkins, to sit in on British Cabinet meetings; and, in general, so behaving that the London *Economist*, in a 1945 lead editorial, took Churchill to task for the "humiliation and abasements" that his "policy of appeasement" of the Americans entailed[28]—was his appreciation of the strength of anti-British sentiment in the United States. Indeed, until the Japanese attack on Pearl Harbor and Germany's declaration of war on the United States three days later rendered the entire debate moot, one of the most telling arguments employed by American isolationists was that for America to go to war to save the British Empire would be the height of immorality and hypocrisy.

To a considerable degree, Roosevelt shared these anti-British sentiments. Although he had the greatest respect for Churchill's moral and intellectual qualities, he nonetheless regarded Churchill's conservatism—and particularly his devotion to Empire—as hopelessly antiquated. Roosevelt objected to imperialism on practical as well as moral grounds. "The President said he was concerned about the brown people in the East," recalled his adviser, Charles Taussig. "He said that there are 1,000,000,000 brown people. In many Eastern countries, they are ruled by a handful of whites and they resent it. Our goal must be to help them achieve independence—1,000,000,000 potential enemies are dangerous."[29]

Roosevelt also objected to Churchill's devotion to what Americans referred to disparagingly as "power politics." In Roosevelt's view, Great Power rivalries, rooted in Europe's obsession with the balance of power, spheres of influence, and colonial expansion, had resulted in two terrible wars in the course of his lifetime. For the world to avoid similar calamities in the future, the postwar international order would have to be recast along radically new lines. Thus, when Roosevelt said of Churchill, "Isn't he a wonderful old Tory to have on our side," the implication was clear: So long as war continued to rage, Churchill's virtues outweighed his vices; once the war was over, however, and a new world order had to be fashioned, the qualities that had made the "old Tory" such a splendid comrade-in-arms would transform him into a political embarrassment.

But while Roosevelt knew exactly what he was *against*—colonialism and Great Power politics—he was much vaguer about what he was for. In May 1942, during Molotov's visit to the White House, Roosevelt told him that "the United States, England, and Russia and perhaps China should police the world and enforce disarmament by inspection." When an incredulous Molotov asked Roosevelt whether that was "a final and considered judgment," Roosevelt assured him that it was.[30]

Roosevelt's proposal must have struck Molotov as a transparent attempt to carve up the postwar world, and there were indeed serious difficulties with the Four Policemen concept that lent credence to such an interpretation. The first, and most obvious, problem was how to guarantee that the four Great Powers adhered to the liberal-democratic values that Roosevelt himself cherished. In other words, "Who would police the policemen?" The second problem, inherent in the first, was how to prevent Roosevelt's idealistic plan for perpetual peace from degenerating into a traditional spheres-of-influence arrangement whereby the major powers, each staking out a part of the world as its special "beat," ended up dominating and exploiting the now-disarmed smaller states entrusted to their tender mercies.

Roosevelt never answered these questions satisfactorily. He remained convinced, however, that transforming the Soviet Union from a revolutionary power intent on overthrowing the international order into a status quo power devoted to policing it was a key—perhaps *the* key—to a lasting peace. As he cabled Churchill on September 28, 1944,

> I think we are all in agreement…as to the necessity of having the USSR as a fully accepted and equal member of any association of the great powers formed for the purpose of preventing international war. It should be possible to accomplish this by adjusting our differences through compromises by all the parties concerned.[31]

"I Am Trying to Restrain Stalin"

Churchill, however, was not at all convinced "as to the necessity" of admitting the Soviet Union into the circle of peace-loving states. On the contrary, as he told General Charles de Gaulle on November 12 in newly liberated Paris,

> At present Russia is a great beast which has been starved for a long time. It is not possible to prevent her from eating, especially as she is now in the middle of the herd of her victims. But she must be kept from devouring everything. I am trying to restrain Stalin, who has a large appetite, but is not devoid of common sense.[32]

Churchill's apprehensions about the Soviet Union's "large appetite" had grown more acute as Germany's defeat drew closer. In the early stages of the war, he tried to dismiss such concerns, arguing that the United States and Great Britain, working together, could easily contain the Russians if the need arose. "No one can foresee how the balance of power will lie or where the winning armies will stand at the end of the war," he told his Foreign Minister, Anthony Eden, in 1942. "It seems probable, however, that the United States and the British Empire, far from being exhausted, will be the most powerfully armed and economic *bloc* the world has ever seen, and that the Soviet Union will need our aid for reconstruction far more than we shall need theirs."[33]

Churchill's basic assumption—that the United States and Great Britain would concert their policies toward Moscow—proved mistaken. The first indication that Roosevelt intended to pursue an independent line occurred on March 18, 1942. "I know you will not mind my being brutally frank when I tell you that I think I can personally handle Stalin better than your Foreign Office or my State Department," he wrote Churchill. "Stalin hates the guts of all your top people. He thinks he likes me better and I hope he will continue to do so."[34]

Relying on the dubious expertise of advisers like Joseph E. Davies,[35] a former American ambassador to the Soviet Union, Roosevelt persuaded himself that the anti-Western features of Stalinist rule were essentially defensive in character. Besieged from birth by formidable enemies, not the least of whom was Winston Churchill, the Bolsheviks had naturally come to distrust, and even hate, the "imperialist" powers. If Roosevelt hoped to win Stalin's trust and transform him into one of his Four Policemen, he would have to distance himself from Churchill's Britain.

In May, Roosevelt wrote a letter, addressed to Stalin and delivered personally by Davies, suggesting a meeting "on either side of the Bering Straits" between Stalin and himself, but without Churchill. It was to be "an informal and completely simple visit for a few days between you and me," Roosevelt proposed, to achieve "a meeting of minds."[36] When Churchill learned of Roosevelt's attempt to exclude him and expressed his distress, Roosevelt simply lied. "I did not suggest to U.J. ["Uncle Joe" Stalin] that we meet alone," he wrote to Churchill on June 28— even though that was precisely what he had suggested.[37]

Teheran: "A Bloody Lot Has Gone Wrong"

Roosevelt's cold-shouldering of Churchill came at the worst possible moment. With the surrender of German forces at Stalingrad in February 1943 and Russia's victory in the great tank battle of Kursk in July, it became increasingly evident to Churchill that Hitler's downfall was only a matter of time and that Stalin's Russia would emerge as the dominant

European power unless it were contained by countervailing Anglo–American might. Yet all of Churchill's efforts to meet with Roosevelt to forge a common policy toward Russia in advance of the Teheran Conference, where the Big Three were to meet from November 28 to December 1, 1943, to begin addressing postwar issues, were rebuffed by the suddenly elusive American President. As Churchill told British diplomat and future Prime Minister Harold Macmillan while en route to Teheran:

> Cromwell was a great man but he had one failing. He had been brought up in the tradition of the Armada to believe that Spain was still a great power. He made the mistake of supporting France against Spain and thereby establishing France as a great power. Do you think that that will be said of me? Germany is finished, though it may take some time to clean up the mess. The real problem now is Russia. I *can't* get the Americans to see it.[38]

Churchill's frustrations were echoed by his personal physician, Charles Wilson, later Lord Moran. "What I found so shocking," wrote Lord Moran in his diary, "is that to the Americans the P.M. [Prime Minister] is the villain of the piece; they are far more skeptical of him than they are of Stalin. Anyway, whoever is to blame, it is clear that we are going to Teheran without a common plan."[39]

The Teheran Conference confirmed Churchill's worst fears. Not only did Roosevelt immediately arrange a private meeting with Stalin, but he even accepted a Soviet invitation to take up residence in the Russian embassy compound. Although this was a remarkable demonstration of trust in Stalin's good offices—in striking contrast to Molotov's insistence, during his visit to Chequers the previous year, that a gun be placed at his bedside—it is unlikely that the paranoid Stalin appreciated Roosevelt's gesture. According to former Soviet Foreign Minister Andrei Gromyko, Stalin once asked him, "Is Roosevelt clever?" This suggests that he viewed Roosevelt's attempts to ingratiate himself as a mark of naiveté, not statesmanship.[40]

Roosevelt also did not hesitate to joke with Stalin at Churchill's expense. On one such occasion, Roosevelt later recalled,

> Winston got red and scowled, and the more he did so, the more Stalin smiled. Finally, Stalin broke into a big hearty guffaw, and for the first time in three days I saw light. I kept it up until Stalin was laughing with me, and it was then that I called him "Uncle Joe."… The ice was broken and we talked like men and brothers.[41]

By such childish pranks did an American President seek to gain a cruel tyrant's trust.

Finally, and perhaps most alarmingly to Churchill, it was at Teheran that Roosevelt, at Stalin's insistence, decided against Churchill's proposal for an invasion of Europe through the Balkans and opted for a cross-Channel operation instead. Churchill's controversial plan, which envisioned opening a second front in Southeastern Europe through Italy, would have ensured that Allied troops arrived in the Balkans ahead of Soviet forces. The plan for an Allied invasion of Europe that Stalin and Roosevelt adopted, on the other hand, virtually sealed the fate of the Balkans as a zone of Soviet influence. No wonder that when asked whether the sessions at Teheran had gone well, Churchill replied, "A bloody lot has gone wrong."[42]

The 1943 Teheran Conference marked a crucial turning point in Anglo–American relations. Until Teheran, Churchill could continue to believe that the Anglo–American–Soviet alliance was an association of equals; after Teheran, it was clear that Roosevelt and Stalin dominated the alliance and that Churchill was, at best, a junior partner. Even worse, from Churchill's point of view, was the fact that the senior American partner was pursuing a policy—appeasing Stalin—that was bound to end in disaster. What, then, was Churchill to do? Should he confront Roosevelt and risk losing whatever remaining influence he still enjoyed with the Americans, or should he play along, try to conclude the best deals possible with Stalin, and hope for the best?

Churchill found it exceedingly difficult to resolve this dilemma. As his personal physician, Lord Moran, noted in his diary in October 1944:

All this havering, these conflicting and contradictory policies, are, I am sure, due to Winston's exhaustion. He seems torn between two lines of action: he cannot decide whether to make one last attempt to enlist Roosevelt's sympathy for a firmer line with Stalin, in the hope that he has learnt from the course of events, or whether to make his peace with Stalin and save what he can from the wreck of Allied hopes. At one moment he will plead with the President for a common front against Communism and the next he will make a bid for Stalin's friendship. Sometimes the two alternate with bewildering rapidity.[43]

Poland and Yalta

Nowhere was Churchill's ambivalence more evident than in his approach to Poland's postwar future. At the second gathering of the Big Three at Yalta in February 1945, Churchill succeeded in persuading himself that Stalin's pledge to hold free elections in Poland "within a month" meant that Poland would regain her independence after the war. In exchange for this pledge, both Roosevelt and Churchill acceded to Stalin's demand that only those Poles deemed "democratic" should be allowed to join Polish Communists and Communist sympathizers in the current provisional government. Later, when he had returned to England, Churchill tried to put the best face possible on the Yalta accords. He even went so far as to assure the House of Commons on February 27, 1945, that "I know of no government which stands to its own obligations, even its own despite, more solidly than the Russian Soviet Government."[44]

In private, however, Churchill was far less certain about the worth of Stalin's Polish promises. On February 25, Colville recorded in his diary that

The Prime Minister was rather depressed, thinking of the possibilities of Russia one day turning against us, saying that Chamberlain had trusted Hitler as he was now trusting Stalin (though he thought in different circumstances), but taking comfort, as far as Russia went, in the proverb about the trees not growing up to the sky.

Two days later, wrote Colville, "The P.M. made a speech in the House about the Crimea [Yalta] Conference and in particular about Poland.... He is trying to persuade himself that all is well, but in his heart I think that he is worried about Poland and not convinced of the strength of our moral position." And on February 28, upon learning that Stalin had just imposed a Communist government on Romania, Churchill assured Colville that things would work out differently in Poland: "As we went to bed, after 2:00 a.m., the P.M. said to me, 'I have not the slightest intention of being cheated over Poland, not even if we go to the verge of war with Russia.'"[45]

On March 6, 1945, Churchill learned that only Moscow's nominees were being allowed to join Poland's new government, contrary to Stalin's promise at Yalta that all three Great Powers would have to agree on the "democratic" credentials of the handful of non-Communist Poles to be included. Churchill realized that he had been duped. "This made it clear," he informed the Cabinet, "that the Russians were not going to carry out the conditions on which we had agreed."[46] The next day, when he discovered that in newly "liberated" Poland two sealed trains, each filled with 2,000 Polish priests, teachers, and intellectuals, had been sent by the Russians to labor camps on the Volga, Churchill asked that the information be sent on to Roosevelt. The long debate that he had conducted with himself over whether he should seek Stalin's friendship or try to enlist Roosevelt in an Anglo–American bid to contain Stalin was concluded. The old British lion had decided to have it out at last with the rampant Russian bear.

Once Churchill decided that Roosevelt must be persuaded to join him in an anti-Soviet coalition, he pursued his goal with Churchillian tenacity, bombarding the American President with so many alarming cables that on March 17 he felt constrained to apologize to a grievously ill Roosevelt for his persistence. Typical of Churchill's messages was a

March 13 telegram deploring the "great failure and…utter breakdown of what was settled at Yalta," but arguing that through "combined dogged pressure and persistence" America and Britain might yet save the day.[47]

Roosevelt, however, was extremely reluctant to get drawn into a confrontation with Stalin over Poland. His basic approach was expressed by his Secretary of State, Cordell Hull, during an October 1943 conference of foreign ministers in Moscow. Pressed by the American ambassador to Russia, Averell Harriman, to discuss Poland's eastern borders with Molotov, Hull replied, "I don't want to deal with these piddling little things. We must deal with the main issues."[48] To Roosevelt, the "main issues" in 1945, as in 1943, concerned the establishment of a new world order based on cooperation between the Four Policemen; compared with that glittering vision, Poland and her problems truly were "piddling little things."

Thus, far from sharing Churchill's alarm at Stalin's misbehavior, Roosevelt counseled patience. "I would minimize the general Soviet problem as much as possible," he wrote Churchill on April 11, "because these problems, in one form or another, seem to arise every day and most of them straighten out…."[49] This was Roosevelt's final word on Russia. The next day, he died.

Truman and Potsdam

Churchill did not attempt to woo the new American President, Harry Truman, quite so ardently as he had pursued FDR, but his basic message was unchanged: In the face of the utter breakdown of the Yalta accords, Anglo–American unity was essential for the preservation of world peace. Churchill spelled out his concerns to Truman most clearly in a May 12 message. Expressing his "deep anxiety" over Russia's "attitude towards Poland, their overwhelming influence in the Balkans…and above all their power to maintain very large armies in the field for a long time," Churchill urged Truman to join him in reaching a "settlement" with Russia now, "before we weaken our armies mortally" through withdrawal and demobilization and "our strength is gone."[50]

But while Churchill believed that the best route to a settlement with Russia was through the coordination of Anglo–American approaches, Truman was persuaded by his advisers that Churchill was merely trying to upgrade his status from junior to senior partner by displacing Stalin. He therefore dispatched the ubiquitous Joseph E. Davies to London to convince Churchill that it would be best if Truman and Stalin first met alone. An indignant Churchill immediately informed Truman "that I should not be prepared to attend a meeting which was a continuation of a conference between you and Marshal Stalin…. I consider that at this Victory meeting…at which subjects of the greatest consequence are to be discussed, we three should meet simultaneously and on equal terms."[51]

When the Big Three met for the third and last time at Potsdam from July 17 to August 2, 1945, no common Anglo–American understanding had been reached, despite all of Churchill's urgings to the contrary. To his credit, Truman did not seek to ingratiate himself with Stalin the way Roosevelt had, but neither did he lend strong support to Churchill in his verbal duels with Stalin. Instead, he fell naturally into the role of mediator between the Russians and the British. When, for example, Churchill and Stalin clashed over the demarcation of Poland's western boundary (the Eastern Niesse vs. the Western Niesse), Truman opined that he "could not understand the urgency of the matter" and suggested that the issue be given over to the foreign ministers for further discussion.[52] Churchill did not agree and resumed his attack, leading a British observer, Admiral Cunningham, to note in his diary that "The PM is certainly keeping up his end but Truman is holding back and not giving him much support."[53]

In the midst of these proceedings, Churchill announced that he and Clement Attlee, the Labor Party leader who accompanied him to Potsdam, would return to England so they could be present when the results of the general election were announced on July 26. Churchill's renewed confrontation with the Soviet Union had re-ignited his loathing for socialism, and he made anti-socialism a centerpiece of his re-election campaign. "No socialist government conducting the entire life and industry of the country," he warned in a June 4 political broadcast, "could afford to allow free, sharp or violently-worded expressions of public discontent. They would have to fall back on some form of Gestapo, no doubt very humanely directed in the first instance."[54] Fortunately for Labor, the notion that Attlee, Churchill's mild-mannered deputy, was a potential Heinrich Himmler struck most British voters as preposterous: Labor won the 1945 election by a landslide.

Labor's victory meant that Attlee, Britain's new Prime Minister, returned to Potsdam without Churchill. He and Truman subsequently agreed to a far greater enlargement of Soviet-dominated Poland than Churchill thought wise. On August 7, the day after the United States dropped an atomic bomb on Hiroshima, Churchill told a friend that had he been re-elected, he could have persuaded the Americans to use their new weapon "to restrain the Russians." He also would have provoked "a show-down with Stalin and told him he had got to behave reasonably and decently in Europe, and would have gone so far as to be brusque and angry with him if needs be." Truman and his advisers, Churchill claimed, had shown "weakness in this policy."[55]

"An Overwhelming Assurance of Security"

When Churchill, now out of office, looked back at Potsdam, he could not help but regard it as a historic opportunity gone awry. At the opening of the conference, it appeared to him that all the pieces were in place for a major showdown with Stalin. The American and British armies were still in Europe; the new American President was not nearly as enamored of Stalin as his predecessor had been; and the atomic bomb, a weapon of unprecedented power, had just been tested successfully in New Mexico. All that remained was for Churchill, with his incomparable persuasive power, to bring these pieces together to yield a "settlement" with Stalin that acknowledged Russia's genuine security needs but prevented her from surrounding the states of Eastern and Central Europe with an Iron Curtain.

Yet just as Churchill was about to make his move, an ill-informed electorate (Churchill had always been skeptical of universal suffrage) yanked him rudely off the stage of history, leaving it to what Churchill must have considered two well-meaning mediocrities—Truman and Attlee—to handle Stalin on their own. Naturally, they fumbled it, and it therefore became Churchill's task, as leader of the opposition, to advocate a course of action that would complete the unfinished business of Potsdam.

When President Truman invited him to lecture at Westminster College in Fulton, Missouri, Churchill seized the opportunity to make his case. Echoing and enlarging on many of the themes in his May 12 telegram to Truman, Churchill's famous "Iron Curtain" speech, delivered on March 5, 1946, was essentially a plea for Anglo–American unity in a forthcoming showdown with Stalin.

"From Stettin in the Baltic to Trieste in the Adriatic," Churchill declared, "an iron curtain has descended across the Continent. Behind that line lie all the capitals of the ancient states of central and eastern Europe." Preventing this unnatural division of Europe from exploding into a third world war, he warned, meant reaching a "settlement" with Russia *now*:

> Our difficulties and dangers will not be removed by closing our eyes to them. They will not be removed by mere waiting to see what happens; nor will they be relieved by a policy of appeasement. What is needed is a settlement, and the longer this is delayed the more difficult it will be and the greater our dangers will become.

The key to an overall settlement, Churchill continued, was Anglo–American strength:

> From what I have seen of our Russian friends and allies during the war, I am convinced that there is nothing they admire so much as strength, and there is nothing for which they have less respect than for military weakness. For that reason the old doctrine of a balance of power is unsound. We cannot afford, if we can help it, to work on narrow margins, offering temptations to a trial of strength.

Instead, the Soviets would have to be confronted with an overwhelming display of Anglo–American resolve and strength. Only then would they agree to "the establishment of freedom and democracy as rapidly as possible in all countries":

> If the population of the English-speaking Commonwealth be added to that of the United States, with all that such cooperation implies in the air, on the sea, and in science and industry, there will be no quivering, precarious balance of power to offer its temptation to ambition or adventure. On the contrary, there will be an overwhelming assurance of security.... If all the British moral and material forces and convictions are joined with your own in fraternal association, the highroads of the future will be clear, not only for us but for all, not only for our time but for a century to come.[56]

Churchill's Iron Curtain speech is sometimes taken to mark the onset of the Cold War, but its immediate impact on the conduct of U.S. foreign policy was actually rather limited. In the aftermath of the Second World War, as of the First, the last thing most people on either side of the Atlantic wanted was a major showdown with Russia. President Truman in particular still believed that, as Roosevelt's successor, he was duty-bound to carry out Roosevelt's foreign policy, and that meant Soviet–American cooperation, not confrontation. Shortly after Churchill's Fulton address, he therefore wrote a letter to Stalin offering to accompany him to Missouri, where he might present his side of the story. The Soviet dictator—perhaps wondering whether *all* Americans were children—declined Truman's invitation.[57]

Recreating the European Family

But if Churchill's Fulton speech was less influential than is commonly thought, the address he delivered in Switzerland six months later had a major impact. Speaking at the University of Zurich on September 19, 1946, Churchill called for the creation of "a kind of United States of Europe." The question, he told his audience, was where to

start. Churchill answered his own query with a proposal "that will as-
tonish you.... The first step in the re-creation of the European family
must be a partnership between France and Germany. In this way only
can France recover the moral leadership of Europe. There can be no
revival of Europe without a spiritually great France and a spiritually
great Germany."[58]

When Churchill delivered these remarks, what struck most observers
was his willingness, as *The Times* put it, to include Germany "within the
unity he postulates."[59] Even more important was his conclusion. After
calling on France and Germany to take the lead in creating a United
States of Europe, Churchill said that Britain and the British Common-
wealth, as well as "mighty America, and I trust Soviet Russia—for then
indeed all would be well"—must be the "friends and sponsors of the
new Europe, and must champion its right to live and shine."[60] These
words, it turned out, had an important influence on the formation of
the Marshall Plan:

> [O]n June 12, [1947], in introducing his Plan at a news
> conference, General [George C.] Marshall...declared
> that it was Churchill's call for a United Europe, in his
> Zurich speech in September 1946, that had influenced
> Marshall's belief that the European states could work
> out their own economic recovery, with financial help
> from the United States.[61]

Indeed, the way Churchill proposed to create a United Europe—by
having the Europeans settle their differences first and then look to the
U.S. for support—was precisely the way the Marshall Plan approached
Europe's economic reconstruction. And when NATO was created, the
same Churchillian pattern was followed: Only after the West Europeans
formed their own defense organization—the Western European Union—
did they turn to the U.S. for support.[62] Churchill thus emerges as a
prime mover in two of the West's most important Cold War initiatives:
the Marshall Plan and NATO.

As far as Western policy toward the Soviet Union was concerned, however, Churchill's was still a voice in the wilderness. Nonetheless, Churchill continued to press his case, both privately and publicly, for a diplomatic showdown with the Russians as soon as possible, while the West still enjoyed a fleeting atomic monopoly. For example, after a meeting with the former Prime Minister on April 17, 1948, the American ambassador to Great Britain, Lewis Douglas, reported to Washington that "[Churchill] believes that now is the time, promptly, to tell the Soviets that if they do not retire from Berlin and abandon Eastern Germany, withdrawing to the Polish frontier, we will raze their cities."[63]

In his public remarks, Churchill was more circumspect, but his meaning was still clear. In a speech at Llandudno, Wales, on October 9, 1948, he explained why it was essential for the West to settle with Russia quickly, while it still had the power:

> The question is asked: What will happen when they [the Russians] get the atomic bomb themselves and have accumulated a large store? You can judge yourselves what will happen then by what is happening now. If these things are done in the green wood, what will be done in the dry?... No one in his senses can believe that we have a limitless period of time before us. We ought to bring matters to a head and make a final settlement. We ought not to go jogging along, improvident, incompetent, waiting for something to turn up, by which I mean waiting for something bad for us to turn up. The Western Nations will be far more likely to reach a lasting settlement without bloodshed, if they formulate their just demands while they have the atomic power and before the Russian Communists have got it too.[64]

That time was working against the West, and that it was necessary to force a diplomatic showdown with Russia quickly, was also the theme of a major speech Churchill delivered to the House of Commons on November 30, 1950:

> [W]hile it is right to build up our forces as fast as we
> can, nothing in this process, in the period I have men-
> tioned, will deprive Russia of effective superiority in
> what are called now the conventional arms. All that it
> will do is to give us increasing unity in Europe and
> magnify the deterrence against aggression.... There-
> fore I am in favor of efforts to reach a settlement with
> Soviet Russia as soon as a suitable opportunity pre-
> sents itself, and of making those efforts while the im-
> mense and measureless superiority of the United States
> atomic bomb organization offsets the Soviet predomi-
> nance in every other military respect.[65]

Even after being elected Prime Minister again in 1951, Churchill continued to dream of picking up where he had left off in July 1945 and bringing the Potsdam Conference to a successful conclusion through a grand diplomatic showdown with Stalin. "W[inston] has several times revealed to me his hopes of a joint approach to Stalin," Colville re-corded in his diary on August 25, 1952, "proceeding perhaps to a con-gress in Vienna where the Potsdam Conference would be reopened and concluded. If the Russians were uncooperative, the Cold War would be intensified by us."[66]

The Ultimate Vindication

Despite Churchill's immense prestige, however, neither Harry Truman nor his successor, Dwight Eisenhower, was prepared to follow his lead. From their point of view, Churchill's call for a showdown culminating in a grand diplomatic settlement was both too hard and too soft. It was too hard in the sense that public opinion in the United States would never tolerate a policy of deliberate nuclear saber rattling. It was too soft because, given the Soviet Union's ideologically based hostility to the West, no diplomatic settlement with Moscow was likely to endure. Far better, they reasoned, to adopt a policy of containment which promised to bring about a major ideological change of heart in the Soviet leader-ship without committing the United States to futile negotiations on the one hand or dangerous brinksmanship on the other.[67]

But Churchill had a powerful case. The containment policy developed by Truman and subscribed to (despite some rhetorical bluster to the contrary) by Eisenhower initially depended on America's nuclear superiority, which could be used to offset the Soviet Union's conventional supremacy. Nuclear superiority, however, was a wasting asset. Sooner or later, the Soviet Union would acquire its own threatening nuclear arsenal, at which point the West would be forced to offset Soviet conventional forces with similar forces of its own.

Did the indolent, pleasure-loving Western democracies have the stomach for such a course? Churchill doubted it. He had seen how they had sought to appease Hitler rather than risk a conventional war against Germany, and he had no reason to suppose that they would behave any differently toward Stalin's heirs. Better, then, to force a settlement now, before the inevitable rot set in.

The questions Churchill raised about the strategy of containment were never put to rest intellectually during his lifetime; even Churchill, old and ailing, set them aside during his lackluster second term. But in 1981, the newly elected American President, Ronald Reagan, accepted the validity of Churchill's critique. It was clear to him that containment had not succeeded either in preventing Soviet expansion or in modifying Soviet ideology. On the contrary, when Reagan came into office it seemed as though the global balance of power was beginning to tilt in Moscow's favor—a perception eagerly exploited by Soviet spokesmen as proof of "socialism's" superiority.

As for détente, the policy the United States had adopted in the hope containing Soviet adventurism, it struck Reagan as little more than a contemporary version of appeasement. It followed that if the United States ever hoped to win the Cold War, it had to adopt a Churchillian course by renewing its faith in the righteousness of its cause; playing to its economic, technological, and political strengths; and seizing the initiative *now*, before Soviet gains became truly irreversible.

That is precisely what Ronald Reagan did.

3 Konrad Adenauer

Opting for the West

Konrad Adenauer: Opting for the West

On September 25, 1944, a distinguished, elderly German who had served as the Lord Mayor of the great Rhineland city of Cologne throughout the ill-fated Weimar Republic's brief existence was hauled into Brauweiler prison by the Gestapo. The warden of Brauweiler, who had known the new arrival in earlier times, accompanied him to the clothing depot, where the prisoner was deprived of his suspenders, shoelaces, and pocket knife. "Now please don't commit suicide," the warden mockingly told his new charge. "You would only cause me no end of trouble. You're 68 years old, and your life is over anyway."[1]

The aged ex-mayor was then placed in a cell directly above the room where prisoners were tortured. As he lay on his straw mattress at night, drenched in sweat, he could hear their screams. During the day, he was able to observe the constant round of executions from his window, including the hanging of a 16-year-old boy. Although the old man himself escaped execution, these events traumatized him. Years later, on his deathbed, he would imagine that he was back in Brauweiler: "Now they are locking an old man in prison," he would cry out in his delirium.[2]

In 1944, however, Konrad Adenauer's death was still 23 tumultuous years away. In 1949, at the age of 73, he became Chancellor of West Germany, and he held that office for 14 years—longer than the entire span of the Weimar Republic. During this period, he presided over West Germany's transformation from international pariah into respected member of the Western alliance. He helped spark the "economic miracle" that turned West Germany into the economic powerhouse of Western

Europe. He was personally responsible for West Germany's effort to make financial amends to Israel and the Jewish people for the Holocaust.

And perhaps most important, at the height of the Cold War, when West Germany might well have adopted a neutralist or even pro-Soviet foreign policy orientation, it was Konrad Adenauer who ensured that his nation would be aligned, closely and unambiguously, with the West. "Whoever has Germany has Europe," Lenin had said in 1918.[3] Adenauer kept West Germany, and therefore Western Europe, out of Soviet hands.

Friend and foe alike attributed Adenauer's stance to a harsh and unbending anti-Communism. He was regarded as the ultimate Cold Warrior, and there was much truth in this contention: Adenauer despised the Soviet Union with every fiber of his being. But at the heart of his approach to foreign policy was a distrust of nationalism. To Adenauer, nationalism was a modern form of idolatry: the worship of a man-made object—the state—instead of God. Having seen how nationalism had encouraged the Germans to ignore God's laws and commit unspeakable crimes during Hitler's Third Reich, he was determined to stamp out the nationalist temptation once and for all by anchoring post-World War II Germany firmly within a wider community—the democratic, Christian West.

It was, therefore, anti-nationalism as much as anti-communism that made Adenauer such a firm Western ally. And in 1989, when the Berlin Wall collapsed and serious negotiations over German reunification began, it was Adenauer's policy that finally prevailed: West Germany absorbed East Germany without surrendering her membership in NATO or any of her other ties to the West.

"Do Your Duty!"

Konrad Adenauer was born in the old fortress-city of Cologne in Germany's Rhineland on January 5, 1876. His parents, Johann and Helene, were far from well-off, and until he was 17 years old, Konrad shared a bed with his brother Hans. (He also had another brother, August, and a sister, Louise.) The Adenauers were strict, hard-working, deeply pious Catholics, and throughout his long life, Adenauer would

go to Church on Sunday, fast on Lent, and—even during trips abroad—
try to attend Mass. According to his principal German biographer, Hans-
Peter Schwarz,

> References to hell-fire and purgatory were a frequent
> part of his parental discipline. His children were con-
> vinced that their father retained a literal faith in these
> terrors for many years. Fear of God and God's wrath
> were a cardinal element of his religious beliefs, and it
> was only in later years that he began to question the
> truth of at least some of these dogmas.[4]

Adenauer was born in the midst of the *Kulturkampf*, or Culture War,
waged by the Iron Chancellor, Prussian aristocrat Otto von Bismarck,
against Germany's Roman Catholic Church, which Bismarck regarded
as a state within a state and a threat to the new Reich's unity. Many of
Adenauer's critics have argued that this struggle left the devoutly Catholic Adenauer deeply embittered against "heathen," Protestant Prussia
and that anti-Prussianism (the belief that the largely Catholic Rhineland
had more in common with Catholic France than with Protestant Prussia
and was in fact better off with historic Prussia under Soviet control) was
the key to his foreign policy.[5]

This reading of Adenauer's career, however, is almost surely wrong.
True, he did tell British military intelligence officer Noel Annan (later
Lord Annan) in 1945 that "the greatest mistake that the English ever
made in their relations with Germany" had been "at the Congress of
Vienna, when you so foolishly put Prussia on the Rhine as a safeguard
against France and another Napoleon."[6] But this also was Adenauer's
first known anti-Prussian outburst and, coming at the age of 69, hardly
suggests a life-long antipathy.

The truth is that, despite considerable resentment against Bismarck
and Prussian Protestantism, there was no "break away from Prussia
movement" in the Catholic Rhineland during the *Kulturkampf*. Most
Rhinelanders were loyal subjects of Prussia and the Reich who hoped,
through the formation of the Catholic Center Party, to reform the Prussian state, not to leave it. And when Bismarck abandoned his anti-Catho-

lic campaign in 1886, Rhineland Catholics came to regard the conservative Prussian throne as a valuable ally against their secular Liberal and Social Democratic opponents.

Moreover, whatever resentment the Adenauers may have felt toward Prussia was more than offset by the fact that the head of the family, Johann Adenauer, was a proud veteran of Prussia's wars, having fought in both the Austro–Prussian War of 1866 and the Franco–Prussian War of 1870–1871. In the Austro–Prussian War, Sergeant Adenauer distinguished himself during the battle of Königgrätz, becoming one of only three non-commissioned officers to receive a battlefield promotion to full officer status.

After leaving the army to marry Helene, Johann became a mid-level civil servant in the justice administration of Cologne. His colleagues regarded him as a stern, conscientious man who, though not particularly likable, was "the very model of a Prussian civil servant."[7] Deeply ambitious for his three sons, he continually stressed the importance of doing one's duty. When his eldest son, August, abandoned his homework one day to observe a fire that raged through Cologne, the old soldier took him sharply to task: "Even if they fire guns beside you, you have to stay with your work."[8] As an old man, Konrad Adenauer would attribute his success in life to his father's undeviating rule: "Do your duty!"

The youthful Konrad Adenauer was neither brilliant nor self-confident. On the contrary, both as a child and as a young man, he was painfully shy, and his face reddened when he was spoken to. Despite considerable effort, his grades were generally mediocre. "The two factors which do stand out in his childhood, as in later life," writes Schwarz, "were religious conviction and a capacity for hard work."[9]

Had Adenauer followed his natural inclinations, he probably would have become either a botanist or a professional gardener, since he retained a passion for flowers throughout his life. Instead, he followed his brother August into the legal profession (brother Hans became a priest). Unlike August, Adenauer showed no particular aptitude for the law, but he pursued his course work at the universities of Munich and Freiburg with his characteristic diligence, sometimes placing his bare feet into a bucket of ice water to avoid dozing off over his books. In 1901, he was licensed to practice law, after which he spent four and a half years training for the Prussian civil service. Finally, in 1906, he obtained a position in the justice administration of his native Cologne. Like his father, he became a model Prussian civil servant. Unlike his father, he was a *senior* civil servant.

Thus far, Adenauer's life resembled that of countless other young men of lower middle-class origins who, through sheer perseverance and sacrifice, succeed in making their way into the professional classes. But in 1906, he did something most unusual for a Prussian civil servant: He decided to enter politics.

In those days, both the Lord Mayor of Cologne and his dozen adjuncts, or deputies, were elected by the City Council, which was dominated by local representatives of the Center and Liberal parties. Learning that one of these deputies had suddenly resigned and that Dr. Kausen, the leader of Cologne's Center Party, was planning to replace him with a young judge from Saarbrucken, Adenauer entered Kausen's office and asked, "Why not take me, Herr *Justizrat*? I'm sure I'm just as good as the other fellow."[10] Impressed by the young man's boldness, Kausen supported Adenauer's candidacy, and on March 7, 1906, Konrad Adenauer became the youngest of the Lord Mayor's adjuncts.[11]

By this time, Adenauer was not only married, but also a proud young father. His wife, Emma, came from one of Cologne's best families, and it was through his in-laws' connections, as well as Dr. Kausen's efforts, that Adenauer was elected adjunct. But Emma's health was precarious, and in 1910, after she had given birth to their third child, the doctors told Adenauer that she was terminally ill. Not wanting to worry Emma, he kept the news to himself.

He now taxed his considerable powers of self-discipline to their utmost, putting in 12-hour days at the office, looking after his increasingly helpless wife in the evenings, and then working on his papers into the early hours of the morning. In 1916, Emma died, leaving Adenauer a widower with three young children to raise. Many years later, Adenauer's brother-in-law recalled that "the way this man, overburdened with work as he was, stood by my sister during her illness was in my view a greater achievement than anything he's ever done in politics."[12]

Adenauer's capacity for hard work was duly noted by members of Cologne's City Council, and when Lord Mayor Max Wallraf resigned in 1917, they decided to offer Adenauer the job. As it happened, he was in the hospital at the time, recovering from a serious car accident, so two members of the Council were dispatched to the hospital to ascertain whether the accident had affected Adenauer's mental powers. Sensing their concerns, he said, "Gentlemen, it's only outwardly that my head isn't quite right."[13] Everyone laughed, Adenauer was offered the job, and the City Council elected him by an overwhelming vote. On September 18, 1917, at the age of 41, Konrad Adenauer became Lord Mayor of Cologne and the youngest mayor in all of Prussia.

Adenauer came into his own during the brief revolutionary upsurge at the end of World War I. In November 1918, Cologne was occupied by mutinous German soldiers and sailors who sought to govern the city through "Workers' and Soldiers' Councils." Adenauer entered into negotiations with the rebels and, through sheer force of character, managed to dominate them. Working 18 to 20 hours a day, he saw to it that law and order were maintained, that field kitchens operated around the clock, and that soldiers returning from the front surrendered their arms before receiving their pay and discharge papers.

Throughout this ordeal, according to one military observer, "Adenauer remained absolutely calm and unruffled.... This man, I felt, was a true Commander-in-Chief."[14] In the end, Adenauer's self-image was transformed. As Hans-Peter Schwarz writes,

> Adenauer's self-assurance, which was so obvious to observers in the years to come, appears to have developed as a result of these experiences. During the upheaval, both the public and Adenauer himself came to recognize his leadership qualities. Subsequently his sense of superiority was marked; his cool and pitiless observation of human beings in action convinced him

that, in times of crisis, most people were either foolish, emotional or doctrinaire—or a combination of the three.[15]

"A Fair and Just Game"

Shortly after Germany's defeat in World War I, Cologne was occupied by the British, and Adenauer's relationship with the occupiers was often tense. Nevertheless, when British troops left Cologne in 1926, Adenauer called on his countrymen to recognize, "despite the many troubles we've had to bear, that in the political field our departed adversary has played a fair and just game."[16]

But if Britain's policy during its occupation of the northern Rhineland was, in Adenauer's view, "fair and just," the same could not be said of France's policy in the southern Rhineland. The French were convinced that their future security required detaching the Rhineland from Germany and bringing it, either directly or indirectly, under French control. Recognizing that this policy posed a mortal threat to the Rhineland's German identity, in January 1919 Adenauer convened a conference in Cologne to develop an appropriate response. A record of the three-hour speech he delivered to this conference survives, and while the course of action he demanded was not adopted, it is significant nonetheless, for it illustrates Adenauer's intuitive grasp of foreign affairs and foreshadows, in many respects, the approach he would take as Chancellor of West Germany.

Adenauer began by telling his audience that one should approach questions of foreign policy as clinically and objectively as possible:

> It is necessary for us to put ourselves in the place of our opponents and, first of all, try to follow their thoughts and reasoning. Considerations of foreign policy quite generally will lead to reasonable conclusions only if one tries to think with the other fellow's mind, if one asks himself the question: how would I act if I were, at this moment, in the position of France, Britain or the United States?

He then proceeded to look at Germany through French eyes, concluding that, from France's point of view, nothing was more certain
than that a "resurgent Germany" one day would seek to "avenge" her
current defeat.

> Any responsible French statesman must endeavor, there-
> fore, to get hold of real and tangible guarantees. For
> him, by far the most desirable guarantee would un-
> doubtedly consist in making the Rhine France's strate-
> gic frontier with Germany. That is how France really
> feels. Differences of opinion only exist with regard to
> the best way of carrying out this plan. While the chau-
> vinists would like to make the Rhine the political fron-
> tier between France and Germany, the moderates aim
> at turning the Rhineland into a buffer state under
> French influence.

Adenauer went on to argue that while Germany had to defeat French
designs, there was no reason to be indignant about them—especially
since, until recently, Germany had pursued a similar policy. "There was
a time," Adenauer reminded his audience,

> when people in Germany, believing victory to be within
> their grasp, declared we must have safeguards against
> France and England. These safeguards were to be pro-
> vided by Belgium. There were those who wanted to
> incorporate Belgium into Germany and annex her al-
> together, and there were the moderates who proposed
> to keep Belgium under German domination by main-
> taining military garrisons there and placing her rail-
> ways under German management.

This, then, was how the world worked, and Germans should not
grow either too self-righteous about their own grievances or too indif-
ferent to the grievances of their neighbors.

The key question was, "Is there any solution available which would
satisfy the claims of France and yet avoid such damage to Germany as
would necessarily be caused by a cession of the left bank of the Rhine?"

Adenauer thought there was. He proposed that the left bank of the Rhine should be detached from Prussia and united with adjacent areas on the right bank. Only if the forthcoming constitutional assembly decided to partition Prussia could the Rhineland be saved for Germany. "In the opinion of our former enemies," he explained,

> it was Prussia who drove the world into this war. They believe that Prussia is dominated by a military and Junker caste, and that Prussia in turn dominates the rest of Germany, including the people of Western and Southern Germany with whose general outlook and temperament the Entente nations are basically in sympathy. Public opinion abroad therefore demands: Prussia must be partitioned.
>
> Now, if this were done, if the western provinces of Germany were joined together in a federal state, it would no longer be possible for Prussia, in the opinion of other countries, to dominate Germany.... This could, and should, satisfy France.[17]

In the event, nothing came of Adenauer's proposal until August 1946, when Britain, once again occupying Germany, established the new *Land* (province or state) of North Rhine Westphalia—precisely the large West German state that Adenauer had advocated in 1919! But the basic approach that Adenauer laid out in his maiden foreign policy speech would continue to characterize his thinking more than 30 years later, when he assumed almost exclusive responsibility for West Germany's foreign affairs.

Thus, in his relations with France, England, and the United States during their occupation of the Federal Republic of Germany between 1949 and 1955, Adenauer did everything he could "to think with the other fellow's mind" and to imagine "how I would act if I were, at this moment, in the position of France, Britain or the United States." His willingness to do so, and to recognize that these nations had more than sufficient grounds to distrust Germany, infuriated his German opponents, who scornfully called him the "Chancellor of the Allies."

Recognizing the legitimacy of certain Allied concerns, however, did not keep Adenauer from also realizing that West Germany had legitimate demands of her own that she was entitled to press—including the right to rejoin, as quickly as possible, the family of sovereign nations. This put him at odds with many of his neighbors, who believed that in light of her atrocious behavior during World War II, Germany should not be allowed to regain full sovereignty under any circumstances.

Adenauer firmly rejected this view. Deeply ashamed of Germany's conduct during World War II, he nonetheless pursued Germany's postwar interests with patience and tenacity. Moreover, he sought invariably to advance these interests in ways that took his neighbors' concerns into account: after World War I by advocating the partition of Prussia, and after World War II by integrating the Federal Republic economically and militarily with the West. Both in 1919 and after 1949, Adenauer sought to chart a patriotic middle course between total national assertion and complete national abnegation.

"To Support and Help Each Other"

As Adenauer developed into a strong and self-confident leader, his personal life also took a sharp turn for the better. In 1919, he married Gussie Zinsser, the daughter of his next-door neighbors. Konrad and Gussie were to have five children together, and, amazingly, both they and Adenauer's three children from his first marriage survived the Second World War.

As Lord Mayor of Cologne, Adenauer proved that he could "think big." Shortly after Germany's political collapse in 1918, he observed that "Times of political catastrophe are especially suitable for building something new."[18] He then set out to make Cologne one of Germany's great cities with a series of ambitious building projects that included a new university, an enlarged harbor, and a "Green Belt" of trees, more than half a mile wide and over 10 feet long, surrounding the city.

To implement his plans, he sought to enlist the help of Protestant as well as Catholic Rhinelanders. "In our fight for the recognition of Christian principles in public affairs," Adenauer told the Munich Catholic Conference in 1922, "we must seek allies among non-Catholics.... As far as we possibly can, we must join the efforts of the people in the Protestant camp who think like us, and we must seek to support and help each other."[19] Twenty-three years later, he put these ideas into practice by working to destroy the old Catholic Center party and replace it with the Christian Democratic Union, a non-sectarian party in which Catholics and Protestants worked side by side on behalf of common Christian ideals.

Like most strong leaders, Adenauer liked having his own way, and he often ran roughshod over his opponents. After 1949, sociologist Rolf Dahrendorf coined the phrase "Chancellor-Democracy" to describe a regime in which Adenauer's iron-handed rule coexisted alongside normal parliamentary procedures. Perhaps Adenauer's years as master of Cologne might similarly be called "Mayoral-Democracy."

In the end, however, for all his autocratic ways, Adenauer was on the side of the angels: Words like "reconciliation," "rapprochement," and "international community" recurred constantly in his speeches. In remarks delivered at the founding of the University of Cologne in 1919, for example, he stated with characteristic insight that

> Whatever the shape of a peace treaty, over the coming decades German culture and the culture of the western democracies will meet here on the Rhine, the old thoroughfare of the nations. If there is no reconciliation, if the European peoples fail to recognize and value the elements common to all European cultures...if they fail to re-unite the peoples through cultural rapprochement, and if they fail to avoid another European war, then Europe's preeminence in the world would be lost forever. It is the special task of the University of Cologne to promote the noble work of lasting international reconciliation and international community for the welfare of Europe.... Above all...it should show the relationship of all European culture; it should show that there is much more that unites the European

> peoples than divides them. Its holy vocation is to serve
> the real league of nations, the progress of the peoples
> to a higher stage of development![20]

After 1945, Adenauer would make it his own "holy vocation" to lead the German people "to a higher stage of development" in which they would come to recognize "that there is much more that unites the European peoples than divides them."

"A Miracle of God"

By the time his 12-year term as Lord Mayor of Cologne expired in 1929, Adenauer had acquired a national reputation. (In 1926, the Center Party had even suggested that he try to head a national unity government in Berlin—an offer that, after considering the matter carefully, he declined.) Despite this, however, and even though he had transformed the city, Adenauer's autocratic ways had won him many enemies, and the City Council reelected him to a second term by a margin of only one vote.

Adenauer's second term coincided with the onset of the Great Depression, the rise of Adolf Hitler, and the downfall of the Weimar Republic, and he found himself helpless in the face of these calamities. In a letter to his close friend, Dannie Heineman, a Belgian–American entrepreneur of Jewish background, Adenauer wrote: "Since 1918 I have never seen a political and economic situation so bungled as the current one. How Germany will come out of it, and how Europe will come out of it, is a complete mystery to me."[21] He might have added that how he personally would come out of the crisis was also a mystery, since he had invested—and lost—his considerable fortune in the American stock market and was now financially ruined.

Like many other Germans, Adenauer despised the Nazis but still hoped that governmental responsibility would somehow tame Hitler. After attaining power on January 30, 1933, however, Hitler dissolved the Reichstag and called for new elections in the hope of obtaining a parliamentary majority. Adenauer's response was exemplary. On February 17, he infuriated Hitler by refusing to greet him upon his arrival at the Cologne airport, arguing that Hitler had come to Cologne as a political candidate, not as Chancellor of Germany. That same day, he antagonized Hitler a second time by ordering two swastika flags removed from the pillars of a Rhine bridge, pointing out that the bridge was city property and could not be used for partisan purposes.

As the pro-Nazi *Westdeutscher Beobachter* observed at the time, these incidents revealed Adenauer's "deepest aversion" to National Socialism. "Herr Adenauer might like to know," it added darkly, "that such challenges will be avenged in the future."[22] Predictably, Nazi vengeance was not long in coming.

On March 13, Adenauer slipped out of his home early in the morning and left for Berlin, having learned the previous day that the Nazis had planned for a mob to break into his office and "spontaneously" throw him out the window. Adenauer complained about his treatment to the Interior Minister of Prussia, Hermann Göring, but Göring, one of Hitler's principal lieutenants, proved unsympathetic. In short order, Adenauer found himself without a job, without money, without prospects, and without friends. Former acquaintances who had fawned on him when he was "King of Cologne" now went out of their way to snub him, leading an embittered Adenauer to observe, "It is really very hard to know the human race and not to despise it."[23]

Adenauer's feelings during this period verged on the suicidal. Fortunately, an old schoolmate of his was now the abbot of the Benedictine monastery of Maria Lach, and it was there—afraid that he would be assassinated by Nazi thugs were he to return to Cologne—that Adenauer remained for nearly a year. Quite suddenly, the man who had grown accustomed to the din and clatter of public life found himself enveloped in monastic silence, with ample time on his hands to read, pray, and reflect. According to his official biographer, Paul Weymar:

> Adenauer read a great deal in these months of seclusion and inactivity, mainly historical works, including ancient Roman history. Art history was another field which interested him deeply, and he made a special study of the life of Rembrandt and his works. But more important than all this were the two great papal encyc-

licals on social questions, *Rerum Novarum* and *Quadragesimo Anno*, which Adenauer encountered for the first time at Maria Lach and which made a decisive impression on him. In these two fundamental papal pronouncements the practitioner of the day-to-day political struggle discovered a comprehensive and coherent program inspired in an order willed by God which was perfectly practicable in terms of modern society. They represented, it seemed to him, an impressive attempt to overcome and defeat the class struggle in the spirit of Christian charity and to release the working masses…from the spiritual and material pressure of their seemingly hopeless situation.[24]

In June 1934, however, Adenauer's reflections were brutally interrupted when he was arrested by the Gestapo during a roundup of all politically suspect Germans. He was detained with a number of German generals, whom he found so unimpressive that three years later, when attempts were made to draw him into an anti-Hitler resistance group that consisted largely of Wehrmacht officers, he declined. "Have you ever seen a general with an intelligent face?" he asked one of the conspirators.[25]

Adenauer was released from detention on July 2, 1934, and succeeded eventually in winning a pension from the City of Cologne. He used the money to acquire a small house in the sleepy village of Rhondorf, not far from Bonn. He did not expect the Hitler regime to last very long.

In a 1934 conversation with Rudolf Amelunxen, a Center Party politician who also had been dismissed from office in 1933, Adenauer asked how long the Nazis were likely to remain in control of Germany. When Amelunxen replied that it might be as long as two years, an appalled Adenauer exclaimed, "Two years! For God's sake! I'll be too old to get back in again! You are still young and will be able to take part in the essential work of reconstruction! But you must be sure to crack down hard."[26] Thirteen years later, both men would indeed crack down hard—

Amelunxen as Minister-President of North Rhine–Westphalia and Adenauer as chairman of the newly established Christian Democratic Union.

The years between Adenauer's release from detention in 1934 and his liberation from the Nazis in 1945 are easily summarized: Adenauer and his family did their best to live as quietly and inconspicuously as possible. In August 1944, however, Adenauer was arrested and sent to a holding area pending transfer to the Buchenwald death camp. With the help of some friends, he managed to escape. Then he was rearrested and sent to Brauweiler prison, where he spent a harrowing two months before being released, thanks to the intervention of his son Max, a German army officer. Finally, on March 23, 1945, Rhondorf was liberated by the Americans, and the 18 members of Adenauer's household—including daughters-in-law, children, grandchildren, and four escaped French prisoners of war—were free. As Adenauer told his son, "It is a miracle of God that I have survived!"[27]

"A New Political Life"

Few of their countrymen were as lucky as the Adenauers. Some five million Germans, military and civilian, were killed during World War II, and millions more were wounded. Great cities like Cologne, Hamburg, and Berlin had become an "abomination of desolation."[28] A quarter of Germany's housing was destroyed or uninhabitable. Nearly a quarter of her pre-1938 territory was in Russian or Polish hands. After her unconditional surrender in 1945, Germany had ceased to exist as a state. She was merely a region in Central Europe occupied by four foreign powers—the United States, the Soviet Union, Britain, and France—who collectively would determine her fate. Worst of all, her very name had become a byword for evil.

How had Germany come to this? During his years of enforced inactivity at Rhondorf, Adenauer had given this agonizing question much thought:

> I asked myself how the Nationalist Socialist Reich had
> come about, welcomed at first with jubilation by many
> ordinary people, then feared by so many because of its

abysmal meanness and malice—feared, despised and
cursed. What made this National Socialist Reich possible among the German people?... How was it possible for miracles of bravery and dedication to duty to
be performed by the same people who carried out
crimes unexampled in number and enormity?... How
did the German people fall into this abyss?[29]

His answer was that Germany's downfall had occurred because millions of ordinary Germans—"farmers, shopkeepers, professionals, intellectuals [and] workers," as well as "the military [and] the big industri-
alists"—had surrendered their Christian values and beliefs and had come
to worship the state: "For many decades, the German people had suffered from a wrong attitude to the state, to power, to the relationship
between the individual and the state. They made an idol of the state and
set it upon an altar; the individual's worth and dignity had been sacri-
ficed to this idol."[30]

This "belief in the omnipotence of the state," Adenauer maintained,
had been facilitated by "Marxist materialism."

Anyone who works for the centralization of political
and economic power in the hands of the state or of
one class, and who therefore advocates the principle of
class war, is an enemy of the freedom of the individual
and is bound to prepare the way for dictatorship in the
minds of his adherents. That such a result is inevitable
is shown by the histories of the countries that regard
Karl Marx as their Messiah and his teachings as gospel.
National Socialism was simply the last logical development—pushed to criminal lengths—of that worship
of power and that scorn for the individual which naturally arises from a materialist ideology.[31]

If a materialist philosophy that culminated in the worship of the state
was the root cause of the German catastrophe, it followed that only a
Christian philosophy that upheld the dignity of the individual against
the state could bring about Germany's reconstruction. "Western Chris-

tianity denies the dominance of the state," said Adenauer, "and insists on the dignity and liberty of the individual. Only this traditional Christian principle could now help us to show the German people a new political goal, to recall them to a new political life."[32]

Thus, the new political goal was a Christian Germany rooted firmly in the Christian West; and the new political life envisioned by Adenauer was one in which the ordinary German would regard his European "citizenship" as no less significant than his German identity, making it impossible for him even to contemplate a war against fellow "citizens" who happened to live in another country. "I am a German," Adenauer declared, "but I am also, and have always been, a European and have always felt like a European."[33] It was now necessary to make Germany an integral part of Europe—economically, politically, and culturally—so that every German would come to feel as European as Adenauer did.

What Adenauer wanted, then, was not simply a return to traditional Christian pieties, but a fundamental transformation of Germany's national consciousness. To borrow a formulation from the American political journalist George Will, Adenauer's "statecraft" was really a form of "soulcraft." And since only "a great party with its roots in Christian–Western thinking and ethics"[34] could accomplish the radical intellectual and moral reorientation he sought, creating and leading such a party became Konrad Adenauer's immediate postwar goal.

"An Integral Part of Western Europe"

But before the septuagenarian Adenauer was able to embark on what he doubtless thought, in 1945, would be his last political crusade, more urgent matters intervened. The American liberators had brought with them both a "Black List" of leading Nazis and a "White List" of anti-Nazi Germans, and Adenauer's name headed the "White List." They therefore requested that he accept immediate reinstatement as Cologne's Lord Mayor. For years, Adenauer had dreamed of returning to Cologne in triumph, yet when the great moment was finally at hand, concern for the fate of his sons, who were still serving in the German army and would be harshly punished were it known that their father was a "collaborator," led him to turn down the American request. He did offer, however, to serve behind the scenes as an unofficial adviser until the war was over, whereupon he would gladly resume his prewar office. The Americans accepted Adenauer's terms, and soon he was back in Cologne, planning his city's recovery.

Adenauer did what he could to allay the suffering of postwar Germany. As soon as conditions permitted, for example, he sent a bus to the liberated Buchenwald death camp to bring Cologne prisoners home. But his view of the Americans soon soured. As Adenauer's good friend, the Swiss consul-general Franz-Rudolph von Weiss, wrote on April 9, 1945,

> [Adenauer] told me in strict confidence that, on the basis of the behavior of the Americans, he saw the future as very black for Germany.... The behavior of the American soldiers had aroused the greatest indignation among the population everywhere. At first they had genuinely welcomed the arrival of the Americans as a liberation and regarded their presence as a deliverance from tyranny. But since their arrival the American troops have made themselves so unpopular by their looting, stealing, and by their arrogant, unworthy conduct that their approach, if it does not change, will breed a new National Socialism, if not Bolshevism....[35]

A month later, when a German friend tried to defend the Americans by arguing that they were just big children, Adenauer grimly replied, "Yes, big, bad children."[36] When, therefore, on June 21, 1946, the British took over from the Americans (Cologne being part of their occupation zone after World War II, just as it had been after World War I), he was far from unhappy.

Yet the British, it soon transpired, were even worse than the Americans. Adenauer was particularly incensed that General Barraclough, the British military governor, had ordered him to cut down the trees in the Green Belt surrounding Cologne and use them for fuel. The lush Green Belt was one of Adenauer's proudest achievements as Lord Mayor of prewar Cologne, and rather than destroy it, he advised the British to release some of the Ruhr coal they had requisitioned. Barraclough responded by accusing Adenauer of gross incompetence and summarily firing him from office and expelling him from Cologne. Even worse, Barraclough's letter of dismissal forbade Adenauer from engaging, "either directly or indirectly, in any political activity whatever. If you fail in any respect to observe the instructions contained in this letter, you will be brought to trial by military court."[37]

Adenauer was bitterly hurt by his dismissal, attributing it to a conspiracy by British Laborites and German Social Democrats against a prominent anti-Socialist. He was also distressed by the failure of his German friends to come to his defense. "When I was dismissed by the British occupation forces...and expelled from Cologne," he later recalled, "my friends, who were afraid of the occupation forces, avoided me. When I left Cologne, nobody said good-bye. The atmosphere around me was very similar to what I remembered when the National Socialists had hounded me out."[38]

Despite these disappointments, Adenauer remained convinced of the urgent necessity of integrating Germany economically, politically, and culturally into Western Europe. In his view, the division of Europe was already a fact: Soviet Russia had succeeded in annexing Eastern Europe and the eastern part of Germany into its sphere of influence. Unless England, France, and the western part of Germany set aside their differences, pooled their resources, and formed a "Union of States of Western Europe," they too would soon fall prey to Soviet imperialism. As Adenauer wrote to a friend in October 1945, shortly after his dismissal by the British,

> Division [of Europe] into Eastern Europe, the Russian territory [eastern Germany], and Western Europe is...a fact.... The part of Germany not occupied by the Russians is an integral part of Western Europe. If it remains sick, that would have the most serious consequences for the whole of Western Europe, including Britain and France. It is in the interests not only of the non-Russian-occupied part of Germany, but also of Britain and France, to combine Western Europe under

their leadership, to bring political and economic health
to that part of Germany that is not occupied by the
Russians.[39]

If one accepted Adenauer's basic premise—that the division of Europe between a predatory East and a vulnerable West was an accomplished fact—then his argument for integrating western Germany into an anti-Soviet bloc made excellent sense. In October 1945, however, this premise was not accepted either by most Western statesmen or by Western public opinion generally. On the contrary, only two months after the conclusion of the Potsdam Conference, hopes still ran high that the Russians, the British, and the Americans would compose their differences and avoid dividing Europe into two opposing camps. At Potsdam, the four occupying powers (the United States, the Soviet Union, Great Britain, and France) had agreed to treat Germany as a single unit economically. So long as Western leaders remained committed to this agreement—and to the broader objective of Soviet–Western friendship—they would reject Adenauer's call to integrate the western zones of Germany with the rest of Western Europe.

Eventually, of course, the Western powers *did* conclude that Soviet expansionism made further cooperation impossible, and that their self-interest required that the western zones of Germany be aligned with the rest of the West. But they did not reach this decision until the summer of 1948. In the meantime, Germany's future was in limbo; her administration remained in the hands of military governors who (on the western side) had no clear sense of their objectives; and her economy—tightly controlled and regulated by the Allies—continued to deteriorate.

"In the Spirit of Western Civilization"

It was in these unpromising circumstances that Adenauer, now relieved of his duties as Mayor of Cologne, embarked on his campaign to organize and lead a new German political party, the Christian Democratic Union (CDU), comprised of Catholics and Protestants and dedicated to the renewal of Germany's domestic and foreign policies on the basis of the Christian ethic. (The British, Adenauer recalled in his memoirs, rescinded their ban on his political activity in December 1945 but viewed the CDU "with great mistrust and seemed to think that its founders were predominantly former Nazis."[40]) This required him to travel to all parts of the British zone of occupied Germany in order to rally supporters, convince waiverers, outwit opponents, and establish the infrastructure of a modern political party. It was a grueling task, but Adenauer saw it through with his customary blend of relentless self-discipline and unwavering sense of duty.

In his efforts to build an effective party machine, Adenauer was assisted by Josef Löns, a 35-year-old former prisoner of war who was employed in the legal branch of the Cologne city administration when Adenauer first spotted his remarkable organizational talents. (Adenauer eventually would appoint Löns ambassador to The Hague.) There was only one problem: Although sympathetic to the idea of rebuilding Germany on a Christian basis, Löns, like many younger CDU members, was a socialist and considered Adenauer a reactionary.

Adenauer, however, succeeded in arguing Löns out of his socialist beliefs. "Do you really believe," he asked, "that a worker or employee enjoys more rights, privileges and liberties in a state-owned industry than under private management?" He continued:

> Is it not a fact, rather, that concentration of economic and political power in one single hand subjects the working man to a form of dependence which goes far beyond his dependence on the private, individual employer? Look at Russia, and you will see how many rights and privileges a worker enjoys in the state-owned industries! Would you not agree that it is better and wiser to separate political power from economic power and have the state function as an arbiter between capital and labor?

Adenauer's reasoning, as well as the force of his character, had a dramatic impact on the younger man. "For the first time," Löns later recalled,

> I felt the effect of [Adenauer's] personality upon me.
> His manner of speech was dry, matter-of-fact, almost
> doctrinaire, and occasionally seasoned with biting irony,
> but his arguments invariably struck home. I fought
> hard to break out of his encirclement, but again and
> again he blocked my escape route. Finally I advanced
> some personal motives. "I cannot accept the post of
> party secretary," I said. "I have lost six years through
> the war and must be thankful for having at least firm
> ground under my feet again...."

At this Adenauer flew into a bit of a temper. "And what are we old ones to say," he asked, "if the young, for purely selfish reasons, keep aloof from political work?" We struggled for a full two hours. At the end of the interview I was no longer a Christian Socialist but secretary general of the CDU.[41]

It was through such prodigious feats of willpower, patience, and persuasiveness that Adenauer succeeded in creating a new political party, the Christian Democratic Union, in his own image: Christian, capitalist, and passionately pro-Western. (His success is all the more remarkable for having been achieved against a backdrop of personal tragedy: On March 3, 1948, Gussie Adenauer died of a bone disease contracted during her brief incarceration in Brauweiler prison.) "The CDU," Adenauer wrote in his memoirs, "wanted the citizens of the new Germany to become Europeans determined to make their contribution to the European community in the spirit of Christianity and Western civilization."[42]

Besides Löns, Adenauer's most valuable political recruit during these early postwar years was Bavarian economist Ludwig Erhard. By 1948, thanks to Erhard, the Western allies had abandoned most of their efforts to regulate the German economy in their zones and had allowed a free market to emerge. The ensuing spurt of spectacular economic growth silenced Adenauer's socialist opponents within the CDU and made it the most popular political party in the western zones of Germany.

The First Berlin Crisis

In June of 1948, having despaired of reaching an accommodation with Stalin, the Western powers agreed at the London Conference to form a single West German government out of the three Allied occupation zones. They did this because they realized, intellectually, that the Soviet Union had become the principal threat to their well-being and that West Germany could make a crucial contribution to the West's defense. Emotionally, however, Germany remained the dreaded enemy, and it was difficult for many in the West to accept yesterday's foe as today's friend. It was not until the conclusion of the Berlin blockade crisis in the spring of 1949 that attitudes changed and—at least in the United States—West Germany began to be accepted, emotionally as well as intellectually, as a legitimate partner in the struggle against Communism.

The Berlin crisis was precipitated by the West's decision, following the London Conference, to introduce a new currency into the western zones of Germany, thereby laying the groundwork for their eventual political consolidation. Although located 110 miles inside the Soviet zone of occupation, the city of Berlin, like Germany herself, was divided into four occupation sectors (three Western and one Soviet). On June 26, 1948, Stalin—still hoping to bring West Germany into the Soviet orbit—imposed a blockade on all access routes to the city. The commandant of the Soviet sector of Berlin informed his Western counterparts that the blockade, which deprived West Berlin of food, fuel, and other necessities, would continue until the West reversed the steps it had taken to create a West German government.

But Western leaders would not succumb to Soviet intimidation. Instead, the United States and Great Britain launched "Operation Vittles"—more commonly known as the Berlin Airlift—and, contrary to nearly everyone's expectations, succeeded in providing West Berliners with all the provisions they required. Additionally, in a subtle but unmistakable warning to Stalin, President Truman dispatched 60 B-29 bombers, capable of dropping atomic bombs on Soviet territory, to former World War II air bases in Great Britain.

Meanwhile, Stalin offered to negotiate. At the end of July 1948, he met with the U.S. ambassador to Moscow, Walter Bedell Smith, and told him that he still regarded the United States and the Soviet Union as allies. What agitated him, however, was the unilateral decision taken by the West at the London Conference to establish a separate West German state. Such a decision, Stalin maintained, was a flagrant violation of the Potsdam accords, which envisaged a common approach to German issues. "If this went ahead," he warned, "the Soviet government would be faced with a *fait accompli* and there would be nothing left to discuss." If the London decisions were revoked, however, Stalin was sure that "after much skirmishing they could return to a basis of agreement."[43]

Ambassador Smith thought that Stalin's ideas were worth exploring, and the director of the State Department's Policy Planning Staff, George Kennan, was even more enthusiastic. Arguing that the creation of a West German state would forever rule out a Soviet–American agreement on Germany, and thus would serve only to perpetuate current tensions, Kennan urged the United States to open negotiations with Stalin on the possibility of creating a united, demilitarized, and neutralized Germany.

Kennan's proposals, known within the State Department as "Plan A," did not go unchallenged. Another State Department paper warned that "A segregated [neutralized] Germany would be under irresistible temptation to seek, through its central geographic position and potential strength, to achieve dominance in Europe, playing off the East against the West." It also would "have a great tendency to revert to extreme authoritarian rule." Finally, a neutral Germany "would provide a fertile field for the rebirth of aggressive German nationalism and permit a rapprochement with the Soviet bloc. The fear of these developments constitutes the heart of the German problem."[44]

Robert Murphy, a senior American diplomat who served as political adviser to the chief of the U.S. military government in occupied Germany, General Lucius Clay, also was critical of Plan A. Kennan, he said, was wrong to argue that the only alternative to a united, neutral Germany was an unstable, divided Germany. Rather, a prosperous Western

Germany linked to Western Europe would serve as a "magnet" that ultimately would detach Eastern Germany from Soviet control. The West held the winning hand, provided it did not "fold" prematurely. General Clay concurred. "We have won the battle," he complained, "but [we] are writing an armistice as though we had lost the battle."[45]

Secretary of State Dean Acheson, although initially sympathetic to Plan A, eventually rejected Kennan's proposal. Unlike Kennan, Acheson simply did not believe that the United States could do business with Stalin. "The most dangerous thing in the world we can do," he maintained, "is to again enter into any agreement which depends for its execution upon Russian cooperation and Russian goodwill."[46] Now that progress was being made on integrating West Germany into a free and democratic Europe, the last thing the United States should do was jeopardize that progress by entering into agreements with Moscow that Stalin was unlikely to honor in any case.

What is striking about these early debates among senior American officials is the way they anticipate the positions that the various parties to the German question would take over the next 15 years. Thus, West Germany's principal opposition party during the Adenauer era, the Social Democrats, would come to embrace views virtually identical to Kennan's 1948 proposal. They would argue that, to secure both the peace of Europe and the unity of Germany, West Germany should strive for an agreement with Moscow that exchanged its close alignment with the West for Soviet acquiescence in a united, disarmed, and neutral Germany.

For his part, Adenauer would counter these views by advancing arguments that echoed the analysis put forward by Kennan's critics. He would contend that a neutralized Germany—that is, a Germany torn loose from its close association with Western Europe—would face irresistible temptations to return to an aggressive, nationalistic course. Such a Germany could not be trusted to remain democratic and would end up either dominated by or aligned with the Soviet Union. If Germany pursued a "policy of strength," however, and remained firmly allied with the West, the Soviet Union sooner or later would be forced to agree to unification on West German terms.

Adenauer's refusal to negotiate with Russia would attract strong support from President Dwight Eisenhower's Secretary of State, John Foster Dulles, who, like Acheson, did not trust the Soviets and believed in creating what Truman's Secretary of State had called "situations of strength." Later, when President Kennedy came into office, the United States, to Adenauer's great displeasure, would adopt a position very much like Ambassador Smith's—that is, a willingness to explore alternative arrangements with Moscow.

But while all of these developments stand out clearly in retrospect, the future of Germany was very uncertain in 1948. In July, as the Berlin airlift was just getting underway, the British, French, and American military governors passed on the London Conference proposals for a separate West German state to the Minister-Presidents of the 11 West German provinces (*Länder*). These officials, in turn, agreed to the formation of a Parliamentary Council, which was tasked with drafting a Basic Law, or provisional constitution, for the new government. (The constitution was considered provisional because about one-third of Germany was under Soviet control, its people unable to participate in the constitution-making process; only after Germany was united and the entire German people endorsed it would the Basic Law lose its provisional status.) The president of the new council was Konrad Adenauer.

After much deliberation, the Parliamentary Council adopted the Basic Law on May 8, 1949, only four days before the Soviets had agreed to lift the Berlin blockade and a little more than a month after the signing of the North Atlantic Treaty by 12 states of Western Europe and North America on April 4. On May 24, after the Basic Law was approved by the Western occupying powers and ratified by the West German state parliaments, the Federal Republic of Germany (FRG) came into being. Though only semi-sovereign—a Western-drafted Occupation Statute that went into effect at the same time as the Basic Law reserved "supreme authority" over key aspects of economic and foreign policy to three Western High Commissioners—the FRG was clearly on the road to full independence.

On August 14, 1949, in the first truly free elections that had been held in their country since 1932, the citizens of West Germany voted for members of the West German Bundestag (Parliament). The largest bloc of votes was won by Adenauer's CDU and its Bavarian affiliate, the CSU (Christian Social Union). The Social Democrats came in second, and the liberal Free Democratic Party (FDP) was third. On September 17, the Bundestag elected Adenauer Chancellor by exactly one vote— his own. He would preside over a coalition government made up of the CDU/CSU and the FDP.

At this point, Adenauer was 73 years old, and no one imagined that he would remain in office for more than a year or two. They were wrong. He served Germany as Chancellor for 14 years, and by the time he finally stepped down in 1963, he had accomplished his primary mission: Both at home and abroad, the Federal Republic of Germany was fully accepted as an inseparable part of the democratic West.

A Reversal of Historic Proportions

On October 15, 1949, in response to the birth of the FRG, the Soviet Union created the German Democratic Republic (GDR) out of the eastern zone. It appears that Stalin undertook this move reluctantly, since it ended his ambitious scheme to dominate the whole of Germany. His plan has been summarized concisely by historian John Lewis Gaddis:

> New evidence reveals that Stalin met with the leaders of the German Communist Party (KPD) as early as 4 June 1945, to lay out plans for incorporating a reunified Germany within Moscow's sphere of influence. Two principal instruments would accomplish this: The Red Army would control the Soviet occupation zone, while the KPD would seek popular support beyond the reach of Soviet military authority. Germany would at first be divided, with its eastern territories administered by the Russians, the remainder by the Western allies. Within the east the KPD would merge with the Social Democrats (SPD) to form the Socialist Unity Party (SED), thus following the example of other East-

ern and central European communist parties which
were, under Soviet instructions, organizing "national
fronts" with non-communist parties on the left. Having consolidated its position in the east, the SED, operating under KPD control, would then solicit the al-
legiance of Social Democrats and other sympathetic
Germans in the west, and by these means bring about
unification. "[A]ll of Germany must be ours," Stalin
assured the Yugoslavs in the spring of 1946, "that is,
Soviet, Communist."[47]

Two things spoiled Stalin's plan. First, Kurt Schumacher, the anti-
Communist leader of the Social Democrats in the western zones of occupied Germany, refused to go along with the decision of his comrades
in the eastern zone (made under Soviet duress) to merge with the Communists. (When told that Communists and socialists were "ideological
brothers", the sharp-tongued Schumacher replied, "Yes, just like Cain
and Abel."[48]) Hence, Stalin did not succeed in forming a "national front"
in the western zones.

Even more important, the behavior of Soviet forces in eastern Germany—where up to 2 million German women were raped by Red Army
troops in 1945 and 1946—was so barbaric that, for most Germans, the
notion of supporting a pro-Soviet party was simply unthinkable. As
Colonel S. I. Tiul'panov, a Soviet propaganda officer in East Germany,
admitted in 1948, "[T]he Soviet occupation force in Germany has made
incredible…mistakes, which unfortunately can only be rectified with
great difficulty."[49]

Despite these setbacks, Stalin remained optimistic. After all, had not
President Roosevelt assured him at Yalta that American troops would
depart from postwar Europe after two years? And without American
troops to protect them, how could the western zones of Germany *not*
fall into Soviet hands?

The Berlin airlift demonstrated to Stalin that—FDR's assurances to
the contrary notwithstanding—the Americans were not about to abandon Western Germany. His subsequent failure to lure the West into

negotiations to forestall the creation of a West German state left him with no choice but to create an East German state. The result, as historian Martin Malia has observed, was that "Germany was partitioned, and soon the whole of Europe was divided as well: behind the Soviet lines there was socialism, and on the far side there was what the Soviets called 'capitalism' and the West called 'democracy.'"[50]

But if Stalin had failed in his bid to control all of Germany, his domination of eastern Germany had important consequences for western Germany. If they truly wanted to be reunited someday with their eastern kinsmen, many West Germans concluded, they had better refrain from antagonizing Stalin by aligning themselves with the West, and strive instead for a general European settlement acceptable to Stalin: creation of a unified, disarmed, and *neutral* Germany. Such a solution to the German problem was exactly what Kurt Schumacher, the formidable leader of West Germany's Social Democrats, advocated.

Though firmly anti-Communist, Schumacher was also a Marxist and a German nationalist. As a prewar Social Democrat whose outspoken opposition to Nazism had landed him in the infamous Dachau concentration camp in 1933, he was convinced that the Social Democrats had failed to defeat the Nazis because they were perceived as insufficiently nationalist. Determined not to repeat this mistake, he made the reunification of Germany his top priority; and if this required that the FRG refrain from allying itself with the West, that was fine with him. As a Marxist, Schumacher feared that a close association with the West would turn the FRG into "a clericalist and capitalist state," ruling out eventual unification with the Protestant and socialist East. What he favored, therefore, was for the FRG to adopt a "third way" by remaining proudly aloof from *both* the Communist and capitalist camps.[51]

Schumacher's commitment to a third way, even more than his Marxism, was anathema to Adenauer. In Adenauer's view, Germany's search for a third way—her traditional belief that she belonged neither to the East nor to the West, but was fated to play some extraordinary, exceptional role—was what had gotten her into so much trouble in the first place. In the words of political scientist Wolfram F. Hanrieder,

The possibility of a neutralist and drifting Germany in the heart of Europe raised for Adenauer (and of course others) the specter of a repetition, or perpetuation, of Germany's historic *Sonderweg*—its singular and autonomous path through European history, which had brought such misfortunes to Germany's neighbors and to the Germans themselves. Adenauer was determined to obviate such future calamities. But he was also aware that in seeking to prevent Germany from embarking in the future upon a neutral and independent diplomatic course in Europe, he aimed for a reversal of truly historic proportions that might not take hold unless it were enforced by restraining Germany through international commitments and integrative institutions.[52]

Der Alte Fuchs

In his effort to end Germany's commitment to a third way and anchor her firmly in the Western camp, Adenauer had to overcome not only the weight of German history, and not simply the opposition of the Soviets and Social Democrats, but also the hostility of the French. On the face of it, French opposition to Adenauer made no sense. After all, what he sought was to prevent the outbreak of another Franco–German war by integrating Germany into Western Europe. The problem was that he sought to do so on the basis of the equality of all participants, including Germany, and this was unacceptable to many French figures.

Like the Arabs in relation to Israel today, the French had acquired an unspoken, unacknowledged, but very real sense of inferiority *vis-à-vis* the Germans. They feared that if they entered into any relationship—however peaceful—with Germany on the basis of equality, superior German discipline and organization would lead eventually to German hegemony. Rather than face such a distasteful prospect, France preferred to maintain the status quo—whereby the FRG remained a semi-sovereign country, no longer under military occupation but nonetheless answerable to three High Commissioners, one of them French—in perpetuity.

Fortunately for Adenauer, he did have one very powerful ally: the United States. The American Secretary of State, Dean Acheson, was profoundly anti-Russian and believed that what John Maynard Keynes had written about Germany after World War I applied equally well after World War II: "Round Germany as a central support the rest of the European economic system grouped itself, and on the prosperity and enterprise of Germany, the prosperity of the rest of the Continent mainly depended."[53] In order to prevent Moscow from exploiting Europe's economic misery, it was necessary to restore Germany's prosperity as soon as possible; if France objected, then so much the worse for France.

Acheson met Adenauer for the first time in November 1949 and was deeply impressed. As he later recalled in his memoirs,

> One's first impression of the Chancellor was as the human embodiment of the doctrine of the conservation of energy. He moved and spoke slowly, gestured sparingly, smiled briefly, chuckled rather than laughed, was given to irony.... I was struck by the imagination and wisdom of his approach. His great concern was to integrate Germany completely into Western Europe. Indeed, he gave this end priority over the reunification of unhappily divided Germany, and could see why her neighbors might look upon it as almost a precondition to reunification.... He wanted Germans to be citizens of Europe, to cooperate, with France especially, in developing common interests and outlook and in burying the rivalries of the past few centuries.[54]

Acheson's growing friendship with Adenauer naturally alarmed France. It also, however, led her more realistic leaders to conclude that it was better for them to arrive at an understanding with West Germany now, while she was still relatively weak, than to wait until the United States—

thoroughly exasperated by French delaying tactics—reached a deal with the Germans on her own that might prove disadvantageous to France. Among these more realistic French leaders was the brilliant Jean Monnet.

In 1950, Monnet, who was in charge of supervising the modernization of French industry, foresaw a bleak future for his country:

> The United States, he claimed, would insist on granting Germany a place in the Western camp, partly because they could see no other solution and partly because they doubted French stability and dynamism.... The United States would dominate, pulling the British along in [their] wake; the Americans would set Germany more or less free, in order to gain an ally in the Cold War; and France would be left behind.[55]

To avert such a calamity, Monnet argued, it was vital that France seize the initiative and offer her own plan for the economic revival of Europe. He therefore proposed "to place the whole of Franco–German coal and steel production under an international authority open to participation of other countries of Europe." The new institution, which later became known as the European Coal and Steel Community (ECSC), would be established by international treaty and directed by a High Authority, and "the whole enterprise will be based on equal Franco–German representation...."[56] Monnet persuaded French Foreign Minister Robert Schuman to adopt his initiative, and on May 9, 1950, Schuman informed Adenauer of the "Schuman Plan."

Konrad Adenauer was not called *Der Alte Fuchs* ("the old fox") for nothing. He realized immediately that the French had not proposed the Schuman Plan out of altruism. On the contrary, he recognized that

> the French wanted to obtain a larger market area through the fusion of markets while retaining their current lead. The development of German steel industry was to be geared to French needs. Equally, the French wanted to share German coal resources on favorable terms, having failed in the attempt to make their own coal mines competitive by means of increased invest-

ment.... From the German point of view, it could be argued that Monnet's failure with his ambitious modernization plans had persuaded him to attempt an eleventh-hour "flight forwards," undertaken in an attempt to disguise the bad investment policies over which he had presided.[57]

Nonetheless, Adenauer decided to accept the Schuman Plan. He did so because it seemed to him that the plan's political advantages—integrating West Germany with the rest of Western Europe and beginning the process of Franco–German reconciliation—far outweighed its economic drawbacks. As Adenauer explained in his memoirs, "Schuman's plan corresponded entirely with the ideas I had been advocating for a long time concerning the integration of the key industries of Europe. I informed Schuman at once that I accepted his proposal wholeheartedly."[58] When he met Jean Monnet on May 23, he went even further. "Monsieur Monnet," he said, "I regard the French proposal as the most important task before me. Should I succeed in handling it well, I believe I will not have lived in vain."[59]

Predictably, the Social Democrats objected to the Schuman Plan, seeing in it a capitalist conspiracy to undermine the rights of German labor. More surprisingly, the United States also was initially suspicious, with Secretary of State Acheson, who had cut his teeth as a trust-busting New Deal lawyer, sensing in the coal and steel pool the makings of a dangerous "supercartel." Eventually, however, Acheson came to support the Schuman Plan. (According to Adenauer, U.S. High Commissioner John J. McCloy told him that "Nobody [in Washington] knew what [the Schuman Plan] meant, but the general notion connected with it that it would combine Germany and France in a way that would exclude warlike conflict for all time was enough."[60]) Not so the British, who refused to subordinate their own heavy industry to a European High Authority.

Nevertheless, on April 18, 1951, Italy and the Benelux countries (Belgium, the Netherlands, and Luxembourg) joined France and the FRG in signing the treaty that created the European Coal and Steel Community. "For France and West Germany," write historians Dennis Bark and

David Gress, "this agreement filled many of the functions of a peace treaty."[61] And although not many Germans shared Adenauer's optimistic conviction that the ECSC "would lead Europeans out of the straits of their national lives into the broad field of Europe which would bring to the life of the individual a greater and richer meaning,"[62] it has, at the very least, helped to reconcile the French and the Germans, just as Adenauer hoped it would. In the words of historian Alan Milward:

> The Franco–German association which it created was in many respects a shotgun wedding. The German bride, although her other choices were not very enticing, had nevertheless to be dragged protesting by her aged father [Adenauer] to the altar while numerous members of her family staged noisy protests on the way and an equally large number of the bridegroom's friends and relations prophesied disaster. Yet the knot once tied, this surprising union soon settled into a safe bourgeois marriage in which the couple, rapidly becoming wealthy and comfortable as passions cooled, were held together, as such couples are, by the strong links of managing their complex joint economic affairs.[63]

"We Have Duties to Fulfill"

On June 25, 1950, in the midst of the negotiations over the Schuman Plan, North Korean troops invaded South Korea. Throughout the FRG, it was widely assumed that East Germany would soon follow suit and attack West Germany. Since the FRG was forbidden by the Occupation Statute from fielding an army and the lightly armed Western occupation troops were not considered militarily effective, it was also widely believed that an East German invasion was bound to succeed. The result was widespread panic. As Charles Thayer, an American diplomat attached to the U.S. High Commissioner's Office, later recalled:

> The reaction of the Bonn politicians...verged on the hysterical.... A dozen of them hurried to my office requesting Allied permits requesting firearms with

which to shoot the Communists or, if necessary, themselves. "There's not a grain of cyanide to be bought,"
one member of Parliament told me in high alarm. "My
colleagues have cleaned out the market to be prepared
to take their lives when the Communists come."[64]

The Korean War scare made West Germans realize how militarily
vulnerable they were. As Chancellor, Adenauer could not tolerate such a
situation. He demanded that Allied occupation forces either assume
full responsibility for West Germany's defense or allow West Germans
to defend themselves. The first alternative—having American, French,
and British troops fight the Red Army while Germans sat disinterest-
edly by—was an obvious non-starter. But in view of recent history, the
second alternative—allowing the Germans to re-arm—was equally unacceptable.

Adenauer offered the Allies a way out of their dilemma. The army he
proposed to raise would not be a national fighting force, but would be
integrated into a European army. This proposal, however, had a political condition attached to it: If the FRG did join a European army, it
would have to do so on the basis of equality—that is, as a sovereign
state. And that, in turn, meant abrogating the Occupation Statute.

The Truman Administration proved quite receptive to Adenauer's
ideas. In April 1950, NSC 68, drafted primarily by Paul Nitze (who had
replaced George Kennan as head of the State Department's Policy Planning Staff), had endorsed West Germany's rearmament. Initially, its recommendations were set aside by President Truman. North Korea's attack on South Korea, however, caused Truman to change his mind. It
now seemed to him that West German rearmament was essential and
that NATO was the perfect vehicle for integrating West German forces
into a wider Western defense structure.

Before the outbreak of the Korean War, NATO was more of a political than a military alliance: a pledge made by the U.S. in 1949 to regard
an attack on any of NATO's member states as an attack on itself. But a
unified military command had not been established for NATO, and
American troops had not been dispatched to Europe as part of a NATO

army. Now, however, the U.S. proposed to lend NATO some military muscle. On September 12, 1950, Acheson told his French and British counterparts (who, like the Germans, feared that North Korea's attack on South Korea was the prelude to a Soviet attack on Western Europe) that the United States was prepared to make a major troop commitment to NATO, as well as to provide a Supreme Commander (General Eisenhower), on condition that they permit German troops to serve in such a force.

At first, the French were adamantly opposed to Acheson's proposal; but they quickly realized that, as in the case of Europe's economic recovery, the Americans were determined to cooperate with the Germans in Europe's military defense. Rather than offer futile opposition, it would be wiser to propose an initiative that met French as well as American concerns. Predictably, Jean Monnet came up with a plan: Create a supranational political authority—the European Defense Community (EDC)—to supervise a future European army that would be distinct from, though subordinate to, NATO forces.

This time, however, when French Prime Minister René Pleven floated his plan for the EDC, Adenauer's reaction was sharply negative. It seemed to him that by making the creation of a European army hinge on Europe's political integration, the Pleven plan was simply a French ruse to delay German rearmament indefinitely. As usual, Acheson agreed with the Germans. Though he welcomed the Pleven plan publicly, privately "He did not much like this baroque idea, in which French acceptance of the unthinkable depended on the achievement of the politically utopian."[65]

That the Americans eventually came around to support the EDC is a tribute to the remarkable persuasiveness of Jean Monnet. At the age of 16, Monnet had left school to become a salesman in the family brandy business, and all his life he remained a pitchman of genius. He convinced the U.S. High Commissioner to Germany, his old friend John J. McCloy, and NATO's designated Supreme Commander, General Eisenhower, that the creation of a powerful European army as envisaged by the Pleven plan was very much in America's interest, since it would permit the eventual withdrawal of American troops from Europe. (Eisenhower was so impressed by Monnet's presentation that he volunteered to serve a future European Defense Community as its Defense Minister.[66]) Together, McCloy and Eisenhower convinced Acheson to support the EDC, and Acheson in turn convinced Adenauer.

It turned out that convincing Adenauer was one thing, but convincing the West Germans was something else again. Throughout the FRG, anti-rearmament sentiment ran high, expressed in the popular slogan *"Ohne Mich!"* ("Count Me Out!"). The Social Democrats argued that since the Western Allies had forced the FRG to disarm and had repeatedly condemned German militarism, protecting the Federal Republic was an Allied, not a German, responsibility. Leading figures of the Protestant establishment, including the highly respected anti-Nazi pastor, Martin Niemöller, agreed with the socialists, as did Adenauer's Minister of the Interior, Gustav Heinemann. Referring to World Wars I and II, Heinemann wrote Adenauer that "God has twice taken the weapons from our hand, we may not take them into our hands a third time but must wait patiently."[67]

Adenauer strongly opposed such arguments. In the Bundestag, he declared that the entire Western world, not merely Germany, was profoundly threatened by Soviet expansionism and that Germany could not avoid rearming because "we have duties to fulfill to Europe and the people of Western civilization."[68] To Heinemann, meanwhile, he drafted the following reply, which made the Christian case for rearmament:

> While you take the view that we must hold back and wait, even in the face of the threat from Soviet Russia, in the hope that God will guide everything toward peace, I take the view that it is precisely as Christians that we are also obliged to use our strengths in order to defend and save the peace. I take the view that a passive attitude towards Soviet Russia from our side will virtually encourage Soviet Russia not to keep the peace. From the experiences we have had with totalitarian National Socialism, I think it must be clear that a totalitarian state is never persuaded to refrain from its goals of conquest by patient waiting, but only by the

establishment of forces which show it that it can only achieve its goals of conquest by endangering its own existence.[69]

But although Adenauer was deeply disturbed by the "*Ohne Mich*" movement, he also realized that it gave him a powerful argument with which to press for the total abrogation of the Occupation Statute. As he wrote in his memoirs,

> In order to overcome the negative attitude of the German people [toward rearmament] it seemed to me necessary to convince them that we were free or that at least there were prospects that the Federal Republic would soon be completely free and that it was therefore worth making sacrifices for this freedom. I believed that generous gestures by the Western Allies toward the Federal Republic were urgently needed. Otherwise I could not see how we could win over the German people to cooperate voluntarily in the defense of Europe.[70]

Acheson agreed with Adenauer on the need for "generous gestures." Otherwise, he feared, popular resistance to rearmament might lead to Adenauer's replacement by Schumacher's Social Democratic Party in the upcoming 1953 German elections. Having met Schumacher in 1949, and having been repelled both by his "harsh and violent nature" and his "nationalistic and aggressive ideas,"[71] Acheson believed that a socialist victory in West Germany would be a disaster for the United States. He therefore pressed for the Western Allies and the FRG to enter into two parallel sets of negotiations—one to focus on replacing the Occupation Statute with a series of treaties or "contractual" agreements and the other to determine the structure of the European Defense Community—with Western willingness to ratify the results of the first set of negotiations contingent on the successful completion of the second. By March 1952, both sets of negotiations appeared headed for success.

A Diplomatic Bombshell: The Stalin Note

At this point, the Soviet Union suddenly dropped a diplomatic bombshell. Noting that "seven years have passed since the end of war in Europe, and a peace treaty with Germany is not yet concluded," the so-called Stalin Note proposed four-power negotiations to create an all-German government and conclude a peace treaty. Though this was by no means the first time the Soviets had proposed four-power negotiations over Germany, the Note's non-polemical tone and offer of new concessions made it seem as though, this time, Stalin might be seriously interested in reaching an agreement.

Among the most striking reversals from previous Soviet positions was the Note's assurance that "Germany will be permitted to have its own national armed forces (land, air and sea) which are necessary to the defense of the country." By contrast, the proposed EDC forbade a national German army. Additionally, Germany would be permitted its own armament industry, no limits would be placed on German trade or economic development, and a reunited Germany would be allowed full membership in the United Nations. In what appeared to be a bid for the Nazi vote, the Note even called for the restoration of civil and political rights to "all former Nazis, excluding those who are serving court sentences for the commission of crimes."

The one demand upon which the Note insisted was that a reunited Germany not be allowed to join "any kind of coalition or military alliance directed against any power which took part with its armed forces in the war against Germany."[72] In other words, German participation in the EDC would be forbidden.

A few days after receiving the Stalin Note, U.S. High Commissioner McCloy told an aide that it was a move "I have been expecting for a long time.... The Soviets are playing their heaviest cards as one expected they would do to deflect our policy of European integration." McCloy called on Adenauer to remain steadfast and not to be swayed by Soviet propaganda. "If the Germans were now to delay [joining the EDC], the American reaction might be to wash our hands of the entire project and let the Germans fend for themselves.... Germans must now give evidence of which side they were on."[73]

It did not take much American urging for Adenauer to demonstrate which side he was on. Although Social Democrats and religious pacifists implored him to suspend negotiations over the EDC until Soviet intentions on German reunification were clarified, Adenauer refused. The extent to which that the Stalin Note included concessions, Adenauer argued, demonstrated that his "policy of strength" was working: "If we continue in this way, if the West including the United States is as strong as it must be, if it is stronger than the Soviet government, that will be the time when the Soviet Union starts to listen."[74] The correct response to the Stalin Note was for Germany to continue along the path of strengthening the West by joining the EDC.

Besides, Adenauer did not believe that the Soviet offer to dismantle the GDR and reunite Germany was genuine. If the Soviet Zone (the GDR) were liberated, other Soviet satellites would be encouraged to demand their freedom as well—and Moscow could not tolerate that. As Adenauer explained in a background conversation with the editors of *The Times* of London on June 3, 1952:

> If we were to accept that the Soviet Union would set free the Soviet Zone [the GDR], restore the unity of Germany by means of free, secret elections, and abandon the idea of creating a sphere of influence in this newly-created Germany, then they would also have to abandon their policy in the satellite states. Such conduct would kindle the spirit of resistance and the hope of liberation among the many opponents of Bolshevism in Poland, Czechoslovakia and Hungary, and would be bound to produce a complete change in Soviet policy which would run counter to developments since 1945 and bring the Soviet Union no tangible return.

It followed that Germany would be reunited only within the context of an overall settlement that also restored a measure of freedom to the other satellite states. Such a solution, in turn, could come about only when Soviet internal problems were so pressing, and the West was so strong, that Soviet leaders would have no choice but to make major concessions. When one of his British interlocutors mockingly asked whether this denouement would take place in 25 years or 100 years, Adenauer cooly replied, "In my view, 5 to 10 years."[75]

Adenauer was wrong about the time frame; it took 38 years for Germany to be reunited. But he was absolutely right in insisting that German reunification would take place only as part of a wider settlement that included the other satellite states. He also was right both in predicting that such a settlement would be reached when the Soviet Union was in the midst of a major internal crisis and in dismissing the Stalin Note as nothing more than a propaganda ploy.

This last assertion—that Adenauer was correct not to take the Stalin Note seriously—has long been a matter of dispute. In particular, many West German scholars have maintained that Adenauer's failure to enter into negotiations with the Soviets on the basis of the Note constituted a "lost opportunity" for German reunification. In his memoirs, former Soviet Foreign Minister Andrei Gromyko repeated these charges: "[Adenauer] was impervious to reason; once West Germany had been drawn into the Western military bloc, it was almost as if the Federal Republic had become more important to Adenauer than the idea of reunification."[76]

Since the fall of the Soviet Union, however, new information has come to light. This new evidence demonstrates conclusively that the Stalin Note was part of a propaganda offensive designed by the Soviet Foreign Ministry to prevent German accession to the EDC by bringing down the Adenauer government. A particularly revealing insight came from former Soviet diplomat Vladimir Semyonov, who recalled Stalin's asking him whether it was certain that the Americans would reject the note. "Only when assured that it was did the Soviet leader give his approval, but with the warning that there would be grave consequences for Semyonov if this did not prove to be the case."[77] The last thing Stalin wanted was to enter into genuine negotiations that might bring about the end of the GDR, for that could easily give others the dangerous idea that "socialist gains" were not "irreversible."

Thanks to Adenauer's steadfastness, the Stalin Note did not succeed in slowing down the negotiations between the FRG and the Western allies; on the contrary, fearing that new Soviet initiatives might be in the works, Acheson ordered that the pace of the negotiations be accelerated. The result was that on May 26, 1952, the "contractual" agreements were signed in Bonn, and on May 27, the EDC treaties were signed in Paris. All that remained was for the parliaments of the signatory states to ratify the accords, and the FRG would rejoin the family of nations as a sovereign state.

But matters did not proceed as smoothly as Adenauer and Acheson had anticipated. Many French leaders proved unable to rise above the traumas of the past—among them General Charles de Gaulle, who declared his total opposition to the EDC. The French National Assembly kept delaying the ratification of the EDC treaty by demanding one change after another. Finally, on August 23, 1954, the Assembly voted to set the treaty aside, effectively killing it.

A devastated Adenauer was convinced that Moscow was somehow behind this defeat, and he may well have been right. According to Soviet expert William Hyland, after France's defeat at Dien Bien Phu in 1954, Soviet Foreign Minister Molotov offered the new French Prime Minister, Pierre Mendès-France, a "crude but effective" deal: "[T]he Soviet Union would use its influence with Ho Chi Minh to permit the French to save face and withdraw gracefully from Indochina, but the price would be paid in Europe, the French defeat of the EDC."[78] Mendès-France took the bait and allowed the EDC to be defeated.

Adenauer, who believed that Germany's own best interests required that her institutions be integrated into a broader European framework, took the news of the EDC's defeat very badly. "It is madness," he told Luxembourg's Prime Minister, Joseph Bech,

> that I should be forced to create a German national army, it is grotesque.... I am firmly convinced, one hundred percent convinced, that the national army to which M. Mendès-France is forcing us will be a great

danger for Germany and Europe—once I am no longer
here I have no idea what will become of Germany if
we are not able to create Europe in due course.[79]

At this point, British Foreign Minister Anthony Eden stepped in for-
tuitously with an initiative of his own. In 1948, five West European
nations—Britain, France, Belgium, the Netherlands, and Luxembourg—
had set up a military alliance known as the Western European Union
(WEU) as a precursor to NATO. The WEU had established a supranational council to regulate the rearmament of its neighbors. Now Eden
proposed bringing the FRG into both the WEU and NATO, thereby
satisfying French demands for some kind of European control over
Germany's armed forces while also satisfying American demands for a
major German troop contribution to NATO. He also promised to maintain a permanent British military presence on the European continent,
further reassuring the French against possible German aggression. To
their own surprise as well as everyone else's, the French found Eden's
proposals acceptable. On May 5, 1955, the Western occupation of Germany ended. On May 9, West Germany joined NATO.

From America's point of view, West Germany's admission to NATO
was an extraordinary triumph, for it meant that a balance of military
power had finally been established in Europe, thereby making a Russian
attack extremely unlikely and freeing Western Europe from the threat of
Soviet hegemony. For precisely these reasons, the Soviet Union sought
to undermine NATO by splitting the FRG away from its Western allies.
Its most sustained effort to do this provoked the second Berlin crisis,
which lasted from 1958 to 1962.

The Second Berlin Crisis

Ironically, it was West Germany's economic and political vitality that
precipitated this crisis. Exactly as Robert Murphy predicted during the
1948–1949 Berlin blockade, the FRG had become a "magnet" attract-
ing disgruntled East Germans in growing numbers, and the vast majority of these new arrivals came to the FRG through Berlin. As the Soviet
ambassador to the GDR, Mikhail Pervukhin, explained candidly in a
1959 report to Moscow, "The presence in Berlin of an open and, to

speak to the point, uncontrolled border between the socialist and capitalist worlds unwittingly prompts the population to make a comparison between both parts of the city which, unfortunately, does not always turn out in favor of Democratic Berlin."[80]

By 1958, Soviet leader Nikita Khrushchev recognized that this massive exodus, which included highly skilled members of the intelligentsia as well as ordinary Germans, posed a long-term threat to the existence of the GDR. The danger, however, extended well beyond the GDR. As Khrushchev acknowledged in his memoirs, the end of the GDR "would have been the beginning of a chain reaction, and it would have encouraged aggressive forces in the West to put more and more pressure on us. Once you start retreating, it's difficult to stop."[81]

Of course, the Soviets could have stanched the flow of refugees quite easily by building a wall between East and West Berlin. A plan for such a wall had been drawn up by the East German State Police, the *Stasi*, in 1952,[82] and it remained only for Khrushchev to approve it. But recognizing that construction of such a wall would be a tacit admission of the "socialist camp's" inability to compete with the West, Khrushchev declined to give his approval. Instead, he chose to follow Ambassador Pervukhin's advice: "[T]he Berlin question can be solved...by the gradual political and economic conquest of West Berlin."[83]

To achieve the gradual conquest of West Berlin, on November 27, 1958, the Soviet Union delivered formal notes to the United States, France, and Great Britain declaring that the Four Power Accord on Berlin was null and void and calling for the transformation of Berlin into a "free city." If no agreement on Berlin's status was reached within six months, the Soviet Union would conclude a separate peace with the GDR and give it control over the access routes to Berlin. Thereafter, the Allies would have to negotiate directly with the East Germans.

In issuing these demands, Khrushchev hoped both to force the Western powers to recognize the GDR and to bring about a process of Western disengagement from Berlin that would lead ultimately to its absorption by the GDR. Had he succeeded, it is almost certain that most West Germans, convinced that the West had "sold them out," would have turned against Adenauer and his pro-Western policies.

"If Berlin were to be lost," Adenauer told Charles de Gaulle in 1959, "my political position would at once become untenable. The Socialists would take over power in Bonn. They would proceed to make a direct arrangement with Moscow, and that would be the end of Europe."[84] Adenauer's position would become equally untenable if the Western powers recognized the existence of the GDR, for that would signal their acquiescence in the permanent partition of Germany—something all West Germans opposed passionately. Either possibility—Western recognition of the GDR or Western acceptance of the Soviet conquest of West Berlin—carried with it the risk of undermining NATO by bringing the neutralist Social Democrats to power in West Germany.

It followed, then, that it was in the West's interest, no less than in Adenauer's, to reject Khrushchev's demands categorically. But when Adenauer looked to the United States and Great Britain for support, he found them less than enthusiastic about confronting the Soviets over Berlin. Such a confrontation inevitably posed the risk of a nuclear war, and risking war for the sake of Hitler's former capital seemed grotesque. Both President Eisenhower and Prime Minister Macmillan therefore began to cast about for some sort of compromise with Khrushchev, despite Adenauer's heated objections. As de Gaulle summarizes their position in his memoirs:

> On the question of Berlin, Eisenhower and Macmillan inclined towards a compromise but without specifying what it should be. The President and the Prime Minister believed that Khrushchev, in spite of his well-intentioned airs, was really determined to ensure that the city was cut off from the West and would, if necessary, take active steps to bring this about. They agreed that in such an eventuality decisions would have to be taken. But they were extremely reluctant to define them, and made no secret of the fact that if it came to the point they would be even less willing to put them into

effect. Fundamentally, both were inclined to do anything to avoid the worst. Macmillan, in particular, declared with feeling that he could not conceive of himself taking the responsibility for leading his country to
appalling destruction simply for the sake of the future—
in any case highly problematical—of a German city.[85]

If Charles de Gaulle, who had come to power in France in 1958 after
12 years in the political wilderness, were a typical French leader, he
undoubtedly would have joined Eisenhower and Macmillan in urging
some sort of deal with Khrushchev to cut the feared and hated Germans
down to size. But de Gaulle was an unconventional statesman. He recognized that if Adenauer were humiliated by the Western allies, the result might well be the repudiation of his Western orientation, a revival
of German nationalism, and the end of NATO—a course fraught with
peril for all of Europe, but especially for Germany's French neighbor.
De Gaulle therefore sided with Adenauer, urging Macmillan and
Eisenhower not to negotiate with Khrushchev:

> I for my part considered that if we yielded to the threat,
> the psychological balance would be upset. Then the
> natural trend of things would lead the Soviets to de-
> mand more and more, and the Western powers to make
> more and more concessions, until the moment when,
> withdrawal becoming unacceptable for the latter and
> conciliation impossible for the former, flashpoint was
> reached. "You do not wish to die for Berlin," I told my
> two friends [Eisenhower and Macmillan], "but you may
> be sure that the Russians do not wish to either. If they
> see us determined to maintain the status quo, why
> should they take the initiative in bringing about con-
> frontation and chaos? Moreover, even if any complai-
> sance on our part did not lead immediately to a gen-
> eral aggravation of the crisis, the final consequence
> might be the defection of Germany, who would go and
> seek in the East a future she despaired of being guaran-
> teed in the West."[86]

In the end, although Eisenhower and Macmillan entered into negotiations with Khrushchev and persuaded him to revoke his six-month deadline, they conceded nothing of substance. When President John Kennedy (who found Adenauer "old, unimaginative and excessively prone to recall agreements that he had made with Kennedy's predecessors"[87]) came into office, Khrushchev renewed his threats over Berlin, and Kennedy urged his advisers to develop new initiatives, thereby seriously straining German–American relations. But Adenauer remained firm, de Gaulle stood staunchly by his side, and Khrushchev played his cards poorly. As a result, on August 13, 1961, it was Khrushchev who "blinked" by finally giving East Germany's leader, Walter Ulbricht, permission to build the Berlin Wall, which saved his tottering regime but was a major propaganda setback for the Communist cause.

Initially, the Kennedy Administration believed that the Berlin Wall would have a stabilizing effect on Soviet–American relations, and it issued no protest as the Wall went up. (The Wall, Kennedy told his aide Kenneth O'Donnell, was "not a very nice solution but...a hell of a lot better than a war."[88]) Yet even after the Wall had been completed, the President and his advisers still feared that the unresolved situation in Berlin someday might ignite an all-out war. They therefore decided to offer the Soviet Union major concessions—including recognition of the GDR and the transfer of control over American access rights to West Berlin to a neutral international authority—in exchange for a final settlement of the Berlin problem.

When Kennedy revealed his intentions to Adenauer, the Chancellor was furious. Shortly thereafter, an accurate account of Kennedy's proposals appeared in the German press and *The New York Times*. Kennedy accused Adenauer of leaking the information; Adenauer denied any wrongdoing. Whoever was responsible for the revelations, however, had succeeded in scuttling Kennedy's initiative. As William R. Smyser has written, "The proposals to recognize the GDR and transfer American rights to a neutral international access authority generated such an uproar in the United States, in NATO and in Berlin that Kennedy had to withdraw them."[89] Once again, Adenauer had prevailed.[90]

"I Have Not Given Up Hope"

In 1963, the 87-year-old Adenauer stepped down from office—or rather, his colleagues, exasperated by his autocratic ways, forced him out. He remained chairman of the CDU until a year before his death in 1967 but was very bitter. He continued to believe, as he told his aide Herbert Blankenhorn in 1962, that the Germans are "politically imprudent, political dreamers!"[91] They still needed his firm guidance, yet they had rejected him in favor of Ludwig Erhard, a brilliant economist but not, in Adenauer's view, a gifted leader. This rejection so rankled Adenauer that when his secretary remarked in 1966 that the memoirs he was writing read like a novel, a furious Adenauer replied, "A novel. It is not a novel. It is a terrible tragedy."[92]

Yet for all his bitterness, Adenauer never lost his remarkable clarity of vision. In 1966, at his final CDU party conference, he assured his audience:

> We believe that Germany should be reunited in peace.... I have not given up hope. One day Soviet Russia will recognize that the division of Germany, and with it the division of Europe, is not to its advantage. We must be watchful for when the moment comes. But when the moment comes, or appears to be coming, providing a favorable opportunity, then we must not let it go by unexploited.

At that same party conference, Adenauer almost casually passed on his political testament: "Our basic principle was incorporation among the free peoples of the West."[93]

Seated in the audience listening to Adenauer was a 34-year-old CDU delegate named Helmut Kohl. Twenty-three years later, when the Berlin Wall fell and the reunification of Germany suddenly became a very real possibility, Chancellor Kohl proved himself a loyal "Adenauerian." ("Kohl's great political model and inspiration has been Konrad Adenauer," writes Henrik Bering. "Throughout his career, he presented himself as Adenauer's grandson."[94]) He would not allow the prospect of reunification to go by unexploited, but neither would he agree to any Soviet demands—such as withdrawing a united Germany from NATO—that might compromise Germany's ties to the West.

Most West Germans heartily approved of Kohl's determination to press ahead with reunification, but there was widespread opposition to his insistence that a united Germany remain in NATO. Many Germans, including Kohl's Foreign Minister, Hans-Dietrich Genscher, maintained that Moscow would never accept the GDR's membership in NATO and that Kohl's unrealistic demand jeopardized reunification. These arguments deeply worried American policymakers, because "if Germany left the alliance, it would be difficult if not impossible to retain American troops in Europe."[95] But Kohl, like Adenauer before him, was adamant. "A united Germany will be a member of NATO," he assured President Bush when they met at Camp David in February 1990.[96]

And so it came to pass: On October 3, 1990, East Germany's parliament voted to unify with West Germany, and a united Germany remained in NATO. The internal crisis of the Soviet system that Adenauer had foreseen in his interview with the editors of the London *Times* back in 1952—and which Bush's predecessor, Ronald Reagan, had done so much to exacerbate during his eight years in office—was so severe that Soviet leader Mikhail Gorbachev was unable to prevent unification on Kohl's terms, especially since Kohl accompanied his demands with 60 billion deutsche marks in aid and credits.[97]

The United States thus has two reasons to honor the memory of Konrad Adenauer. It was Adenauer's vision of a revived and renewed Western Europe—with, first, western Germany and then all of Germany as an integral part—that led to the FRG's vast economic and military potential being placed, at the height of the Cold War, entirely on the Western scale of the East–West balance; and it was his political legacy that convinced another Christian Democratic leader, Helmut Kohl, not to sever Germany's links with NATO in exchange for reunification, thereby allowing the United States to retain her all-important NATO bases in Germany even after the Cold War had ended.

What Konrad Adenauer accomplished after World War II would be a titanic achievement for any statesman; for someone whose life seemed to have ended when he entered a Nazi prison at the age of 68, it was almost miraculous.

4 Alexander Solzhenitsyn

Re-Moralizing the Struggle

Alexander Solzhenitsyn: Re-Moralizing the Struggle

S hortly after his 1974 expulsion from the Soviet Union, the great Russian novelist Alexander Solzhenitsyn received an invitation from George Meany, president of the AFL–CIO, to visit the United States as the guest of the American labor movement. Although Solzhenitsyn initially declined Meany's offer, a year later—convinced that the Ford–Kissinger policy of Soviet–American détente was endangering the very survival of the West—he accepted it.

Thus it happened that on June 30, 1975, at a gathering sponsored by the AFL–CIO, Solzhenitsyn issued his powerful *Warning to the West*. He began by tracing the history of the West's seeming inability to grasp the reality of the Communist threat:

> For decades on end, throughout the 1920's, the 1930's, the 1940's, and 1950's, the Soviet press kept writing: Western capitalism, your end is near. We will destroy you. But it was as if the capitalists had not heard, could not understand, could not believe this. Nikita Khrushchev came here and said, "We will bury you." They didn't believe that either. They took it as a joke. Now, of course, they have become more clever in our country. Today they don't say "We are going to bury you," now they say, "Détente." Nothing has changed in Communist ideology. The goals are the same as they were, but instead of the artless Khrushchev, who couldn't hold his tongue, now they say "Détente."[1]

Unfortunately, Solzhenitsyn continued, many Americans had decided, for the sake of peace and a quiet life, to appease the Soviet Union. They refused to recognize that Communism is an evil force that must be resisted firmly:

> In the twentieth century it is almost a joke in the Western world to use words like "good" and "evil." They have become old-fashioned concepts, yet they are very real and genuine. These are concepts from a sphere which is above us. And instead of getting involved in base, petty, shortsighted political calculations and games we must recognize that a concentration of evil and a tremendous force of hatred is spreading throughout the world. We must stand up against it and not hasten to give, give, give, everything that it wants to swallow.[2]

When Solzhenitsyn delivered this searing critique of détente, his views were considered so far beyond the pale of respectable opinion that then-President Gerald Ford refused to meet with him in the White House. Yet only six years later, during his first presidential press conference, Ronald Reagan declared that "the only morality [the Soviets] recognize is what will further their cause, meaning that they reserve unto themselves the right to commit any crime, to lie, to cheat."[3] During those six years, American attitudes toward the Soviet Union clearly had undergone a sea change, and the man most responsible for that reorientation was Alexander Solzhenitsyn.

An "Unprompted Inclination Toward Writing"

"I was born on December 11, 1918 in Kislovodsk," wrote Solzhenitsyn in the autobiographical statement he submitted to the Nobel Foundation after winning the Nobel Prize for Literature in 1970.

> My father, a student in the Department of Philology at Moscow University, failed to complete his studies because he volunteered for the armed forces in the war of 1914. He became an artillery officer on the German front, served for the duration of the war, and died in

the summer of 1918, six months before I was born. I was brought up by my mother. She was a typist and stenographer in Rostov on the Don, where I spent my entire childhood and youth. It was there I finished secondary school in 1936. From childhood on I experienced an entirely unprompted inclination toward writing and produced a great deal of the usual adolescent nonsense.[4]

"Nonsense" Solzhenitsyn's juvenilia may have been, but "usual" they were not. In 1928, when he was only 9 years old, he began a journal called "Twentieth Century" and subtitled "On the Meaning of the Twentieth Century." In 1936, when he was not quite 18, Solzhenitsyn narrowed his focus somewhat by resolving to write "a big novel about the Revolution." He tentatively called it *R–17*. Thirty years later, while writing *August 1914*—the first novel in his *Red Wheel* series on the Russian Revolution—he found that he could include whole scenes from *R–17* practically unaltered.

Solzhenitsyn and his mother lived in a one-room shack in a dead-end street near the center of Rostov. As he told a French interviewer in 1976,

From the end of 1918, the year I was born, until 1941, I didn't know what a house was. We lived in huts which were constantly assailed by the cold. Never enough fuel to keep us warm. No water in the room where we lived—we had to go out and fetch it some distance away. A pair of shoes or a suit of clothes had to last for several years. As for the food, don't mention it. After the starvation of the 1930s, ordinary shortages were a minor evil. In some mysterious way, all these things struck me as more or less normal.[5]

When Solzhenitsyn was born, his recently widowed mother, Taissia, was 23 years old. (His father, Isaaki, had died in a hunting accident.) Her background—she came from a wealthy peasant family—made her suspect in the eyes of Soviet officialdom, and no sooner would she find a job than a colleague would denounce her as a "class alien" and she would be dismissed. That Solzhenitsyn's father had been an officer in the Tsar's army and had served in an "imperialist" war only worsened matters. The young Solzhenitsyn helped his mother bury Isaaki's medals lest they draw further adverse attention to the family's background.

Under these circumstances, it is hardly surprising that, as Solzhenitsyn later recalled, "Everyone was anti-Bolshevik in my circle." What *is* surprising is that neither Taissia nor any of Solzhenitsyn's other relatives sought to conceal their anti-Bolshevism from the boy. The sharp contrast between what Solzhenitsyn heard about the regime at home and what he was taught at school—what psychologists call cognitive dissonance and Solzhenitsyn, perhaps drawing on his physics background, refers to as social tension—had a decisive impact on his development:

> The fact that they [Solzhenitsyn's relatives] used to say everything at home and never shielded me from anything decided my destiny. Generally speaking…if you want to know the pivotal point of my life, you have to understand that I received such a charge of social tension in childhood that it pushed everything else to one side and diminished it…. And for this I have been frequently and cruelly punished in life. But that's the way I am and was, because inside me I bore this social tension—on the one hand they used to tell me everything at home, and on the other they used to work on our minds at school. Those were militant times…. And we used to listen with such wide eyes to the exploits of the Reds, wave flags, beat drums, blow trumpets…. "We'll complete the Revolution."… And so this collision between two worlds gave birth to such internal tension within me that it somehow defined the path I was to follow for the rest of my life…. Even now it is the same social tension that drives me on.[6]

Despite this social tension—or perhaps because of it—Solzhenitsyn was a brilliant student. "I had intended to acquire a literary education," he informed the Nobel Foundation in 1971, but the kind I desired was unavailable in Rostov, and our modest means, together with the fact that my mother was ill and alone, did not permit me to depart for Moscow. I therefore enrolled in the Department of Mathematics at Rostov University. I had considerable aptitude for mathematics and mastered it with ease, but did not feel it to be a life-long vocation. Yet mathematics was to play a beneficial role in my fate, saving my life on at least two occasions: I would probably not have survived the eight years of camps, had I not, as a mathematician, been removed for four years to a so-called *sharashka* [a research institute staffed by scientifically trained prisoners]. And later, in exile, I was permitted to teach mathematics and physics, which made my life more bearable and made it possible for me to pursue writing. Had I received a literary education, I could scarcely have survived my trials.... Later on, it is true, I did take up literary studies as well: Between 1939 and 1941, and concurrently with my studies in physics and mathematics, I took courses in the correspondence division of the Institute of History, Philosophy and Literature in Moscow.[7]

In addition to his course work in mathematics and physics and his literary studies, Solzhenitsyn was deeply immersed in the study of Marxism, which he believed was necessary for a proper understanding of the Revolution. By this time, Solzhenitsyn had become a convinced Communist—a member of the *Komsomol* (Young Communist League), an editor of the student newspaper, and the proud holder of a Stalin scholarship. He had also married a fellow student, Natalya Reshetovskaya, but did not fail, during their brief honeymoon in 1940, to continue studying the works of Lenin. Of this period in his life, Solzhenitsyn later said, "The Party had become our father and we, the children, obeyed. So when I was leaving school and embarking on my time at university, I made a choice: I banished all my memories, all my childhood misgivings. I was a Communist. The world would be what we made of it."[8]

There were, however, limits to Solzhenitsyn's devotion to the Party. While he was still a university student, representatives of the NKVD (secret police) tried to recruit him. He turned them down, but one of the most powerful and moving passages in his great book, *The Gulag Archipelago*, makes it clear that it was a close call:

> I remember my third year at the university, in the fall of 1938. We young men of the Komsomol were summoned before the District Komsomol Committee not once but twice. Scarcely bothering to ask our consent, they shoved an application form at us: You've had enough physics, mathematics and chemistry; it's more important for your country to enter the NKVD school. (That's the way it always is. It isn't just some person who needs you; it is always your Motherland. And it is always some official or other who speaks on behalf of your Motherland and who knows what she needs.)
>
> One year before, the District Committee had conducted a drive among us to recruit candidates for the air force schools. We avoided getting involved that time too, because we didn't want to leave the university— but we didn't sidestep recruitment then as stubbornly as we did this time....
>
> It would be hard to identify the exact source of that inner intuition, not founded on rational argument, which prompted our refusal to enter the NKVD schools. It certainly didn't derive from the lectures on historical materialism we listened to: it was clear from them that the struggle against the internal enemy was a crucial battlefront, and to share in it was an honorable task. Our decision even ran counter to our material interests: at that time the provincial university we attended could not promise us anything more than the chance to teach in a rural school in a remote area for miserly wages. The NKVD school dangled before us special rations and double or triple pay. Our feelings

could not be put into words—and even if we had found
the words, fear would have prevented our speaking
them aloud to one another. It was not our minds that
resisted but something within our breasts. People can
shout at you from all sides: "You must!" And your own
head can be saying also: "You must!" But inside your
breast there is a sense of revulsion, repudiation. I don't
want to. *It makes me feel sick.* Do what you want without me; I want no part of it.

Still, some of us were recruited at that time, and I think
that if they had really put the pressure on, they could
have broken everybody's resistance. So I would like to
imagine: if, by the time the war broke out, I had already been wearing an NKVD officer's insignia on my
blue tabs, what would I have become? What do shoulder boards do to a human being? And where have all
the exhortations of grandmother, standing before an
ikon, gone? And where the young Pioneer's [the Pioneers were Soviet Boy Scouts] daydreams of future sacred Equality?

…So let the reader who expects this book to be a political exposé slam its covers shut right now.

If only it were all so simple! If only there were evil
people somewhere insidiously committing evil deeds,
and it were necessary only to separate them from the
rest of us and destroy them. But the line dividing good
and evil cuts through the heart of every human being.
And who is willing to destroy a piece of his own heart?[9]

"I Will Not Swerve from My Path"

When Germany invaded the Soviet Union in June of 1941,
Solzhenitsyn, who had just completed his studies, immediately volunteered for military service. Rejected at first because of an improperly
treated groin condition, he was finally accepted by an artillery school in
Leningrad, from which he graduated in October 1942 with the rank of

second lieutenant. He was eager for combat. "One cannot be a great Russian writer," he told his wife Natalya, "without having been at the front."[10]

By the summer of 1943, Solzhenitsyn was in the thick of the fighting. An artillery commander, he participated in the battle of Kursk, was awarded the Order of Patriotic War for gallantry, and was promoted to captain. A colleague, Captain Melnikov, later recalled that Solzhenitsyn "fought courageously on several fronts, repeatedly displayed personal heroism, and inspired the devotion of the section he commanded. Solzhenitsyn's section was the best in the unit for discipline and battle effectiveness."[11]

Solzhenitsyn later recalled that during this period, "My power convinced me that I was a superior human being."[12] As such, he had little patience with Natalya's desire for children and the comforts of domesticity. After all, he wrote her, anyone can have a child, "but to write a history of the post-October years as a work of art is something that perhaps I alone can do.... I love you, I love nobody else. But just as a train cannot move off the rails for a single millimeter without crashing, so it is with me—I will not swerve from my path at any point."[13]

In fact, Solzhenitsyn already had begun to swerve from a purely literary path. "For a long time," he later recalled, "I had been sending a friend letters clearly criticizing Stalin without mentioning his name. I thought he had betrayed Leninism and was responsible for the defeats in the first phase of the war, that he was a weak theoretician, and that his language was primitive." Eventually, Solzhenitsyn and his school friend, Nikolai Vitkevich, who served on the Ukrainian front, agreed on "Resolution Number 1," which called for the establishment of a new Leninist political party in the Soviet Union. To deceive the military censors, they referred to Stalin as "the whiskered one," *Khozyain* ("master"), and *balabos* (Yiddish for boss).[14] But the censors were not deceived, and on February 9, 1945, Solzhenitsyn was arrested.

"I Have Served Enough Time There"

Ironically, Solzhenitsyn's arrest was a blessing in disguise. As they fought their way to Berlin, nearly all the members of his unit were killed, and he almost certainly would have lost his life as well had he not been arrested and sent to Moscow for interrogation and sentencing. But as Solzhenitsyn entered the fearsome Lubyanka prison, the blessing the authorities had conferred on him was well-disguised indeed.

Initially, Solzhenitsyn was placed in a tiny cell of his own, where he barely had room to move and where a 200-watt bulb that was never turned off, along with warders who constantly checked up on him, made sleep impossible. Later on, he was transferred to a cell with four other prisoners. Interrogations always occurred at night.

Solzhenitsyn was horrified to discover that his interrogator had copies of all his letters to Natalya, Vitkevitch, and other friends. By Soviet standards, he was clearly guilty under Article 58 of the Criminal Code, which made it illegal to engage in "propaganda or agitation containing an appeal to overthrow, undermine or weaken the Soviet regime, or to commit individual counter-revolutionary acts." But what his interrogator wanted was for Solzhenitsyn to name all the other "conspirators" involved in the new political organization mentioned in Resolution Number 1. "Looking back on my interrogation from my long subsequent imprisonment," Solzhenitsyn later recalled,

> I had no reason to be proud of it. I might have borne
> myself more firmly; and in all probability I might have
> maneuvered more skillfully. But my first weeks were
> characterized by a mental blackout and a slump into
> depression.... The only reason that these recollections
> do not torment me with remorse is that, thanks to God,
> I avoided getting anyone else arrested. But I came close
> to it.[15]

Eventually, he was convicted of conspiring to establish an anti-Soviet organization and sentenced to eight years of servitude in the Soviet concentration camp system now known as the Gulag. When Solzhenitsyn protested that two people—himself and Vitkevich—hardly constituted an organization, his interrogator shrugged his shoulders and replied, "What is there to say? One person is a person, but two persons are…people."[16]

Solzhenitsyn was relatively lucky. Eight years was a singularly mild sentence by the standards of the time. (In *The Gulag Archipelago*, he recounts the grimly humorous story of a *zek* [prisoner] who was asked by a guard why he had received his 25-year sentence. "For nothing at all," answers the *zek*. "You are lying," says the guard. "The sentence for nothing at all is ten years."[17]) During his interrogation, Solzhenitsyn was subjected to only the mildest of tortures: sleep deprivation. Others were not so fortunate, and it is of them that he writes in *The Gulag Archipelago*:

> If the intellectuals in the plays of Chekhov who spent all their time guessing what would happen in twenty, thirty, or forty years had been told that in forty years interrogation by torture would be practiced in Russia; that prisoners would have their skulls squeezed with iron rings, that a human being would be lowered into an acid bath; that they would be trussed up naked to be bitten by ants and bedbugs; that a ramrod heated over a primus stove would be thrust up their anal canal (the "secret brand"); that a man's genital would be slowly crushed beneath the toe of a jackboot; and that, in the luckiest possible circumstances, prisoners would be tortured by keeping them from sleeping for a week, by thirst, and by being beaten to a bloody pulp, not one of Chekhov's plays would have gotten to its end because all the heroes would have gone off to insane asylums.[18]

Amazingly, from his earliest days in the Lubyanka, and despite his depression at being unjustly arrested, Solzhenitsyn "had this consciousness that prison was not an abyss for me, but the most important turning point in my life."[19] When his ordeal was over and he had survived, he would even come to see his time in prison as a blessing, an opportunity for profound spiritual development:

Lev Tolstoi was right when he *dreamed* of being put in prison. At a certain moment that giant began to dry up. He actually needed prison as a drought needs a shower of rain!

All the writers who wrote about prison but who did not themselves serve time there considered it their duty to express sympathy for prisoners and to curse prison. I...have served enough time there. I nourished my soul there, and I say without hesitation:

"Bless you, prison, for having been in my life!"

(And from beyond the grave come replies: It is very well for you to say that—when you came out of it alive!)[20]

"The Most Important Years in My Life"

After being sentenced, Solzhenitsyn was moved to another Moscow prison called Krasnaya Presnya, where his belongings were stolen by young thieves on his first day in the cell they shared. Then he was sent to a camp called New Jerusalem, 30 miles outside of Moscow, and forced to dig clay from a pit for bricks. At yet another camp, Kaluga Gate, he barely avoided becoming a prison "stool pigeon." Fortunately, in a burst of inspired cunning, he listed his occupation on the camp's registration form as "atomic physicist." This led to his being transferred out of Kaluga Gate to Special Prison No. 16—a former theological seminary, located in an area of Moscow called Marfino, that now served as a *sharashka*, a research institute where scientist-*zeks* worked on state-assigned projects.

Solzhenitsyn has provided a fictionalized account of his four years at Marfino in his novel, *The First Circle*. Gleb Nerzhin, the novel's main protagonist, is modeled closely on Solzhenitsyn himself. Once a committed Communist, he has resolved to "Think! Draw some conclusions from your misfortune."[21] With the possibility of death ever present, he wants desperately to understand the meaning of the Revolution, of the suffering that has engulfed him, even of life itself. Nerzhin's favorite activity is "contemplation," and "when the squall of work passed, he would sit for hours hardly changing his position." Sometimes he records his reflections on tiny scraps of paper. These writings constitute "his first coming of age in thirty years."[22]

In Marfino, Solzhenitsyn came across two remarkable characters: the "devout" Stalinist, Lev Kopelev, and the devout Christian, Dmitri Panin. In Mavrino, where the *sharashka* in *The First Circle* is located, Nerzhin meets two brilliant *zeks*, Lev Rubin and Dmitri Sologdin, clearly modeled on Kopelev and Panin. Rubin is an unusually warm and generous human being, but a diehard Stalinist. Sologdin is a philosopher and mystic, but far more self-centered than Rubin.

Though Nerzhin admires Rubin's character, he learns to think critically from Sologdin and is influenced gradually by his ardent Christianity. This becomes obvious during his brief, supervised meeting with his wife Nadia, a character modeled on Solzhenitsyn's wife, Natalya. Nerzhin tells Nadia that he may soon be transferred out of the *sharashka*. When Nadia asks him where he will go, Nerzhin replies, "God only knows!" "Don't tell me you've started to believe in God!" exclaims a shocked Nadia, to which Nerzhin only smiles and replies, "Pascal, Newton, Einstein,"—three great scientists who were also believers.[23]

When he finally is taken from Mavrino to a "special regime" camp (established by Stalin in 1948 exclusively for political prisoners rather than the more favored common criminals), Nerzhin is a changed man. As a student, "he reasoned that the only people of any consequence were those who carried in their heads the legacy of world culture: encyclopedists, scholars versed in antiquity, devotees of fine art—versatile men with a multifaceted education. These were the elect and one must belong to them."[24] But in prison, he realizes that these "delicate, sensitive, highly educated persons who valued beauty often turned out to be cowards, quick to cave in, adroit in excusing their own vileness. They soon degenerated into betrayers, beggars and hypocrites. And Nerzhin had barely escaped becoming like them."[25]

In May 1950, Solzhenitsyn was transferred from Marfino—the relatively benign "First Circle" of the Gulag—to Ekibastuz, its hellish seventh circle. Located in the arid plain of Kazakhstan, Ekibastuz was broilingly hot in the summer, ice-cold in the winter. Prisoners were referred to not by their names, but by their numbers—in Solzhenitsyn's case, Shch–262. With its barbed wire fencing, its all-night use of floodlights, its guard dogs and sentries armed with machine guns, Ekibastuz, writes David Aikman, "was emblematic of the Gulag as it has become known to us."[26] *One Day in the Life of Ivan Denisovich*, the work that brought Solzhenitsyn fame, is based on his experiences in this camp.

In Ekibastuz, Solzhenitsyn later recalled, "I worked as a common laborer, a bricklayer, a foundryman. There I developed a malignant tumor which was operated on but not cured: its true nature was discovered only later."[27] While recovering from his cancer operation in the camp hospital, he became a Christian. He describes the events leading up to his conversion in *The Gulag Archipelago*:

> Following an operation, I am lying in the surgical ward of a camp hospital. I cannot move. I am hot and feverish, but nonetheless my thoughts do not dissolve into delirium—and I am grateful to Dr. Boris Nikolayevich Kornfeld, who is sitting beside my cot and talking to me all evening. The light has been turned out—so it will not hurt my eyes. He and I—and there is no one else in the ward.
>
> Fervently, he tells me the long story of his conversion from Judaism to Christianity. This conversion was accomplished by an educated, cultivated person, one of his cellmates.... I am astonished at the conviction of the new convert, at the ardor of his words.
>
> We know each other very slightly, and he was not the one responsible for my treatment, but there was simply no one here with whom he could share his feelings. He was a gentle and well-mannered person.
>
> It is already late. All the hospital is asleep. Kornfeld is ending up his story thus:

"And on the whole, do you know, I have become convinced that there is no punishment that comes to us in this life on earth which is undeserved. Superficially it can have nothing to do with what we are guilty of in actual fact, but if you go over your life with a fine-tooth comb and ponder it deeply, you will always be able to hunt down that transgression of yours for which you have now received this blow."

I cannot see his face.... But there is such mystical knowledge in his voice that I shudder.

These were the last words of Boris Kornfeld. Noiselessly he went out into the nighttime corridor and into one of the nearby wards and there lay down to sleep. Everyone slept. And there was no one with whom he could speak even one word. And I went off to sleep myself.

And I was wakened in the morning by running about and tramping in the corridor; the orderlies were carrying Kornfeld's body to the operating room. He had been dealt eight blows on the skull with a plasterer's mallet while he still slept.... And he died on the operating table without regaining consciousness.

And so it happened that Kornfeld's prophetic words were his last words on earth. And, directed to me, they lay upon me as an inheritance. You cannot brush off that kind of inheritance by shrugging your shoulders.[28]

Solzhenitsyn goes on to relate how, pondering Kornfeld's words during long, sleepless nights in the hospital recovery room, he comes to accept their essential truth. He sets down his thoughts in verse, and they are the reflections of a man who has finally found his God:

When was it that I completely

Scattered the good seeds, one and all?

For after all I spent my boyhood

In the bright singing of Thy temples.

Bookish subtleties sparkled brightly,

Piercing my arrogant brain,

The secrets of the world were…in my grasp,

Life's destiny…as pliable as wax.

Blood seethed—and every swirl

Gleamed iridescently before me,

Without a rumble the building of my faith

Quietly crumbled within my heart!

…And now with measuring cup returned to me,

Scooping up the living water,

God of the Universe! I believe again!

Though I renounced You, You were with me![29]

Solzhenitsyn calls his period of incarceration at Ekibastuz "the most important years in my life, the years which put the finishing touches to my character. From then onward there seem to have been no upheavals in my life, and I have been faithful to the views and habits acquired at that time."[30] Alexander Solzhenitsyn had entered the Gulag on February 9, 1945, the date of his arrest on the front in East Prussia, a committed Marxist–Leninist; he left it in Kazakhstan on February 13, 1953, the date of his release, a pious Christian.

A Life "Built Around a Purpose"

Solzhenitsyn's release from Ekibastuz was not unconditional. He was sentenced to "perpetual exile" in southern Kazakhstan. In *The Gulag Archipelago*, he describes how every fiber of his being sang "I am free!" after he left the camp. Soon he had another reason to rejoice. On the morning of March 6, shortly after his arrival in the tiny town of Kok–Terek that was to be his final earthly abode (so he then believed), the loudspeaker in the central square announced that Stalin was dead:

> This was the moment that my friends and I had looked
> forward to even in our student days. The moment for
> which every *zek* in the Gulag (except the orthodox com-
> munists) had prayed! He's dead, the Asiatic dictator is

dead!... I could have howled with joy there by the loudspeaker; I could even have danced a wild jig! But alas,
the rivers of history flow slowly. My face, trained to
meet all occasions, assumed a frown of mournful attention. For the present I must pretend, go on pre-
tending as before.[31]

On May 3, 1953, Solzhenitsyn became a mathematics and physics
teacher at the local high school. "Shall I describe the happiness it gave
me to go into the classroom and pick up the chalk? This was really the
day of my release, the restoration of my citizenship: I stopped noticing
all the other things which made up the life of an exile."[32]

This was not entirely true, however, for there was one thing—or rather,
one person—whom Solzhenitsyn missed terribly: his wife Natalya. When
he was a *zek* at Marfino, he had urged her to divorce him and make a
new life for herself. Initially, she had refused, but eventually she did file
for divorce, and when Solzhenitsyn was released from Ekibastuz, his ex-
wife, now a successful chemistry professor, was living over 1,500 miles
away in Ryazan with her new common-law husband and her stepchil-
dren. It seemed unlikely to Solzhenitsyn that they would ever be reunited.

Nevertheless, he soon settled into a reasonably satisfactory routine at
Kok–Terek, spending his days teaching and his nights writing. By all
accounts, Solzhenitsyn was a gifted and inspiring teacher. As for his
writing, in the Gulag he had acquired enough material to last a lifetime.
Solzhenitsyn was also befriended by two elderly exiles, Nikolai and Elena
Zubov, and they became "like father and mother to me."[33]

Then, in December 1953, disaster struck. His cancer had returned,
and the pain was agonizing. A local physician advised Solzhenitsyn to
seek radiation therapy at a hospital in Tashkent. (Solzhenitsyn's experiences in Tashkent would later form the basis of his novel, *Cancer Ward*.)

Convinced that he had only a brief time left to live, Solzhenitsyn
copied his manuscripts onto tiny scraps of paper, placed them in metal-
lic containers, and buried them in the yard of his mud hut before leaving for Tashkent. "It seemed as though for me life, and literature, were

ending right there. I felt cheated."[34] To his doctors' astonishment, however, the radiation treatment worked. After a few weeks, the tumor shrank; Solzhenitsyn felt better and even started putting on weight.

For Solzhenitsyn, this recovery was proof of divine intervention. "With a hopelessly neglected and actively malignant tumor," he later wrote in his literary memoir, *The Oak and the Calf*, "this was a divine miracle; I could see no other explanation. Since then, all the life that has been given back to me has not been mine in the full sense: it is built around a purpose."[35] That purpose was to bear witness to the horrors of the Gulag and explain how such a tragedy had befallen the Russian people.

With his cancer in remission, Solzhenitsyn now returned to his teaching and writing. He was eager to remarry, but his style of courtship was unique to say the least. Solzhenitsyn would ask his prospective brides to read Chekhov's short story, "The Darling," about a woman who allows herself to be dominated by each of her successive husbands. Chekhov wrote "The Darling" as a satire, but Solzhenitsyn took it quite seriously and informed the ladies he was seeing that Chekhov had captured his conception of the ideal wife. Apparently, it was not theirs: Solzhenitsyn remained single.

"The Kind of Day That Will Add Up to Years"

In February 1956, the Soviet Union's new leader, Nikita Khrushchev, initiated the period in Soviet history known as "The Thaw" with his famous secret speech to the Twentieth Communist Party Congress denouncing Stalin's "cult of personality." Millions of former political prisoners were granted amnesty, including Solzhenitsyn. No longer doomed to perpetual exile, he set out immediately for Moscow to renew old friendships, especially with Lev Kopelev and Dmitri Panin.

In the Panins' apartment, Solzhenitsyn also was reunited with his ex-wife Natalya. By December, they had remarried and were living in Ryazan. Natalya even agreed to model herself on the submissive wife in "The Darling." Solzhenitsyn returned to his Kok–Terek routine, teaching during the day and writing at night, with Natalya copying and helping to conceal his drafts. Between 1957 and 1961, he wrote several plays, *The First Circle*, and some chapters of *The Gulag Archipelago*.

Then, in 1959, Solzhenitsyn composed a novella based on camp life in Ekibastuz. Initially, he called it *Shch–854*, but the world would come to know it as *One Day in the Life of Ivan Denisovich*. The basic idea had come to Solzhenitsyn at Ekibastuz in 1950–1951. As he told the BBC in a 1982 interview,

> On one long winter workday in the camp, as I was lugging a handbarrow [filled with mortar] together with another man, I asked myself how one might portray the totality of camp existence. In essence it should suffice to give a thorough description of a single day, providing minute detail and focusing on the most ordinary kind of worker: that would reflect our entire experience. It wouldn't even be necessary to give examples of any particular horrors. It shouldn't be an extraordinary day at all, but rather a completely unremarkable one, the kind of day that will add up to years. That was my conception, and it lay dormant in my mind for nine years.[36]

In 1959, Solzhenitsyn began fleshing out his conception in earnest, and it took him only 40 days to complete it. "I sat down, and the story simply gushed out with tremendous force! That's because there were so many of these days all penned up inside me. And it was simply a question of making sure that nothing would be left out."[37]

The story takes place in a Special Camp for "politicals" in Central Asia early in 1951. Stalin—referred to as "Old Man Whiskers"—is in power; the Korean War is raging; and Ivan Denisovich Shukhov is trying to get through another day. He is a Russian peasant who, as an ordinary soldier in World War II, was unfortunate enough to fall briefly into German hands; this led to his incarceration in the Gulag as a German spy.

Uneducated, unsophisticated, but possessing sturdy common sense and a robust humanity, Shukhov is a Russian Everyman. As Solzhenitsyn later explained, "When I hit upon the idea of describing a day in the life of a *zek*, it was of course clear that he would have to be the most ordinary of rank and file members in the Gulag army."[38] But Shukhov—a composite character based on several individuals whom Solzhenitsyn encountered in the army and the camps—is only one of many vividly drawn portraits. For example:

- Captain Buynovsky—based largely on Solzhenitsyn's campmate, Boris Burkovsky—once served as a Soviet liaison officer on a British naval vessel, thereby incurring a 25-year sentence for treason.

- Tyurin, the camp-savvy foreman of Shukhov's work gang—based on someone Solzhenitsyn identifies in *The Gulag Archipelago* only as Nikolai Kh____v—is serving a 19-year sentence for being a kulak, a broad term used to describe peasants suspected of opposing Stalin's policy of enforced collectivization.

- Tzesar Markovich—based on film director Lev Grossman—is a film-maker accused of being a "rootless cosmopolitan," as Jewish victims of Stalin's anti-Semitic purge of the late 1940s and early 1950s were called.

These characters, along with many others, all reflect Solzhenitsyn's artistic determination to reflect reality as accurately as possible. As he has explained,

> I can really see no task higher than serving reality, that is, revealing a reality trampled, destroyed and maligned in our country. I do not consider invention as such to be my main task or goal, and I never seek to dazzle my readers with my fancies. For a writer, invention is simply a means of concentrating reality.[39]

Because his writings faithfully depicted Soviet reality, Solzhenitsyn never expected any of them to be published during his lifetime. Instead, he wrote out of an inner compulsion, a certainty that this was the path God intended him to take. By 1960, however, he began to feel oppressed by a growing sense of claustrophobia. "For twelve years," he later recalled,

> I quietly wrote and wrote. Only in the thirteenth did I
> falter. This was in spring 1960. I had written so many
> things, all quite unpublishable, all doomed to com-
> plete obscurity, that I felt clogged and supersaturated,
> and began to lose my buoyancy of mind and move-
> ment.… When you have been writing for ten or twelve
> years in impenetrable solitude, you begin without re-
> alizing it to let yourself go, to indulge yourself, or sim-
> ply to lose your eye for jarring invective, for bom-
> bast.…[40]

Solzhenitsyn desperately needed some intelligent criticism, and
Natalya suggested that he show *Shch–854* to some friends of hers,
Veniamin and Susanna Teusch. Solzhenitsyn did so, and Veniamin
Teusch's reaction was so enthusiastic—"There are three atom bombs in
the world," he told Solzhenitsyn; "Kennedy has one, Khrushchev another, and you have the third!"—that Solzhenitsyn was encouraged to
believe that a wider audience might prove receptive to his works.

Certainly, the political and cultural climate in the Soviet Union was
changing. At the Twenty-Second Congress of the Communist Party of
the Soviet Union, held in October 1961, Khrushchev renewed the campaign he had initiated in 1956 to discredit Stalin. Also at that Congress,
Alexander Tvardovsky, editor of the liberal Soviet literary journal, *Novy
Mir*, hinted broadly that his magazine would welcome bolder literary
works. To Solzhenitsyn, all of this verged on the miraculous:

> In my little room in a decaying wooden house where
> one unlucky match might send all my manuscripts,
> years and years of work, up in smoke, I read and reread
> those speeches, and the walls of my secret world swayed
> like curtains in the theater, wavered, expanded and car-
> ried me queasily with them: had it arrived, then, the
> long-awaited moment of terrible joy, the moment when
> my head must break water? I must make no mistake! I
> must not thrust out my head too soon. But equally, I
> must not let this rare moment pass me by![41]

In November 1961, Solzhenitsyn decided to submit *Shch–854* to *Novy Mir*. His friend, Lev Kopelev, brought the manuscript—single-spaced, marginless, using both sides of the page—to the magazine's editorial offices. Solzhenitsyn spent the next month in an agony of suspense awaiting a response. Finally, in early December, he received word that Tvardovsky loved the story. Would he please come to *Novy Mir*'s offices in Moscow to discuss it?

Thus began a most complicated relationship between Tvardovsky, a gifted poet and dedicated Communist, and the fiercely anti-Communist Solzhenitsyn. Tvardovsky, who genuinely loved Solzhenitsyn and was in awe of his literary talent, was also a loyal Party member and would not countenance the publication of anything in *Novy Mir* that called Lenin's revolution into question. In the case of *Shch–854*, Tvardovsky was convinced that Solzhenitsyn had produced a story that was not anti-Communist but merely anti-Stalinist, and therefore wholly in accord with Khrushchev's anti-Stalin crusade.

The question, of course, was whether Khrushchev would agree. To find out, Tvardovsky submitted Solzhenitsyn's manuscript to Khrushchev's adviser, Vladimir Lebedev, who in turn showed the work to his boss. Khrushchev's reaction was quite positive. Calling it "a life-affirming work," he went so far as to say "that it expresses the Party spirit. If it had been written with less talent it would perhaps have been an erroneous thing, but in its present form it has got to be beneficial."[42]

Once Khrushchev had given his approval, Tvardovsky felt free to publish *Shch–854*—which, however, he now renamed (with Solzhenitsyn's consent) *One Day in the Life of Ivan Denisovich*. In November 1962, *Novy Mir* printed some 750,000 copies of the story, and another publishing house brought it out in book form, with an initial run of 100,000 copies. All were quickly snapped up.

One Day in the Life of Ivan Denisovich was a runaway best-seller because it dealt with a central, but hitherto unacknowledged, reality of Soviet life—the Gulag. It was also written in a lively, even racy style that made liberal use of camp slang and was light-years removed from stodgy Stalinist prose. Deluged with letters from Soviet readers thanking him for *Ivan Denisovich*, Solzhenitsyn compared its publication

> to a phenomenon that defies physical laws, a situation where objects would rise instead of falling, or cold stones would grow hot of their own accord. It was impossible, simply impossible! The system was designed in such a way that for forty-five years it let nothing through, but there it was, confronted by this sudden breach. So it is clear that Tvardovsky, Khrushchev, and the specific circumstances had to interact in just the right way for the publication to take place.[43]

Solzhenitsyn was now a famous Soviet writer, a newly installed member of the prestigious Writers' Union, and the darling of the editor of one of the Soviet Union's most important literary journals. He was also a crafty ex-*zek* leading a double life. On the surface, he pretended to be a loyal "Soviet man," critical of Stalin but not of the system he created; in reality, he was a committed Christian secretly at work on *The Gulag Archipelago*, a book that he was rightly convinced would shake the system to its very foundations.

"A Government Without Prospects"

Solzhenitsyn maintained this deception until 1965, continuing his work on *The Gulag Archipelago* and enlisting a handful of trusted collaborators to help him type and hide his bulky manuscripts. (Like the overwhelming majority of Soviet citizens, Solzhenitsyn lacked access to a Xerox machine.) He microfilmed his major works and succeeded in having them transferred to the West for safekeeping and possible publication. After "lightening"—or toning down—sections of *The First Circle*, he also managed to convince Tvardovsky that it, too, was an anti-Stalinist work of art that deserved to be published.

This time, however, Tvardovsky failed to obtain Khrushchev's consent. Lebedev told Tvardovsky that Khrushchev "is no longer enamored of Ivan Denisovich; he thinks [Ivan has] brought him a lot of trouble."[44] Stalinist elements had begun to reassert themselves, and in October 1964, a successful coup headed by Leonid Brezhnev brought an end to Khrushchev's halfhearted experiment with liberalization. The Stalinist cabal led by Brezhnev feared (not unreasonably) that Khrushchev's de-Stalinization campaign eventually would spin out of control and undermine the entire Soviet system.

Almost a year later, in September 1965, having heard that a political and ideological crackdown was imminent, Solzhenitsyn removed his drafts of *The First Circle* from Tvardovsky's safe at *Novy Mir*, where they had been deposited pending publication, and placed them in the Teusches' Moscow apartment, where he believed the KGB would never find them. Just a few days later, however, the KGB (in connection with an entirely different case) raided the apartment and seized not only *The First Circle*, but also several earlier manuscripts that Solzhenitsyn had left there, including a play called *The Feast of the Victors* that was openly and unmistakably anti-Communist.

Solzhenitsyn was grief-stricken when he learned of the raid and immediately went into hiding. It was not so much arrest he feared as the possibility of going to his grave without completing *The Gulag Archipelago*—and it was all his fault for removing the manuscripts from Tvardovsky's safe! This self-inflicted wound, he later wrote, was

> the greatest misfortune in all my forty-seven years.... I had been an underground writer for eighteen years, weaving my secret web and making sure that every thread would hold.... My plan was an immensely ambitious one; in another ten years' time I should be ready to face the world with all that I had written, and I should not mind if I perished in the flames of that literary explosion—but now, just one slip of the foot, one careless move, and my whole plan, my whole life's work had come to grief. And it was not only my life's work but the dying wishes of the millions whose last whisper, last moan, had been cut short on some hut floor in some prison camp. I had not carried out their behests, I had betrayed them, had shown myself unworthy of them. It had been given to me, almost alone,

> to crawl to safety; the hopes once held in all those skulls
> buried now in common graves in the camps had been
> set on me—and I had collapsed, and their hopes had
> slipped from my hands.[45]

Had Solzhenitsyn known that KGB agents not only had seized part of his literary "archive," but also—in the course of their "surveillance" of the Teusches—had tape-recorded a number of his conversations, he would have been even more distraught. These tapes, cited by the head of the KGB, Vladimir Semichastny, in his October 5 report to the Central Committee on Solzhenitsyn, contain some remarkably indiscreet observations, any one of which easily could have sent Solzhenitsyn to the Gulag for 25 years or so under Stalin. Speaking of Lenin, for example, Solzhenitsyn said, "Lenin was nothing but a serpent, a man totally without principles. He would literally tell you he was on your side, but when you went to the door, he would shoot you in the back. Totally unprincipled."[46]

Solzhenitsyn was equally unguarded in voicing his opinion of the new Brezhnev regime:

> This is a government without prospects. They have no
> conveyor belts connecting them to ideology, or the
> masses, or the economy, or foreign policy, or to the
> world communist movement—nothing. The levers to
> all the conveyor belts have broken down and don't func-
> tion. They can decide all they want sitting at their desks.
> Yet it's clear at once that it's not working. You see?
> Honestly, I have that impression. They're paralyzed.[47]

Solzhenitsyn even predicted, with obvious approval, the forthcoming breakup of the Soviet Union:

> I'm amazed that liberal Russian people don't under-
> stand that we have to separate from the Republics.... I
> tell them that it's all over for the Ukraine, it has to go.
> "No, no," [they say]. Well, the Ukraine is a controver-

sial issue.... But how could there be any question about
the Caucasus, the Baltics! On the very first day, if you
want—whoever wants to leave, for God's sake, do so![48]

And perhaps most damningly of all, he candidly discussed his ongoing work, *The Gulag Archipelago*:

> But for now I have to gain time in order to write *Archi-pelago*.... I'm writing frantically now, on a binge, I've
> decided to sacrifice everything else.... *Archipelago* will
> murder them. It will be devastating!... I define it this
> way: an experiment in literary investigation. That means
> that where scholarly research can't be carried out, owing to the absence of all the necessary documents, I'll
> apply the methods of literary investigation, i.e., there's
> a great deal of logic in it, a very clear outline and a
> clear construction, but many of the missing links will
> have to be filled in through the use of intuition and
> linguistic imagery.... It's like lava flowing when I'm
> writing the *Archipelago*, it's impossible to stop. I think
> I'll finish the *Archipelago* by next summer.[49]

In addition to these highly incriminating tapes, the KGB chief supplied members of the Central Committee with a brief excerpt from Solzhenitsyn's unpublished play, *The Feast of the Victors*:

> The USSR!... It has no laws. All it has is power—
> power to arrest and torture, with or without laws. Denunciations, spies, filling in forms, banquets and prize-winners.... Applause! For a land of miracles, where
> hymns and odes are sung to hunger and misfortune.
> For the miracles of Communism when whole peoples
> are transported into the depths of Siberia overnight.[50]

All of this material, compiled diligently by the KGB for the enlightenment of the Central Committee, clearly demonstrated that Solzhenitsyn's loyalty to the regime was only a pose, that he was really an embittered enemy of the Soviet system. Under these circumstances, the most natural thing in the world would have been to arrest Solzhenitsyn and sentence him to a spell in the Gulag, just as dissident writers Andrei Sinyavsky and Yuli Daniel were sentenced to seven and five years, respectively, in the labor camps in January 1966 after a major show trial. In Solzhenitsyn's case, however, the only decision taken by the Central Committee was to refer the entire matter to the Writers' Union.

Perhaps Michael Scammell, one of Solzhenitsyn's biographers, is correct when he speculates that Solzhenitsyn's elevation by Khrushchev had endowed him with a special status, a sort of "vestigial respectability…even in the face of overwhelming evidence of his political unreliability."[51] Or perhaps Solzhenitsyn really was right when he concluded that he was the instrument of a Divine Providence. Whatever the reason, he was not arrested.

"I Shall Fulfill My Duty"

Solzhenitsyn, of course, knew nothing of the high-level deliberations that were deciding his fate. Sick with worry, expecting to be arrested at any moment, afraid to return to his apartment in provincial Ryazan, he nonetheless noticed something very strange:

> We were nearing the end of the second month since my novel and my archive had been impounded—and they had not followed through by taking me. They had not merely an adequate but an embarrassingly abundant collection of material on which to base charges against me, ten times more than they had had against Sinyavsky and Daniel—and yet for some reason they didn't take me. Strange times had come upon us!… "Dare is halfway there!" the book of proverbs whispered in my ear. All the circumstances told me that I must be bold and even insolent! But what exactly must I do? "If trouble comes, make use of it." Yes, but how?[52]

An invitation to speak at the Lazarev Institute of Oriental Studies in November 1966 suddenly clarified matters for Solzhenitsyn. He had recently completed *Cancer Ward*—the least politically incorrect of all his novels—yet Tvardovsky refused to publish it. Meanwhile, though

not moving against him officially, the KGB was making it known behind the scenes that Solzhenitsyn was not to be trusted. Solzhenitsyn
responded by taking the KGB to task before an audience of 500 "highly
educated humanists" at the Lazarev Institute:

> There is a certain *organization* which has no obvious
> claim to tutelage over the arts, which you may think
> has no business at all supervising literature—but which
> does these things. This organization took away my novel
> and my archive, which was never intended for publi-
> cation. Even so, I said nothing but went on working
> quietly. However, they then made use of excerpts from
> my records taken out of context to launch a campaign
> of defamation against me, defamation in a new form—
> from the platform at closed briefing stations. What can
> I do about it? Only defend myself! So here I am![53]

Solzhenitsyn's words had an electrifying impact on his audience and
convinced him that God wished him to speak out boldly and fearlessly,
to behave as though he were already a free man living in a free country:

> At last I was beginning to see revealed the higher and
> hidden meaning of that suffering for which I had been
> unable to find justification, that sharp reminder from
> the Supreme Reason which no mere mortal can at first
> understand. This was why my murderous misfortunes
> had been sent to me—to deny me all possibility, snatch
> from me any chance of lying low and keeping quiet, to
> make me desperate enough to speak and act.... Happy
> the man who deciphers more quickly the writing in
> Heaven, but I am slow, I need time—yet I, too, awoke
> one morning a free man in a free country!!!![54]

Having concluded that it was God's will that he go on the offensive
against a Godless regime, Solzhenitsyn became increasingly outspoken.
A particularly important turning point occurred in May 1967 when—
with a recording of Beethoven's Ninth Symphony playing constantly in
the background—he composed a stirring letter to the Fourth Congress

of the Soviet Writers' Union calling on its members to join him in demanding the abolition of all censorship. The distinguished Sovietologist Leopold Labedz has called this letter "the most eloquent plea for freedom of literature that ever appeared in the Soviet Union."[55]

"I am, of course, confident that I shall fulfill my duty as a writer in all circumstances," Solzhenitsyn thundered,

> from the grave even more successfully and incontrovertibly than in my lifetime. No one can bar the road to truth—and to advance its cause I am prepared to accept even death. But may it be that repeated lessons will finally teach us not to stay the writer's pen during his lifetime? This has never yet added luster to our history.[56]

In the eyes of Soviet officialdom, writing the defiant open letter to the Writers' Union was bad enough, but Solzhenitsyn proceeded to compound his offense by sending his letter to the West, where it was broadcast into the Soviet Union by Radio Liberty and the BBC. In 1968, Solzhenitsyn defied the regime even more openly by consenting to Western publication of *The First Circle* and *Cancer Ward*, both of which consolidated his reputation as Russia's greatest living novelist. Also in 1968, he succeeded in smuggling a microfilmed copy of his finally completed masterwork, *The Gulag Archipelago*, to the West, although concern that the regime might retaliate against some of the still-living witnesses quoted in the book led him to postpone publication for the moment.

Faced with this unprecedented offensive against the Soviet regime, Yuri Andropov, who replaced Vladimir Semichastny as head of the KGB in 1967, demanded a stern response. "The question of Solzhenitsyn goes beyond working with writers," he told his fellow members of the Central Committee Secretariat on March 10, 1967. "He has written certain things, like *Feast of the Victors* and *Cancer Ward*, that are anti-Soviet in nature. We should take decisive measures to deal with Solzhenitsyn, for he is involved in anti-Soviet activities."[57] Yet the Central Committee continued to dither, and it was not until November

1969 that he was formally expelled from the Writers' Union—a "disgrace" more than offset by his winning the Nobel Prize for Literature in October 1970.

Being awarded the Nobel Prize should have been one of the high points of Solzhenitsyn's life, but it was overshadowed by domestic tragedy. Starting in 1964, his marriage to Natalya Reshetovskaya had soured, and increasingly he lived apart from her, either just outside Moscow in the *dachas* (cottages) of the esteemed Soviet children's writer, Kornei Chukovsky, and the renowned Soviet cellist, Mstislav Rostropovich, or in his Estonian hideaway, a farmhouse where he completed *The Gulag Archipelago*.

Then, in 1968, he met Natalya Svetlova, a divorced 28-year-old mathematician living in Moscow with her young son, Dmitri, and working toward her doctorate. Initially, their relationship was purely professional. She was one of his trusted helpers—all of them female—who volunteered to type copies of *The Gulag Archipelago*. Soon, however, they fell in love. "The fourth or fifth time we met," Solzhenitsyn recalls, "I put my hands on her shoulders as one does when expressing gratitude and confidence to a friend. And this gesture instantly turned our lives upside down: from now on she was Alya, my second wife."[58]

The trouble was that Solzhenitsyn was still legally married to Natalya, his first wife. Complicating matters still further, Alya informed him in August 1970 that she was pregnant. This led Solzhenitsyn to write a contrite letter to Natalya begging her to grant him a divorce. Instead, on the night of October 14—less than a week after Solzhenitsyn had received a call from a Moscow-based Swedish correspondent informing him that he had won the Nobel Prize—Natalya took an overdose of sleeping pills and tried to commit suicide. Fortunately, he found her in time to save her life.

Solzhenitsyn now faced a serious problem: If he left for Stockholm to attend the Nobel ceremony, would the government allow him to return to the Soviet Union? And if he should request permission to leave with his wife, might not the authorities insist that he go with Natalya rather than Alya? These considerations led him to decide against applying for a travel permit to Sweden.

This proved to be an extremely wise decision, for KGB chief Andropov at that very time was petitioning his Central Committee colleagues to revoke Solzhenitsyn's citizenship and expel him from the Soviet Union. "When analyzing the materials on Solzhenitsyn and his works," read Andropov's "Top Secret" memo of November 20, 1970,

> one cannot fail to arrive at the conclusion that we are
> dealing with a political opponent of the Soviet social
> and state system. His anti-Soviet position has already
> been precisely defined in his novel *The First Circle* and,
> in the opinion of those who have read his unpublished
> work, in *The Gulag Archipelago*.... The deportation of
> Solzhenitsyn from the Soviet Union would deprive him
> of his position as an internal emigré and of all the ad-
> vantages pertaining to that status.[59]

Andropov even included in his memo a proposed draft of a decree depriving Solzhenitsyn of his citizenship. Had Solzhenitsyn gone to Sweden, it might well have triggered the revocation of his citizenship. But with his decision not to do so, Andropov's colleagues once again postponed taking any decisive action against the world-famous author.

The Call to Sacrifice

Andropov's concerns were perfectly valid. During the early 1970s, Solzhenitsyn continued to wage what Andropov called "hostile activity against the land of socialism with impunity," and his criticisms of Soviet–American détente became, as Andropov predicted, "a rallying cry for anti-Sovietism." But what Andropov's memo failed to anticipate was that Solzhenitsyn's devoutly religious views would gradually alienate him from most of the liberal, secular-minded members of the dissident community, and most especially from the one Soviet figure who was Solzhenitsyn's equal, physicist Andrei Sakharov.

The two Russian giants met in August 1968 in the wake of the Soviet invasion of Czechoslovakia and shortly after Sakharov's memorandum, *Reflections on Progress, Coexistence and Intellectual Freedom*, had been published in a Dutch newspaper. "Merely to see him," Solzhenitsyn wrote of their meeting,

> to hear his first words, is to be charmed by his tall figure, his look of absolute candor, his warm gentle smile, his bright glance, his pleasantly throaty voice.... We sat together for four hours that evening, although it was already rather late for me, so that I could not think too clearly or express myself as well as I wished.... And I could not at first get used to the feeling that I could reach out and touch, through that dark-blue sleeve, the arm that had given the world the hydrogen bomb.[60]

Sakharov also has described his first encounter with Solzhenitsyn, and his account focuses on Solzhenitsyn's criticisms of the views expressed in *Reflections*:

> At our first meeting, I listened attentively as he talked away in his usual manner—passionately and with absolute conviction. He began by complimenting me on breaking the conspiracy of silence at the top of the pyramid. Then he voiced his disagreements with me in incisive fashion.... The West has no interest in our becoming democratic. The West is caught up in materialism and permissiveness. Socialism may turn out to be its final ruin. Our leaders are soulless robots who have latched onto power and the good life, and won't let go until forced to do so.[61]

The controversy between Solzhenitsyn and Sakharov, which became increasingly intense over time, has often been interpreted in light of the 19th century debate between Russian "Westernizers," who thought that Russia must model herself on the Western democracies, and "Slavophiles," who believed that Russia should turn her back on the

West and pursue her unique destiny. In fact, both Solzhenitsyn and Sakharov belong morally and intellectually to the West, but Sakharov's philosophy was rooted firmly in the Enlightenment, with its faith in science, rationality, and progress. Solzhenitsyn—a gifted mathematician and physicist—did not discount Sakharov's Enlightenment values, but neither did he award them pride of place. As a fervent Christian, he thought that Sakharov had overlooked the most important value of all: faith in God. In the absence of such an overriding faith, Solzhenitsyn believed, Sakharov's enlightened, democratic society was bound to end exactly as Lenin's had, with "our being suffocated by the smoke and cinders of our cities."

Solzhenitsyn sketched out his Christian vision of a non-communist Russian future in a 1973 essay entitled "Repentance and Self-Limitation":

> After the Western ideal of unlimited freedom, after the Marxist concept of freedom as acceptance of the yoke of necessity—here is the true Christian definition of freedom. Freedom is *self-restriction*! Restriction of the self for the sake of others! Once understood and adopted, this principle diverts us—as individuals, in all forms of human association, societies and nations— from *outward* to *inward* development, thereby giving us greater spiritual depth.[62]

At the forefront of this historic shift from outward to inward development, Solzhenitsyn wrote in a 1974 essay, would be a sacrificial elite willing to "lay aside our material well-being and, if the worst comes to the worst, our lives," to challenge the state.[63] That Solzhenitsyn and his second wife, Alya,[64] took this call to sacrifice with utmost seriousness is evident from their joint decision to part with their children in the event they were taken hostage by the KGB rather than agree not to publish *The Gulag Archipelago*. "Our children were no dearer to us than the memory of the millions done to death," Solzhenitsyn writes in *The Oak and the Calf*, "and nothing could make us stop that book."[65]

Yet for all Solzhenitsyn's sincerity, most of his fellow dissidents were appalled by his extreme religiosity. His exaltation of religious fervor at the expense of scientific and technical expertise struck them as particularly dangerous. Throughout much of its history, the Russian Orthodox Church had been a pillar of reaction, yet here was Solzhenitsyn looking to it for salvation.

In Sakharov's opinion, despite his personal decency Solzhenitsyn was emerging as an ideologist of reaction. "History shows," he wrote, "that 'ideologists' are always milder than the practical politicians who follow in their footsteps."[66] And it was these "practical politicians"—xenophobic, anti-Semitic, and ultra-nationalistic—whom Sakharov believed that Solzhenitsyn, however unwittingly, was encouraging and legitimizing. (After returning to Russia in 1994, however, Solzhenitsyn repudiated the extreme Russian nationalists, and his staunch anti-imperialism served as a moderating force on the Russian right.)

"I Had Glimpsed the Finger of God"

Meanwhile, Soviet rulers continued to debate Solzhenitsyn's fate. Referring to the activities of Solzhenitsyn and other dissidents, Brezhnev opened the discussion at a March 1972 meeting of the Politburo by declaring, "We need to make it clear in a tangible way that we will not allow these people, the scum of human society, to poison our healthy atmosphere.... Our main task, in my view, is to improve ideological work." His fellow Politburo member, Victor Grishin (who reportedly had a brothel connected to his office) agreed, calling Solzhenitsyn "a true degenerate."

Mikhail Solomentsev blamed the whole mess on Khrushchev, who "discovered Solzhenitsyn and raised him up, that scum of society." Party ideologist Mikhail Suslov agreed, noting that "We have not liquidated all the results of Khrushchev's period.... In spite of the fact that the Central Committee Secretariat categorically objected at the time, Khrushchev and Mikoyan insisted on publishing Solzhenitsyn, praising him to the skies, and after that you all know what happened with him."

Andrei Kirilenko called Solzhenitsyn "an anti-Soviet slanderer of the first order," and Alexei Kosygin proposed that "Comrade Andropov himself should decide how to handle these people...." "Correct," said Brezhnev, concluding the discussion. "We will entrust Comrades [Nikolai] Podgorny and Andropov with the responsibility of going through the matter and making concrete proposals on the issue."[67]

As early as 1970, of course, Andropov had advanced a "concrete proposal" to deprive Solzhenitsyn of his citizenship and deport him; but his colleagues had turned it down, and if he simply came back to them with the same proposal, they probably would turn it down again. Andropov knew, however, that Solzhenitsyn had written a viciously anti-Soviet work called *The Gulag Archipelago*. If only he could get hold of a copy and show it to his fellow Politburo members, surely their indignation would overwhelm their caution, and they would finally agree to Solzhenitsyn's deportation.

In August 1973, the KGB obtained a copy of *The Gulag Archipelago* after Elizaveta Voronyanskaya, another of Solzhenitsyn's devoted female assistants, revealed under interrogation where one of the manuscripts was hidden. (Overwhelmed with grief and shame that she had not burned the manuscript as Solzhenitsyn had ordered, Voronskaya subsequently hanged herself.) Upon learning of the KGB's discovery, Solzhenitsyn decided that the time had come to publish—or, as he put it to Alya, to "detonate"—*The Gulag Archipelago*. On September 4, he issued secret instructions to publish the book in the West as soon as possible.

"Not for a single hour, not for a minute, was I downhearted on this occasion," Solzhenitsyn later recalled.

> I was sorry for the poor, rash woman whose impulse—
> to preserve the book in case I could not—had brought
> disaster upon it, upon herself and upon many others.
> But I had enough experience of such sharp bends in
> the road to know from the prickling of my scalp that
> God's hand was in it! It is Thy will! Would I...ever
> have brought myself to it? Would I have realized that
> the time had come to throw in *Gulag*? It is certain that

I would not. I would have gone on postponing it until the spring of 1975, sitting with feigned composure on the powder barrels. But I had glimpsed the finger of God: Sleepest thou, idle servant? The time has long since come and gone; reveal it to the world![68]

"I Have Fulfilled My Duty"

In December, the first volume of the Russian-language edition of *The Gulag Archipelago* was published by the YMCA press in Paris. "I have fulfilled my duty to those who perished," Solzhenitsyn told an interviewer from *Time* magazine on January 19, 1974. "The truth about all this was doomed to perish—*they* had tried to stifle it, drown it, burn it and grind it to powder. But here it is, whole once more, living and in print. And no one can ever wipe it out again."[69]

The Gulag Archipelago proved to be every bit as influential as Solzhenitsyn had hoped. According to British historian Robert Conquest, it has "had an almost unprecedented, worldwide impact on the minds of men."[70] Dissident Soviet historian Roy Medvedev agreed. "I think there are very few people who have not been deeply changed by reading the book," he wrote in 1974. "I can think of no other book, either in Soviet or world literature, with which to compare it."[71]

In the West, *The Gulag Archipelago* "played an enormous role in drawing international attention to political repression in the Soviet Union and to the living conditions of political prisoners."[72] In the East, "[E]xcerpts were broadcast by foreign radio stations into the Soviet Union. Not only dissidents, but common laborers crowded around radios to listen to the terrible truth about their recent past."[73] In retrospect, it is hard to believe that the extraordinary developments that occurred in the Soviet Union in the late 1980s—when intellectuals and journalists, permitted a moderate degree of freedom by reform-minded Soviet leader Mikhail Gorbachev, embarked on a devastating, root-and-branch attack on Soviet history and society that went far beyond anything Gorbachev envisioned—would have taken place had so many Soviet citizens not been "deeply changed" during the 1970s by reading, or listening to, *The Gulag Archipelago*.[74]

Of course, the Soviet media immediately went on the offensive. On January 14, 1974, *Pravda* published an 1,800-word commentary, "The Path of a Traitor," charging that Solzhenitsyn, "a defector to the camp of the enemies of peace, democracy and socialism," was "literally choking with pathological hatred for the country in which he was born and grew up, for the socialist system and the Soviet people." Other Soviet publications echoed *Pravda*, occasionally adding embellishments of their own—that Solzhenitsyn was a Maoist, for example, or an ally of U.S. Pentagon hawks.[75]

What Soviet authorities found especially galling—indeed, unforgivable—about *The Gulag Archipelago* was its contention that the evils it described—the tortures, the executions, the reign of total lawlessness—began not with Stalin, but with Lenin. Compounding Solzhenitsyn's "treachery" was his demonstration that 19th century Czarist Russia, though by far the most despotic state in Europe, was infinitely more humane than its Bolshevik successor. Between 1826 and 1906, for example, 894 people were executed by the czars, but in 1936–1938 alone, just under a million people were killed by the Reds. Moreover, the men and women executed in 19th century Russia actually were guilty of plotting against the regime, but those executed in Soviet Russia were completely innocent.

On January 7, 1974, a furious Politburo met to discuss the publication of *The Gulag Archipelago*. Denouncing the book as "a contemptuous anti-Soviet lampoon," Brezhnev declared that Solzhenitsyn "has encroached on everything that is most sacred: Lenin, our Soviet system, the Soviet government, everything that is so dear to us." Suslov concurred: "Solzhenitsyn has become impudent, he spits on the Soviet system and the Communist Party, he has encroached upon the holiest of holies, Lenin." But it fell to Andropov (who conveniently neglected to mention how his seizure of the manuscript from the luckless Voronyanskaya had triggered its publication in the West) to say, in effect, "I told you so":

> Comrades, since 1965, I have been raising the issue of
> Solzhenitsyn. Today he has gone to a new, higher stage
> in his hostile activities.... He opposes Lenin, the Oc-

tober Revolution and the Socialist system. His *Gulag Archipelago* is not a work of fiction; it is a political document. This is dangerous.... Therefore, we should take all the measures that I wrote about to the Central Committee, i.e., deport him from the country.... I propose that we expel Solzhenitsyn from the country using administrative measures. We should instruct our ambassadors to make the appropriate inquiries in a number of countries, as I stated in my memo, with the goal of having them accept Solzhenitsyn. If we don't take these measures, then all our propaganda work will lead to nothing. If we publish articles in the press, speak about him on the radio, but don't take measures, it will be idle talk. It is necessary to clarify what we do about Solzhenitsyn.[76]

This time, Andropov's colleagues agreed with his plan; and in early February, when Andropov submitted a further memo pointing out that West German Chancellor Willy Brandt had "made a statement that Solzhenitsyn could freely live and work in the FRG [Federal Republic of Germany]," the die was cast. On February 11, the Politburo issued a resolution "agree[ing] with the proposals of Comrade Andropov" to revoke Solzhenitsyn's citizenship and deport him from the country.

The KGB wasted no time. On February 12, six men entered Alya's Moscow apartment, where Solzhenitsyn was staying, and arrested him. "Nothing in my heart warned me," Solzhenitsyn later confessed in *The Oak and the Calf.* "I had lost my tense alertness."[77] Taken to Lefortovo prison, he was searched, stripped, and locked in a cell occupied by two other prisoners. The next morning, he was hauled before the Deputy Prosecutor-General and informed that he was being expelled from the Soviet Union. Shortly thereafter, he was taken to Sheremetyevo International Airport and placed on an Aeroflot jetliner. Within hours, he found himself in Frankfurt, West Germany—a stateless exile.

After staying briefly with his German host, novelist Heinrich Böll, Solzhenitsyn and his family (Alya and his four sons arrived in Zurich in March 1974) lived in Switzerland for over two years before settling in

August 1976 on a 50-acre tract of land in Cavendish, Vermont. Virtually everyone assumed that he would remain an exile for the rest of his life, but Solzhenitsyn believed that one day he would return to Russia. As he told British journalist Malcolm Muggeridge, "In a strange way, I not only hope, I am inwardly convinced that I shall go back. I live with that conviction. I mean my physical return, not just my books."[78]

Solzhenitsyn believed in his eventual return because he had concluded as early as 1965 that the Brezhnev regime was a "government without prospects." Now that Western radio stations were broadcasting excerpts from *The Gulag Archipelago* into the Soviet Union and terrible, long-suppressed truths were finally coming out into the open, it was only a matter of time, he thought, before ordinary Russians would lose their fear of the regime and demand their rights. The Soviet Union was doomed—provided, that is, that the West held firm, prevented it from expanding still further, and refrained from providing the regime with the economic assistance it needed to maintain its precarious hold on life.

Détente: "Giving Up and Giving Up and Giving Up"

There, however, was the rub: The United States and its allies were not resisting the Soviet Union. On the contrary, it seemed to Solzhenitsyn that under the guise of détente, Washington was engaged in "a process of shortsighted concessions; a process of giving up and giving up and giving up in the hope that perhaps at some point the wolf will have eaten enough."[79] Hence his decision to accept George Meany's offer and visit the United States in 1975. He would tell the Americans that détente was a fraud and a sham, alert them to the very real dangers they faced, and try to convince them to side with the Russian people—not their oppressors.

In June of 1975, when he learned that Solzhenitsyn had accepted an invitation to address the AFL–CIO, Secretary of State Henry Kissinger sent a memorandum to President Ford's National Security Adviser, Brent Scowcroft, warning the President not to meet with the Russian dissident. Because the memo became the focus of an intense national controversy, it deserves to be quoted in full:

George Meany has invited the President to attend a June 30 banquet in honor of Solzhenitsyn, which will be an occasion for outspoken anti-Soviet rhetoric. The Soviets would probably take White House participation in this affair as either a deliberate negative signal or a sign of Administration weakness in the face of domestic anti-Soviet pressures. We recommend that the invitation to the President be declined and that no White House officials participate.

During Solzhenitsyn's Washington visit (June 27–July1) another problem may arise: Pressure may be generated by Meany, members of Congress or others for the President to receive Solzhenitsyn in the White House. He is a Nobel Prize Winner, he is widely admired in the United States and the Senate has passed a resolution granting him honorary United States citizenship (if the House follows suit he would be the only person except Churchill so honored). Advocates of a meeting would argue that the President has received a whole range of Soviet visitors ranging from journalists and trans-polar fliers to the Minister of the Food Industry. They would ask: since the White House doors are open to Soviets of this sort, why not also to Solzhenitsyn, the most admired of all Russians? The arguments against such a meeting are as compelling as those against accepting the banquet invitation, but more difficult to defend publicly.

Solzhenitsyn is a notable writer, but his political views are an embarrassment even to his fellow dissidents. Not only would a meeting with the President offend the Soviets, but it would raise some controversy about Solzhenitsyn's views of the United States and its allies (as expressed, for example, in the attached *New York Times* article). Further, Solzhenitsyn has never before been received by a Chief of State and such a meeting would lend weight to his political views as opposed to his literary talent.

We recommend that the President not receive Solzhenitsyn. If significant pressures develop which make it imperative that the White House do something for Solzhenitsyn, we would suggest inviting him to any large social function taking place at the White House while he is in town, or arranging for him to be at a social function attended by the President during that time.[80]

Unfortunately for the Ford Administration, the text of Kissinger's memorandum was leaked to George Meany, who cited it in his testimony before the Senate Foreign Relations Committee in December 1975. "So there it is in black and white," an indignant Meany told the Senators.

We didn't want to offend the Commissars—so we spit in the face of the man our State Department refers to, perhaps sarcastically, as "the most admired of all the Russians." And—most incredible of all—we must not give the Soviets a sign of weakness. Weakness in standing up to the Soviets? No, weakness in standing up to the *anti*-Soviets at home.[81]

The Solzhenitsyn visit and the controversy surrounding it came at an unusually sensitive moment in American political life—a time, in the words of Russia scholar John Dunlop, "when a demoralized and somewhat volatile America was groping around for a proper response to a perceived 'Soviet threat.'"[82] Conservatives, in particular, were casting about for a different approach to Soviet–American relations, since the old approach, "containment," was thought to have been discredited by America's defeat in Vietnam, while the new approach, détente, had not succeeded in constraining Soviet expansionism.

Under these circumstances, the Solzhenitsyn affair became one of those crucial events—like Neville Chamberlain's trip to Munich or Jimmy Carter's "national malaise" speech—that forever define a political era. To anti-Communists on both the right and the left, Ford's refusal to meet with Solzhenitsyn made it abundantly clear that détente really was a form of appeasement—or, even worse, unilateral disarmament. As an editor at *Commentary*, Gabriel Schoenfeld, has observed,

> The Soviet Union, after all, never for a moment ceased to wage ideological warfare against the American "imperialists"; by failing to answer this warfare with our most formidable weapon—the truth—we were, along with everything else, practicing a form of unilateral disarmament in the political sphere…. More than anything else, this was the sum and substance of the neoconservative critique of détente.[83]

"The Overriding Reality of Our Time"

In the wake of the Solzhenitsyn affair, telling the truth about the Cold War became more urgent than ever. And to American anti-Communists, the truth was that Solzhenitsyn was right: The Cold War was not about arms control, or the balance of power, or even containment. It was, instead, a great moral contest between good and evil, right and wrong, freedom and tyranny. If American policy prevented our President from saying so, or even from welcoming someone who said so to the White House, then we obviously needed a new policy.

The most significant conservative political figure to challenge the Ford–Kissinger policy of détente was the former governor of California, Ronald Reagan, who had been eyeing the presidency for some time but was reluctant to challenge Republican incumbent Gerald Ford. A "turning point" for Reagan was Ford's refusal to meet with Solzhenitsyn, which Reagan attacked in his syndicated newspaper column.[84] Declaring that Solzhenitsyn "would be welcome to eat dinner any time at the Reagan White House,"[85] Reagan echoed Solzhenitsyn's criticisms of détente:

Reagan attacked détente as a futile and dangerous attempt to accommodate an adversary bent on achieving military superiority and world domination. He noted that while the United States was busy negotiating "fatally flawed" treaties, the Soviet Union was building its nuclear stockpile, which had become at least as formidable in the mid-1970s as that of the United States. This new preeminence, Reagan argued, was beginning to translate into Soviet military and diplomatic victories in Africa, Asia and South America. "The overriding reality of our time," Reagan said, "is the expansion of Soviet power in the world." He scorned the diplomatic initiatives of Henry Kissinger, whose Machiavellian strategies were, in Reagan's view, diminishing American influence across the globe.[86]

Although Ronald Reagan's attempt to wrest the Republican presidential nomination from Gerald Ford in 1976 failed, his supporters—after a heated fight—were able to add a "Solzhenitsyn plank" to the Republican platform. "We recognize and commend that great beacon of human courage and morality, Alexander Solzhenitsyn, for his compelling message that we must face the world with no illusions about the nature of tyranny," it declared. "Ours will be a foreign policy that keeps this ever in mind."[87]

The Solzhenitsyn plank, which greatly angered Kissinger and reportedly caused him to threaten to resign, was an important step in what might be called the re-moralization of America's policy toward the Soviet Union. But while Solzhenitsyn was the central figure in this process, he was far from the only one. Fearless and outspoken Soviet dissidents such as Andrei Sakharov, Andrei Amalrik, Yuri Orlov, Pyotr Grigorenko, Aleksandr Ginzburg, Anatoly Marchenko, and Natan Shcharansky also helped to focus American outrage at Soviet human rights violations, particularly when they drew attention to such odious Soviet practices as confining normal people to psychiatric hospitals on the basis of their political beliefs. Additionally, the plight of the "refuseniks"—Soviet Jews denied the right to emigrate to Israel—was publicized widely and effectively by American Jewish organizations.

Responding to this growing anger at the Soviet Union that President-elect Jimmy Carter announced his intention to meet with Solzhenitsyn at the White House. But although he did meet with Soviet dissident Vladimir Bukovsky (who was freed from a Soviet jail in exchange for Chile's release of an imprisoned Communist, Louis Corvalan), Carter never quite got around to issuing Solzhenitsyn an invitation.

For his part, Solzhenitsyn felt that, under Carter no less than under Ford, the West was losing the struggle against Communism. He therefore used his 1978 commencement address at Harvard University to deliver yet another warning to the West:

> A decline in courage may be the most striking feature that an outside observer notices in the West today. The Western world has lost its civic courage, both as a whole and separately, in each country, in each government, in each political party, and of course, in the United Nations. Such a decline in courage is particularly noticeable among the ruling and intellectual elites, causing an impression of loss of courage by the entire society. There remain many courageous individuals, but they have no determining influence on public life. Political and intellectual functionaries exhibit this depression, passivity, and perplexity in their actions and in their statements, and even more so in their self-serving rationales as to how realistic, reasonable, and intellectually and even morally justified it is to base state policies on weakness and cowardice. And the decline in courage, at times attaining what could be termed a lack of manhood, is ironically emphasized by occasional outbursts of boldness and inflexibility on the part of those same functionaries when dealing with weak governments and with countries that lack support, or with doomed currents which clearly cannot offer any resis-

tance. But they get tongue-tied and paralyzed when they deal with powerful governments and threatening forces, with aggressors and international terrorists.... Must one point out that from ancient times a decline in courage has been considered the first symptom of the end?[88]

In the editorial pages of *The New York Times* and *The Washington Post*, Solzhenitsyn's speech was dismissed as the raving of an ill-informed, anti-Western religious zealot. In fact, Solzhenitsyn was profoundly pro-Western, and his purpose at Harvard was to help the West avert a looming catastrophe. As the French philosopher Alain Besançon has pointed out,

Solzhenitsyn's message...was that communism has triumphed in Russia because Russia was more vulnerable, but that it had not been born in Russia. The forces that had brought communism to power there were the same ones that had racked Europe in the nineteenth century and that were still at work all over the world. If the West did not heed the warnings of Solzhenitsyn and others, it, too, would be devoured by this anti-life and change its very nature. The decision as to whether this would happen or not lay in the West's own hands.[89]

Having by now delivered his warnings to the West several times over, Solzhenitsyn retired from the public arena to devote himself to his writing. But while he refrained from political comment, he appears to have been gratified by the Reagan presidency. As Solzhenitsyn biographer Edward Ericson has noted, "We know that Solzhenitsyn valued Reagan. We do not know the details of his estimation of the President."[90]

We also do not know very much about Solzhenitsyn's view of the final days of the Soviet Union. It seems reasonable to suppose, however, that while he was profoundly gratified at the Evil Empire's 1991 demise, he also was profoundly disappointed that the spiritual revolution which he had predicted would precede the Soviet Union's collapse had not occurred. "In August of 1991, my wife and I were incredibly excited to watch [Felix] Dzerzhinsky's statue taken down outside the KGB building," Solzhenitsyn told journalist David Remnick. "That, of course, was a great moment for us. But I was asked at the time, 'Why don't you send a telegram of congratulations?' You know, I felt deep inside that this was not yet a victory. I knew how deeply communism had penetrated into the fabric of life."[91]

In a 1994 essay, *"The Russian Question" at the End of the Twentieth Century*, Solzhenitsyn wrote, "We must build a *moral* Russia, or none at all — it would not then matter anyhow."[92] It was to help re-moralize Russia that Solzhenitsyn and his family returned to their homeland in May 1994.

The Enduring Legacy

By all accounts, the results of Solzhenitsyn's efforts have been most unsatisfactory. His books are no longer popular. His TV talk show, "A Meeting with Solzhenitsyn," was canceled after a year due lack of public interest. His relations with the Russian Orthodox Church are strained. He despises the government of Boris Yeltsin. He is disgusted by the West's support for NATO enlargement and infuriated by NATO's bombing of Serbia. And he believes, as he told his family on New Year's Eve 1996, that the Holy Spirit has abandoned Russia.[93]

But whatever one may make of Solzhenitsyn's current positions, it cannot be denied that through his personal example of anti-Soviet defiance and his extraordinarily powerful literary indictment of the Soviet system, Solzhenitsyn helped spark a moral and intellectual revolution in the conduct of American policy toward the Soviet Union. And if the opening volley of that revolution was the Republican Party's 1976 Solzhenitsyn plank, the culminating moment of the re-moralization of American policy came on March 8, 1983, when Ronald Reagan, speaking at the annual convention of the National Association of Evangelicals, declared:

> Yes, let us pray for the salvation of all those who live in
> the totalitarian darkness—pray that they will discover
> the joy of knowing God. But until they do, let us be
> aware that while they preach the supremacy of the state,

declare its omnipotence over individual man, and predict its eventual domination of all peoples on the earth,
they are the focus of evil in the modern world.[94]

It had taken a while, but an American President was finally heeding
Solzhenitsyn's advice and telling the truth.

5 Pope John Paul II

Inspiring the Hopeless

Pope John Paul II: Inspiring the Hopeless

During a visit to Rome in the spring of 1989, Lech Walesa, the leader of the recently legalized Polish trade union movement, Solidarity, met with doctors and medical students associated with the Gemelli Clinic. "We came here to thank you for saving Solidarity," he began. When his audience appeared puzzled, Walesa explained, "It was you who saved the Holy Father after the assassination attempt in 1981. And it's hard to imagine that Solidarity would have survived without him."[1]

No less a figure than Mikhail Gorbachev, former General Secretary of the Soviet Communist Party, echoed Walesa's assessment. "Everything that happened in Eastern Europe in these last few years," he wrote in 1992, "would have been impossible without the presence of this Pope and without the important role—including the political role—that he played on the world stage."[2]

Yet despite his major role in the liberation of Eastern Europe and the demise of the Soviet Empire, the surprising fact is that, until well into his priestly career, Karol Wojtyla, the man who would become Pope John Paul II, disclaimed any interest in politics. According to Jacek Wozniakowski, a prominent Polish liberal Catholic who knew Wojtyla in the 1960s when the future Pope was archbishop of Kraków, "He quite obviously didn't want to get into politics. He thought he should stick to Church matters; he thought that political problems should be left to laymen or to Cardinal [Stefan] Wyszynski." Wojtyla's constant refrain during this period was "I'm not very interested in politics."[3]

Poland's Communist authorities were well aware of this aspect of Wojtyla's character. On August 5, 1967, five weeks after he had been named a cardinal, the UB (Poland's secret police) published a "top-secret" analysis, "Our Tactics Toward Cardinals Wojtyla and Wyszynski," which depicted Wojtyla as a scholarly, basically apolitical cleric: "He has not, so far, engaged in open, anti-state political activity. It seems that politics is his weaker suit; he is over-intellectualized…. He lacks organizing and leadership qualities, and this is his weakness in the rivalry with Wyszynski."[4]

How, then, did this essentially *religious* figure become one of the most remarkable *political* leaders of our time? Perhaps the answer to this question can be found in a distinction that Karol Wojtyla frequently drew when he was a priest in Poland. According to a former parishioner, Wojtyla admonished his flock to differentiate between *politico sensu largo*, "politics in the large sense," and *politico sensu stricto*, "politics in the narrow sense."[5] Politics in the narrow sense had to do with the Communist bosses and their doings, and Wojtyla urged Poles to steer clear of such matters. Politics in the large sense, however, was concerned with the spiritual renewal of the individual and the nation, and this was an issue of intense concern to Wojtyla, both as a priest and, even earlier, as an aspiring actor growing up in the small, southern Polish town of Wadowice, three miles southwest of Kraków.

"It All Comes from There"

Karol Wojtyla, who in 1978 became the first non-Italian pontiff since Adrian VI (a Dutchman who was elected in 1522 and died the following year) was born on May 18, 1920, the third and last child of Karol Sr. and Emilia Wojtyla. Six years earlier, his sister had died in her infancy. In 1929, when Karol was completing third grade, Emilia died of kidney disease. His brother, Edmund, 14 years his senior, died in 1932, shortly after completing his medical studies, of scarlet fever contracted from a patient. "My mother's death made a deep impression on my memory," he later told French journalist André Frossard, "and my brother's perhaps a still deeper one, because of the dramatic circumstances in which it occurred and because I was more mature. Thus quite soon I became a motherless child."[6]

Karol and his father, a retired army lieutenant widely respected for his integrity, occupied a three-room flat across the street from Wadowice's main church. The young Wojtyla was a brilliant student, popular with teachers and classmates alike, but different from the other children. For one thing, like his father, he prayed constantly; for another, he refused to use foul language. Years later, John Paul II recalled that he and his father "never spoke about a vocation for the priesthood, but his example was in a way my first seminary, a kind of domestic seminary."[7]

Also significant about the Wojtyla family was the immunity of both father and son to the anti-Semitic virus that had infected a significant portion of the Polish Catholic Church, including its Primate (or life-time head), Cardinal Augustyn Hlond. About a quarter of Wadowice's population was Jewish, and not only did Karol have close Jewish friends, but when the Jewish soccer team was short a goalie in its contest with the Catholic team, young Karol would gladly play for the Jews. Recalling his Wadowice childhood in 1994, John Paul II observed that "it is from there that I have this attitude of community, of communal feeling about the Jews…. It all comes from there."[8]

"A Passion for Literature"

When he was 14 years old, Karol Wojtyla discovered the theater. It was love at first sight. As a schoolmate later recalled, "His life took a new turn. Lolek [Karol's nickname] now devoted every free minute to the theater."[9] But the philosophy behind the Amateur University Theater of Wadowice was far removed from conventional notions of dramaturgy. The theater's founder, Mieczyslaw Kotlarczyk, believed in using the evocative power of words to convey profound Christian truths.

As an aspiring young actor, Karol immersed himself in the riches of Polish literature. "I was completely absorbed by a passion for literature, especially for dramatic literature, and for the theater," he recalled over half a century later.[10] He was influenced particularly by the great Polish romantic writers of the 19th century—Adam Mickiewicz (1798–1855),

Juliusz Slowacki (1803–1849), and Zygmunt Krasinski (1812–1859)— and their followers, Cyprian Norwid (1821–1883) and Stanislaw Wyspianski (1869–1907). Even after Wojtyla had become an adult, Norwid remained his favorite poet.[11]

Between 1795 and 1918, when Poland was partitioned between Russia, Prussia, and Austria and effectively disappeared from the map of Europe, these poets defended Polish culture against German and Russian efforts to eradicate it. Their key concern was promoting the Polish nation's spiritual renewal. They placed great emphasis on what they called "organic work"—defending the Polish language, culture, and religion against the invaders. They also believed that just as Poland, the "Christ among the nations," had suffered for Europe's sins, so would her spiritual and political rebirth coincide with the moral and political redemption of all mankind.

Concerned as they were about matters spiritual, Mickiewicz and his circle naturally focused on the Catholic Church as the vehicle for Poland's rebirth. Legend has it that after the failure of the revolt of 1831, Mickiewicz told a gathering of his followers in Paris that what was needed now was a religious order dedicated to the spiritual salvation of the Polish nation. "We need a new order," he reportedly said. "There is no other salvation. But how could we found it? I am too proud." Then he pointed to Bogdan Janski, and it was Janski, along with Piotr Semenenko and Hieronim Kajsiewicz, who founded the Order of Resurrectionists.[12]

In their struggle for national survival, the Poles naturally looked to the Holy See for support. To their intense dismay, however, the Roman pontiffs were distinctly unsympathetic to Poland's plight. Indeed, Pope Gregory XVI condemned the 1831 rising as the work of "certain intriguers and spreaders of lies, who under the pretense of religion in this unhappy age, are raising their heads against the power of princes."[13] Pope Pius IX concurred: "The Poles seek Poland above all, not the Kingdom of God, and that is why they have no Poland."[14] This hostility infuriated the poet Juliusz Slowacki, who denounced Pius IX and prophesied his eventual replacement by a Slav:

In the time of quarrels God will choose
A Slavic pope, braver than the Italian
Who came before him. He will be unafraid
To take on a fight.[15]

What makes these words so uncanny is that about 150 years after he wrote them, events turned out pretty much as Slowacki foresaw. As a priest, Karol Wojtyla devoted himself to the "organic work" that Mickiewicz and Slowacki demanded, shunning direct political involvement but defending Christian values against the Soviets and their Polish puppets. "Wojtyla's attitude," said Polish historian Stefan Swiezawski, "was to use each moment to strengthen your orientation, to expand your knowledge, to concentrate on positive work—not wasting your time on political issues and conflicts."[16] Then, "in a time of quarrels" (the Cold War), he became both a "Slavic pope" and a warrior-Pope, "unafraid to take on a fight" with Communist authorities. In this he differed markedly from his predecessor, Paul VI, who favored a more conciliatory approach to the Soviets.

When he graduated from high school in 1938, however, entering the priesthood was the furthest thing from Karol Wojtyla's mind. "Towards the end of my years at the lycée," he told a French journalist some 45 years later, "the people around me thought I would choose the priesthood. As for me, I did not give it a thought. I was quite sure that I would remain a layman. Committed, to be sure, determined without any doubt to participate in the life of the Church; but as a priest, certainly not."[17]

"I Would Be a Priest"

In 1938, after Karol was accepted to the ancient Jagiellonian University (founded in 1364) in Kraków, he and his father left Wadowice and found a tiny basement apartment in a modest section of the city. Karol's courses focused on Polish philology, but the German invasion of Poland in September 1939 interrupted his studies. As part of the German campaign to destroy Poland's intellectual elite and reduce its Catholic population to the status of brute animals—Polish Jews, of course, were slated for extermination from the outset—Jagiellonian University was shut down, its libraries looted, its laboratories destroyed, and 184 members of its distinguished faculty packed off to the Sachsenhausen concentration camp.

As an able-bodied young man, Karol was in danger of being drafted by the Germans for one of their slave-labor battalions. Fortunately, thanks to a friend, he found work at the Solvay Chemical Works just outside of Kraków. This entitled him to a precious *Arbeitskarte*, an identity card indicating that its bearer was engaged in war-related work and was not to be molested. His manual labor at the Solvay plant enabled Karol to earn enough to support himself and his ailing father, who died in 1941.

The shocking ease with which Hitler's Germany conquered Poland led Karol to rethink his country's recent past. In an early letter to Kotlarczyk, he confessed that

> I did not see [Poland] in a fully truthful light. The idea
> of Poland was alive in us, just as it had been in the
> generation of Romanticism. But this Poland was not
> living in the truth, because the peasants were beaten
> and imprisoned on account of their just demand for
> political rights, because they felt their hour of destiny
> approaching, because they were in the right.[18]

These bitter ruminations only reinforced Wojtyla's determination to "build a theater that will be a church where the national spirit will burn."[19]

Meanwhile, his meeting in 1940 with Jan Tyranowski, a tailor and autodidact with a profound grasp of Catholic mysticism and a burning desire to pass that understanding on to others, deepened and enriched Wojtyla's faith by introducing him—via the writings of the 16th century Spanish Carmelite reformer and mystic, Juan de Yepes, better known as St. John of the Cross—to the riches of Carmelite spirituality. After he became Pope, Wojtyla recalled Tyranowski as

> a very simple man who was one of those unknown
> saints, hidden among the others like a marvelous light
> at the bottom of life, at a depth where night usually
> reigns. He disclosed to me the riches of his inner life,

of his mystical life…. I was not yet thinking of the priesthood when he gave me, among other books, the works of St. John of the Cross, of whom he was the first to speak to me.[20]

Although Tyranowski undoubtedly had a major impact on Wojtyla, the younger man's decision to abandon the theater for the priesthood emerged only gradually:

> I was working at the factory and devoting myself, as far as the terrors of the occupation allowed, to my taste for literature and drama. My priestly vocation took shape in the midst of all that, like an inner fact of un-questionable and absolute clarity. The following year, in the autumn, I knew that I was called. I could see clearly what I had to give up and the goal that I had to attain…. I would be a priest.[21]

In the first week of November 1942, Wojtyla and his friend and future fellow seminarian, Mieczyslaw Malinski, went to the priests' residence opposite the Wawel Cathedral in Kraków. A priest poured Malinski some tea while Karol vanished. When Karol returned, he told Malinski that he had decided to become a priest; he had been taken to see Archbishop Sapieha, who interviewed him and then promptly accepted him. Wojtyla became one of seven seminarians who met with their tutors clandestinely in secret locations throughout Kraków, since being caught as a seminarian meant execution or deportation to a Nazi concentration camp.[22]

"The Best Possible Start"

Prince Metropolitan Adam Stefan Sapieha, archbishop of Kraków and a future cardinal, was a complicated man. A descendant of one of Poland's grandest families (and related to Italian nobility, which explains why Hitler, who was cultivating Mussolini, failed to have him arrested),[23] he had sat briefly in his country's parliament during the 1930s as a representative of the far-right National Democrats, a political party not known for its friendship toward Jews or other minorities. During World War II, however, he issued baptismal certificates to Jews hiding from the Germans and on two occasions sent special couriers to the Vatican to inform the Holy See of Nazi atrocities being committed against Polish Catholics and Jews. (The Holy See did not respond.)[24]

Sapieha also oversaw an underground seminary for the training of future priests. With Poland's Primate, Cardinal Hlond, having fled the country in the aftermath of Germany's invasion, Sapieha was widely considered "the head of the Polish nation in both religious and secular matters."[25]

Until the very end of the war—when, to escape increasingly severe Gestapo manhunts, all the seminarians moved into the archbishop's residence—Karol pursued his theological studies while continuing to work at the Solvay factory. He favored the nightshift, which was quieter and gave him more of an opportunity to read. Though they sometimes mocked his piety, his fellow-workers liked the studious lad. They had no idea he was preparing for the priesthood.

Sapieha saw to it that Karol's courses were intellectually demanding—sometimes almost too much so. Years later, the Pope described how he wrestled with a notoriously difficult philosophy text, *Ontology or General Metaphysics*, which he found so impenetrable that "I actually wept over it." But "after two months of hacking through this vegetation I came to a clearing, to the discovery of the deep reasons for what until then I had only lived and felt…. What intuition and sensibility had until then taught me about the world found solid confirmation."[26]

With the end of World War II and the coming to power of Communism in Poland, Archbishop Sapieha understood that the Church would soon be engaged in a desperate struggle that would be as much cultural as political. It followed, therefore, that intellectually gifted seminarians like Wojtyla, capable of engaging the enemy in a future *Kulturkampf*, had to be groomed carefully for battle. Thus, when Father Wojtyla, shortly before his ordination in 1946, approached Sapieha to ask his permission to join a Carmelite monastic order, the archbishop turned him down.

Instead of being allowed to pursue the contemplative life, Wojtyla was sent in 1946 to the Angelicum, the Dominican Theology Faculty in Rome, to obtain his (first) doctorate. He received it in July 1948, after completing his thesis on St. John of the Cross, whose work he first encountered thanks to Jan Tyranowski.

Within two weeks of his return to Poland, Wojtyla was appointed curate (assistant priest) of the rural parish of Niegowic—a surprising choice, given his formidable academic credentials. Here again, Sapieha's hand was to be seen: The parish priest was one of the finest in the diocese. "Valuing Karol as he did," Father Malinski has written, "[Sapieha] wanted to give him the best possible start in his pastoral career."[27]

After Wojtyla had served seven months in Niegowic, Sapieha (who was now a cardinal) decided that his new priest's "basic training" was over. Having experienced a rural apostolate, Karol would now serve as vicar in the university parish of St. Florian's Church in intellectually vibrant Kraków.

Wojtyla was placed in charge of St. Florian's ministry to college students and quickly became hugely popular. A lover of the outdoors, he organized hiking, biking, and canoeing trips with his charges, attempting to create a genuine sense of Christian fellowship. Since so many of his discussions centered on love, marriage, and sex, Wojtyla became quite expert in these areas.

In 1960, this expertise resulted in the publication of *Love and Responsibility*, his first book (not counting his doctoral dissertations). Advocating "the equality of man and woman in marriage," it treated human sexuality as a gift from God and frankly addressed the most intimate matters. Since it was widely believed that only a sexually experienced author could have written *Love and Responsibility*, rumors were rife that Father Wojtyla had once been engaged, or even married. In fact, the evidence is overwhelming that Wojtyla's sexual knowledge is entirely theoretical and derives from countless hours in the confessional, as well as from exhaustive reading and detailed conversations with specialists.

Defensor Hominis

In 1951, Cardinal Sapieha died. His successor, Archbishop Eugeniusz Baziak, ordered Father Wojtyla to begin working on a second doctorate in philosophy, which would enable him to teach at the university level. Though Wojtyla was reluctant to abandon his pastoral duties, he did as he was told and began a two-year investigation of the thought of Max Scheler, a German philosopher described in *The Encyclopedia of Philosophy* as "one of the most insightful, acutely intuitive, and brilliant thinkers of the early twentieth century…. His work has been of significant value in ethics, religion, psychology and sociology."[28] In 1954, Wojtyla's 175-page doctorate, entitled *An Assessment of the Possibility of Erecting a Christian Ethic on the Principles of Max Scheler*, was approved unanimously by the Theological Faculty of Jagiellonian University.[29]

Shortly after Wojtyla completed his doctoral studies, Poland's Communist authorities closed down Jagiellonian University's Theology Faculty. He therefore joined the philosophy faculty of the Catholic University of Lublin, the only Catholic institution of higher learning behind the Iron Curtain, and eventually came to hold its Chair of Ethics.

The Lublin school of philosophy was known for its vigorous defense of human rights—a theme that would become a hallmark of Wojtyla's thought.[30] For Wojtyla, these rights are rooted in the Judeo–Christian belief that man was created in God's image. "God has imprinted his own image and likeness on human beings," he later wrote in his 1991 Encyclical, *Centesimus Annus* (*The Hundredth Year*), "conferring on them an incomparable dignity…. In effect, beyond the rights which one acquires by one's own work, there exist rights which do not correspond to any work performed, but which flow from one's essential dignity as a person."[31]

Wojtyla's belief in human dignity—which implied the right of every person to determine his or her own fate, rather than be told what to do by the state—became the basis of his political philosophy. As one of his philosophical collaborators, Professor Anna-Teresa Tymieniecka, has written,

> [Wojtyla] stressed the self-determination of a human being: that it is in the hands of an individual to delineate his life, to work out his life; and consequently a society and political system have to give the individual the opportunity for self-determination.... If, on the one hand, the social–political system does not give this self-determination its proper rights—as in totalitarianism and communism, which suppress the self-determination of the human being—then the state is pernicious. On the other hand, if societies and cultures allow the individual to become strictly individualistic and oblivious to the community ties which self-determination both calls for and establishes—then social cooperation disintegrates.[32]

If respect for human dignity is based ultimately on belief in God, then the root cause of Communism's denial of human dignity was its atheism. As *Centesimus Annus* proclaims:

> It is by responding to the call of God contained in the being of things that man becomes aware of his transcendent dignity. Every individual must give this response, which constitutes the apex of his humanity, and no social mechanism or collective subject can substitute for it. The denial of God deprives the person of his foundation, and consequently leads to a reorganization of the social order without reference to the person's dignity and responsibility.[33]

Father Wojtyla thrived in the philosophy department at the Catholic University of Lublin. In addition to preparing a major philosophical treatise, *Person and Act* (devoted, as he told Father Henri de Lubac, "to the metaphysical sense and mystery of the PERSON"[34]), he was preoccupied with his research on marriage and sexuality, as well as occasional poems and essays that he published under a pseudonym, Andrzej Jawien, in the highly regarded independent Catholic weekly, *Tygodnik Powszechny*.

Wojtyla also made a point of familiarizing himself with the classics of Marxism–Leninism. "If you want to understand the enemy," he explained to a friend who was astonished to find books by Marx, Lenin, and Stalin on his shelves, "you have to know what he wrote."[35] And, of course, there were his students, on whom he lavished much care. In short, he seemed to have found his niche as a scholarly, non-political priest pursuing some rather esoteric studies on the margins of social and political life in the Polish People's Republic.

Then Archbishop Baziak intervened once again. Recognizing Wojtyla's brilliance, Baziak recommended to Pope Pius XII that he name Wojtyla the suffragan (auxiliary) bishop of Kraków. On July 8, 1958, Pius XII did so. As the influential Polish lay Catholic, Stanislaw Stomma, has observed, "If Baziak hadn't picked him for bishop, Wojtyla would have spent the rest of his life as a distinguished professor at Catholic University in Lublin—he would never have been Pope."[36] But thanks to Baziak, the obscure 38-year-old philosophy professor was now the youngest bishop in Poland, embarked on a path that would bring him, within a relatively short time, to the pinnacle of power in the Catholic Church.

Two things facilitated Wojtyla's rapid ascent in the Catholic hierarchy: Pius XII's death on October 9, 1958, and the decision by his successor, John XXIII, only three months after his enthronement, to convene the Second Vatican Council. Conceived as an *Aggiornamento*, or "bringing up to date," Vatican II, which began on October 11, 1962, and ended on December 8, 1965, brought nearly 3,000 bishops and cardinals to Rome to chart the Church's future course.

In this intellectually demanding milieu, the brilliant Polish bishop-philosopher would have made his mark even if no one were looking after his interests. As it happened, however, a close friend and fellow-seminarian from Kraków, Father (eventually Cardinal) Andrzej Maria Deskur, who had been living in Rome since 1952 and was serving as the Council's press secretary, made a point of introducing Wojtyla to the monsignors and cardinals of the Curia (Vatican bureaucracy), as well as to bishops from abroad. Soon, the young Polish prelate was being widely noticed— particularly since the head of the Polish Church, Cardinal Wyszynski, evinced no great enthusiasm for the Council's reformist agenda, believing that "You don't restructure your army during a battle."[37]

Bishop Wojtyla played an important role in securing passage of two of the Council's most important documents: *Gaudium et Spes* (*Joy and Hope*) and a new *Declaration on Religious Freedom* known as *Dignitatis Humanae*. Both of which were adopted by Vatican II in 1965. In *Gaudium et Spes*, the Council affirmed that "nothing that is genuinely human fails to find and echo" in Christian hearts.[38] In *Dignitatis Humanae*, the Council declared that "the right to religious freedom has its foundation in the very dignity of the human person, as this dignity is known through the revealed word of God and by reason itself."[39]

Both of these documents were major turning points in the history of the Church, and both reflected Karol Wojtyla's deepest beliefs. *Gaudium et Spes* repudiated what Wojtyla called the "ecclesiastical" mentality, with its "lamentations on the…miserable state of the world," and urged the Church to make its case through "the power of arguments" rather than by "moralization or exhortation."[40] *Dignitatis Humanae* broke with the Church's tendency to demand full religious liberty for itself while denying it to others on the grounds that "error" (i.e., other faiths) has no rights. (In the 19th century, for example, Gregory XVI called religious liberty a "delirium," and Pius IX formally condemned the idea that "the Church should be separated from the state."[41])

As Catholic scholar George Weigel has pointed out, *Dignitatis Humane* corrected what Reinhold Niebuhr once called "the root error of Catholicism in the political order," which was "to regard the Church as, on the one hand, a transhistorical institution and, on the other hand, a political force which must be protected and whose interests, including its political interests, must always be paramount."[42] Having once been willing to ally itself with repressive regimes so long as its interests were secured, the Church was now transforming itself into *defensor hominis*: the defender of the rights of man.

"We Cannot Remain Silent"

Nowhere was the Church's transformation more striking than in Poland. Before World War II, about a third of Poland's 30 million people were non-Catholic, yet the Church's insistence that all "true" Poles had to be Roman Catholic morally disenfranchised Poland's Jewish, German, Ukrainian, and Byelorussian minorities. After Marshal Jósef Pilsudski's death in 1935, many elements in the Church openly supported an increasingly repressive military dictatorship that had scant regard for human rights.

So bitter was the memory of those days that after the war, when Polish Stalinists closed Church schools and journals, nationalized Church property, and arrested Poland's Primate, Cardinal Wyszynski, along with scores of other priests and bishops, the Church found few defenders among Poland's secular intellectuals. A striking case in point was Leszek Kolakowski. Today, Kolakowski is an eminent philosopher, outspoken anti-Communist, and friend of John Paul II; as a young Communist in the 1950's, however, he denounced "the curse of clerical fanaticism, mutton-headed Catholicism, which for four centuries has oppressed our national culture and made it sterile."[43]

When Wladyslaw Gomulka became First Secretary of the Polish United Workers' Party (as the Communist Party was formally called) in 1956 in the wake of bloody workers' riots that revealed how unpopular the regime had become, he released Wyszynski from the monastery where he had been confined. In exchange for significant government concessions—including optional religious education in schools, the release of imprisoned clergy, and the reactivation of the Catholic press—Wyszynski urged the workers to return to their jobs. Over the next decade and a half, Gomulka tried to take back the rights he had granted the Church in 1956, and Wyszynski vigorously defended Church interests. But only rarely did the Primate speak out on issues not directly affecting the Church.

In the 1970s, however, the situation changed dramatically. Now the Church refused to confine its demands to strictly "Catholic" issues. Instead, it became the leading advocate of the rights of *all* Poles, and the most outspoken champion of this new approach was Karol Wojtyla,

who by then had become a cardinal. On the Feast of the Epiphany in
1976, for example, in a sermon in Kraków's Wawel cathedral, he declared:

> We cannot remain silent, these anxieties weigh upon
> our hearts; the problem is fundamentally one of social
> ethics.... And so it cannot happen that one group of
> men, one social group—however well-deserving—
> should impose on the whole people an ideology, an
> opinion contrary to the will of the majority. We are all
> Poland, all of us, believers and unbelievers. But it can-
> not be that Poland's destiny should be decided by the
> nonbelievers against the will of the believers. For Po-
> land is not a chance reality. Poland is a thousand years
> of history, Poland is this Wawel Castle, this cathedral,
> these tombs of our Kings. Poland stands for innumer-
> able victories and innumerable sufferings! That is all
> my wish, and the wish is for every man, for every man
> who believes, for every man who is seeking, that he
> may seek without the fear that someone may say to
> him, it is forbidden....[44]

Similarly, during a Corpus Christi Day procession in 1977, Wojtyla
told a gathering of young people that

> Human rights cannot be given in the form of conces-
> sions. Man is born with them and seeks to realize them
> in the course of his life. And if they are not realized or
> experienced, then man rebels. And it cannot be other-
> wise, because he is a man. His sense of honor expects
> it.... And it is impossible to resolve these problems by
> means of oppression. Police and prison provide no
> answer either. They only raise the price that will ulti-
> mately have to be paid.... There is only one road to
> peace and national unity, and that is through unfet-
> tered respect for the rights of man, for the rights of
> citizens and Poles.[45]

As Wojtyla rose in the Church hierarchy, his outspoken defense of human rights, as well as his quiet patronage of intellectual Catholic circles associated with the journals *Tygodnik Powszechny* and *Znak*, expanded the horizons of postwar Polish Catholicism. As Wojtyla's former colleague at the Catholic University of Lublin, Father Józef Tischner, put it:

> There is a great divide between the Catholicism [practiced] between the two world wars and contemporary Catholicism. On the face of it, it was the same dogmas, the same prayers. But in fact, these are two different Catholicisms. The idea of humanity was present in the language of the prewar Church, but it didn't occupy such a prominent place as it does now. This was Wojtyla's contribution.[46]

A Church that defended the human rights of all proved tremendously attractive to Poland's secular *intelligentsia*. Leszek Kolakowski, who had been so scornful of the Catholic Church in the 1950s, declared in the 1970s that "one must be aware that the Church in Poland plays a leading role in the struggle for social rights. The Catholic press is the arena of engagement in the cause of liberty and democracy, unrivaled by anybody in Poland."[47] Similarly, Adam Michnik, a leading dissident intellectual and the son of a Jewish Communist, declared in his influential 1977 book, *Church–Left–Dialogue*, that "For many years now, the Catholic Church in Poland has not been on the side of the powers-that-be, but has stood out in defense of the oppressed. The authentic enemy of the left is not the Church, but totalitarian power, and in this battle the Church plays a role which it is impossible to overestimate."[48]

In the 1930s, historian Timothy Garton Ash has observed, the gap between Polish Catholic and socialist milieux was so great that they constituted "Two Nations."[49] Now, thanks in large part to Wojtyla's influence, the gap was narrowing, and the two nations were becoming one.

"He Is a Poet"

Despite Karol Wojtyla's growing popularity both at home and abroad, however, Cardinal Wyszynski was unimpressed with him initially. When Pius XII, at Archbishop Baziak's urging, had appointed Wojtyla auxiliary bishop of Kraków in 1958, Wyszynski had acquiesced; but when Archbishop Baziak died in 1962 and Wyszynski was called upon to name his replacement, he put six names forward, and Wojtyla's was not among them.

The Primate's lack of enthusiasm stemmed from the fact that Wojtyla was obviously an intellectual, and Wyszynski "didn't trust intellectuals."[50] Moreover, he feared that the scholarly, politically inexperienced young cleric would be subject to manipulation by Communist authorities. "He is a poet," Wyszynski told Bishop Ernest Primeau when the bishop questioned him about "this fellow Wojtyla."[51]

Zenon Kliszko, chief ideologist of the Polish Communist Party, agreed with Wyszynski's assessment of Wojtyla's character—although in Kliszko's view, Wojtyla's alleged susceptibility to Communist blandishments was a point in his favor. According to an agreement worked out in 1956 to govern church–state relations in Poland, Kliszko retained the right to veto Wyszynski's nominations, and he lost no time in doing so. "Wyszynski had already named six candidates to succeed Baziak in Kraków," Kliszko later boasted, "and I didn't approve any of them."[52]

In the end, Wyszynski finally put Wojtyla's name forward. On December 30, 1963, Karol Wojtyla became archbishop of Kraków, much to the satisfaction of Zenon Kliszko, who was convinced he had really put something over on the old cardinal.

Wojtyla's rise was now meteoric. Thanks to his outstanding performance at the Second Vatican Council, he had attracted the favorable notice of Pope Paul VI, who admired the young Pole's ability to embrace the revolutionary innovations stemming from Vatican II without being blown off-course by the fierce winds of change that were sweeping through Catholicism. Vigorous and youthful, Wojtyla increasingly struck the Pope as someone ideally suited to help steer the Church through troubled times, and in 1967 Paul VI made the 47-year-old

Wojtyla a cardinal. (Wojtyla, for his part, later observed that Paul VI had "been like a father" to him.[53]) Eleven years later, his fellow cardinals would elevate him to St. Peter's throne.

"The General Staff of Polish Dissent"

As Karol Wojtyla rose through the ranks of the Church, and as Polish Catholic and secular intellectuals narrowed their differences, relations between Poland's Communist regime and the workers in whose name it claimed to rule deteriorated steadily. Matters finally came to a head on December 13, 1970, a fortnight before Christmas, when the authorities suddenly announced a 36 percent increase in staple-food prices. As historian Adam Ulam has observed, this led to a revolution "in the classical Marxist sense: spontaneous uprisings of the industrial workers against the exploiters."[54] Strikes erupted in the Lenin Shipyard in Gdansk, the Warski Shipyard in Szczecin, and other industrial plants along the Polish seaboard.

Instead of trying to calm the infuriated workers, the Gomulka regime took a hard line. "We are faced with a counterrevolution that must be put down by force," a member of the Politburo declared. "Even if some 300 workers are killed, such measures would be necessary to suppress the uprising."[55]

In the ensuing uprising, which lasted for several days, Polish workers armed with Molotov cocktails battled Polish tanks. The Lenin Shipyard, scene of especially fierce fighting, was cleared of strikers only after the army threatened to bombard the factory with heavy artillery. In all, scores of workers were killed and thousands arrested before the fighting stopped.

Having bungled the price rise badly, Gomulka was expelled from the Politburo and stripped of his Party membership. His successor, Edmund Gierek, tried a more conciliatory approach. Visiting the striking plants early in 1971, he fobbed off the workers' demands for free trade unions with vague promises and appealed to them to call off their strikes. The workers responded by going back to work, but Gierek never honored the commitments he had made to them. It was a bitter lesson. As a worker who participated in these strikes recalled a decade later, "It was a great mistake on our part not to be more unyielding and to make more concrete demands," but "we believed him.... There were tears in his eyes.... We ought not to have yielded unless guaranteed of real changes in the relationship of the authorities to society, between the worker and the employer [i.e., the state]."[56]

Gierek sought to buy off the working class: In return for stable prices and rising wages, workers would set aside their demand for free trade unions and keep the social peace. In order to fund the workers' pay increases, Gierek borrowed massively from the West: In 1973, Poland's debt to the West was $2.5 billion; in 1976, it was $11 billion; in 1980, it was $27 billion—an amount larger than the Soviet Union's Western debt.[57]

In the short run, these funds did lead to a significant increase in the Polish standard of living. Between 1971 and 1976, Poland's GNP rose almost 60 percent, real wages increased 8 percent annually, and per capita consumption of meat went up from 53 kg in 1970 to 70 kg in 1975.[58] Over the long term, however, Gierek's strategy proved unsustainable. Instead of using Western funds to increase the productivity of Poland's agricultural sector—whose products could be exported to the West, thereby earning Poland the foreign exchange necessary to pay off its debts—he invested them in industrial white elephants like the never completed Huta Katowice steelworks. As one Polish wag observed, "Ham and beef are wanted by all, but Polish machine tools and cars will not be bought by anyone who is quite sane."[59] As a result, the Polish debt became unmanageable; by the late 1970s, Poland was borrowing funds from the West just to pay the interest on its outstanding loans.

To cope with this economic crisis, on June 24, 1976—again, without warning—the regime announced food price hikes of about 60 percent. Once more, Polish workers went on strike, even going so far as to set fire to the Party headquarters in Radom. And once again, the authorities withdrew the price increases—but not without taking their revenge on the striking workers, many of whom were arrested, beaten, and fired from their jobs.[60]

The June 1976 strikes seemed at first to be no more than a replay of the risings of December 1970, but they proved far more consequential, for on September 23, 1976, some of Poland's leading intellectuals—including Catholics and non-believers, former Stalinists and former prisoners of Stalin, and even two priests—formed the Committee to Defend Workers, known to the world by its Polish acronym, KOR. The committee's initial purpose was to extend financial and legal support to the workers from Radom and Ursus who were on trial for defying the regime the previous summer, and within a year, KOR was helping 1,000 workers' families throughout Poland, among them the family of an unemployed electrician named Lech Walesa.[61] At the same time, it evolved rapidly into the "general staff of Polish dissent."[62]

The key ideas informing KOR's work were developed by Leszek Kolakowski in a seminal 1971 essay published in the Paris Polish-language journal, *Kultura*. Kolakowski argued that the regime was vulnerable to pressure "from below"—in other words, from society. Therefore, if Polish society organized itself outside of existing Party–state structures and demanded its rights, the regime would be forced to grant them. As summarized by Timothy Garton Ash:

> These "self-organized" social groups and movements would then gradually expand the areas of negative liberty [that is, freedom from coercion] and self-determination open to the citizen. In the end the structures of the Party-state might become little more than stage-sets, the facades of a Potemkin village for the eyes of the new Tsars in Moscow, while behind them Polish society would be reformed in an increasingly open, democratic and pluralist way. The economic success and political stability of relatively autonomous "civil society" would reassure Soviet leaders, whose control of Poland's foreign and defense policy would not be challenged. This strategy was elaborated in a series of essays by Jacek Kuron and Adam Michnik, who christened it "the New Evolutionism." Significantly, in September 1977 KOR rebaptized itself "Committee for

> Social Self-Defense,"…thus expressing the larger aspi-
> ration. In the terminology which now became current,
> they sought the gradual emancipation of "the society"
> from "the power."[63]

In the wake of the KOR's formation, other intellectuals became involved in the process of self-organization. Soon, hundreds of otherwise
inaccessible books, among them George Orwell's *Animal Farm*, were
being published by a vigorous underground press. Uncensored literary
magazines and journals of opinion flourished. And the "Flying University," founded in January 1978, enabled professors, meeting in private
apartments (or, in the case of Cardinal Wojtyła's Kraków archdiocese,
on church premises), to hold unofficial seminars on subjects that otherwise were officially proscribed.

For its part, KOR focused on forging an alliance between the intellectuals and the working class. To that end, in 1977 it founded *Robotnik*
(*The Worker*), a newspaper directed at workers and edited by KOR member Jan Litynski. In 1979, *Robotnik* published a "Workers' Rights Char-
ter" that called for the formation of free trade unions and played a major role in the development of Solidarity. "Only independent trade
unions," it declared, "having the support among the workers whom
they represent, have any chance of opposing the authorities. Only they
will represent a force with which the authorities must reckon and with
which they can deal on equal terms."[64]

Poland's security services, of course, kept a close watch on KOR activists (who made a point, in any case, of shunning underground activity and working in the open) and other dissident groups, and were perfectly capable of rounding up their leading figures if so ordered. But the
Gierek regime, increasingly dependent on Western financial assistance,
feared the adverse publicity that such a repressive campaign inevitably
would generate. It therefore permitted the dissidents to go about their
business unmolested—a stance which, although it won Gierek considerable acclaim in the West (President Gerald Ford even insisted during a
televised 1976 presidential debate with Jimmy Carter that Poland was
independent of the Soviet Union), also disgusted his security chiefs. As
a colonel in the security service responded when asked why the police

did not destroy the underground publishers, "We know all the addresses, we could destroy everything in one night, but the high-ups won't allow us to."[65]

Gierek and his associates were confident that they had nothing to fear from the dissidents. Poland led the world in the per capita consumption of alcohol; its suicide rate was also high. The "civil society" in which the KOR placed so much faith seemed hopelessly dispirited and besotted. How could such a demoralized people mount a serious threat to Communist rule?

Then, on October 16, 1978, Poles watching the evening news heard a brief announcement: On its second day of balloting, the College of Cardinals, meeting in Rome, had elected a new Pope. His name was Karol Wojtyla, archbishop of Kraków, and he was the first Slav ever to be so honored.

"Be Not Afraid!"

If the ascension of the 58-year-old Wojtyla to the throne of St. Peter gave the dispirited Polish people a much-needed injection of national pride, it caused intense dismay in the Kremlin. Although Polish authorities (and their Soviet masters) had believed initially that they could use Archbishop Wojtyla to undermine Wyszynski, they soon learned otherwise. "From the moment his appointment as archbishop was announced," writes Weigel, "Karol Wojtyla was determined not to let a millimeter of distance open between the Primate and himself on Church-state affairs," and this deference eventually won him Wyszynski's respect.[66]

At the same time, Wojtyla developed his own distinct style as bishop, which greatly unnerved Communist authorities. For example, he never tried to be a "player" by mixing with Polish officials, preferring the company of intellectuals and dissidents, whom he regarded as far more important to Poland's future than the Communists. As a result, "with Wojtyla, the regime never knew what was coming next.... They were terrified that Wojtyla might succeed Wyszynski as Primate."[67]

With their worst Polish nightmares now confirmed, Kremlin oligarchs—always inclined to conspiratorial interpretations of Western behavior—leaped to the conclusion that Wojtyla's election had been engineered somehow by President Carter's Polish-born National Security Adviser, Zbigniew Brzezinski, with the help of Polish–American Cardinal John Krol of Philadelphia, to help destabilize the "Socialist bloc."[68] They were totally mistaken, but everything the new Pope did appeared to confirm their suspicions. Even his inaugural sermon of October 22, 1978, seemed ominous. Three times, John Paul II quoted Christ's words: "Be not afraid!" Of whom, suspicious Kremlin leaders may well have asked themselves, was the Pope urging the faithful not to be afraid, if not the Soviets?

On November 4, 1978, a portrait of the new Pope submitted to the Central Committee of the Soviet Communist Party by Oleg Boglomov, director of the Institute for the World Socialist System, confirmed Kremlin fears. Boglomov predicted that under John Paul II, the Holy See's policy toward the Soviet bloc would be characterized by "a new aggressiveness." Specifically, wrote Boglomov,

> According to high-ranking Catholic officials, the election of a Polish cardinal will promote the *universalization* of the Church—that is, its activity in all social-political systems, above all in the socialist system.... It is likely that this dialogue [with the socialist countries] will have, on the part of the Vatican, a more aggressive and systematic character than under Paul VI. Wojtyla will apparently be less willing to compromise with the leadership of the socialist states, especially as regards the appointing [of bishops] to local churches.

Boglomov's report also contained another insightful prediction. Initially, he wrote, "the new Pope will be dependent on the Curia which, without a doubt, will try to subject him to its influence. But the independent temper and energy of John Paul II suggest that he will be fairly quick to get the hang of things and break free from the guardians of orthodoxy in the Curia."[69]

As it happened, John Paul II got "the hang of things" even sooner than Boglomov predicted. "According to one of his close collaborators," writes Weigel, "the first thing the new Pope did after his election was to see the archives on the *Ostpolitik* of Paul VI."[70]

Paul VI's *Ostpolitik*—his Eastern policy, or policy toward the Soviet Union and its satellites—was based on the belief that the division of Europe arrived at by Roosevelt, Churchill, and Stalin at the 1945 Yalta Conference was an immutable fact of international life. Under Paul VI, rather than denounce the Communist regimes as Pius XII had done, the Holy See entered into a "dialogue" with them. In practice, this meant less criticism of the Soviets, more criticism of the Americans (especially over Vietnam), and an attempt to win "breathing space" for churches behind the Iron Curtain through quiet diplomacy rather than public confrontation.

As Boglomov had foreseen, John Paul II quickly scrapped Paul VI's *Ostpolitik* in favor of a more assertive diplomacy. John Paul's policy was based on a conviction shared by virtually every non-Communist Pole: that at Yalta, the Big Three, by sanctioning the spread of totalitarianism to over half of Europe, had committed a great evil to which no moral person—let alone the Catholic Church—could ever become reconciled. As he later put it in his 1991 Encyclical, *Centesimus Annus*, "The [Second World] war, which should have reestablished freedom and restored the right of nations, ended without having attained these goals. Indeed, in a way, for many peoples, especially those which had suffered most during the war, it openly contradicted these goals."[71]

The new Pope did not believe that the Yalta regime could be forcibly overthrown, but neither did he think that the Church should acquiesce in an unjust status quo. His policy was to continue Paul VI's emphasis on negotiations with the Communists but to conduct these negotiations in a new spirit: not as a supplicant begging for concessions, but as *defensor hominis*, the defender of man, asking—even demanding—that Communist regimes fulfill the international commitments they had made to respect basic human rights. "He was determined to give public witness to the truth about the human condition contained in the Gospel of

Jesus Christ—and a deliberately evangelical papacy necessarily confronted the counterclaims about human nature, community and destiny embedded in Communism."[72]

This was how Karol Wojtyla had conducted relations with Communist authorities in Kraków, and it was how he intended to go on conducting them from Rome.

Predictably, the Soviet reaction to the new Pope's policy was extremely hostile. On November 13, 1979, the Secretariat of the Soviet Central Committee approved a "Decision to Work Against the Policies of the Vatican in Relation with Socialist States." Signed by nine members of the ruling Politburo (including future Party chief Mikhail Gorbachev), the document laid out a six-point anti-Wojtyla strategy. Among other things, it:

- Called for the "mobilization" of the Communist parties of Lithuania, Latvia, Ukraine, and Byelorussia (Soviet republics with significant Roman and Uniate Catholic populations) in order to launch "propaganda against the policies of the Vatican";

- Instructed the Ministry of Foreign Affairs "to enter into contact with those groups of the Catholic Church engaged in work for peace" in foreign countries "and to explain to them the policies of the Soviet Union in favor of world peace"; and

- Ordered the KGB "to publicize in the Western countries [the fact] that Vatican policies are harmful" and "above all, to show in the Socialist states that Vatican policies go against the life of the Catholic Church."[73]

Clearly, the Kremlin was girding itself for battle.

In the wake of the May 13, 1981, attempt on John Paul II's life by Turkish terrorist Mehmet Ali Agca, the question has arisen as to whether, in addition to the above points, the Kremlin also considered more "active measures," including assassination, to rid itself of a dangerous enemy. Although the evidence that has emerged to date is inconclusive, many prominent statesmen, including former National Security Advisers Henry Kissinger and Zbigniew Brzezinski, are convinced that the

Soviets were indeed behind Agca's attempt to kill the Pope.[74] "Inside the Vatican," writes Weigel, "a similar view was widespread, if never even hinted at publicly."[75]

"I Ask This of You"

Soviet Party bosses were not the only ones alarmed by the Vatican's new foreign policy; their Polish counterparts were equally apprehensive. Yet when John Paul II, almost immediately after his election, requested permission to visit his homeland in 1979, Polish authorities felt they could not refuse him. As Edmund Gierek later recounted in his memoirs:

> Brezhnev said he heard that the Church had invited the Pope to Poland: "And what is your reaction?" he asked. I said, "We'll give him the reception he deserves."
>
> "Take my advice, don't give him any reception," Brezhnev said. "It will only cause trouble."
>
> "How could I not receive a Polish Pope," I answered, "when the majority of my countrymen are Catholics? They see his election as a great achievement. Besides, what would I say to people about why we're closing the border to him?"
>
> "Tell the Pope—he's a wise man—he can declare publicly that he can't come due to an illness."
>
> "I'm sorry, Comrade Leonid," I said, "I can't do this. I have to welcome John Paul II." Then Brezhnev told me: "Gomulka was a better Communist [than you], because he didn't receive Paul VI in Poland, and nothing awful happened. The Poles have survived the refusal to admit the Pope once; they'll survive it a second time."
>
> "But political reasons dictate that I admit him," I declared.

"Well, do as you wish," Brezhnev said. "But be careful you don't regret it later." And having said that he ended the conversation.[76]

Gierek's willingness to permit John Paul II to visit Poland did not mean that he entertained any illusions about him. On the contrary, a secret set of instructions issued by the Communist Party to teachers in Polish schools revealed what the regime really thought:

> The Pope is our enemy.... Due to his uncommon skills and great sense of humor, he is dangerous, because he charms everyone, especially journalists. Besides, he goes for cheap gestures in his relations with the crowd, for instance, puts on a highlander's hat, shakes all hands, kisses children, etc.... It is modeled on American presidential campaigns.[77]

The Pope lost no time hammering his message home. Arriving at Warsaw airport on June 2, 1979, he politely thanked Gierek for inviting him and then went on the offensive. "Peace and the drawing together of peoples," he declared, depended on "respect for the basic rights of the nation...political self-determination for its citizens and formation of its own culture and civilization."[78]

In city after city, to crowds numbering in the hundreds of thousands, John Paul II announced that "This Polish pope...comes here to speak...before Europe and the world, of those often forgotten nations and peoples. He comes here to 'cry with a loud voice.'" And what his loud voice proclaimed was "the inalienable rights of man, the inalienable rights of dignity."[79]

At times, his voice was anguished, as when he asked at Auschwitz, "Is it enough to put man in a different uniform? To arm him with the apparatus of violence? Is it enough to impose on him an ideology in which human rights are subjected to the demands of the system, completely subjected to them, so in practice not to exist at all?"[80] At other times, his words dripped with sarcasm, as when, after naming Eastern Europe's nationalities, he added, "I trust that they hear me. After all...freedom...of information...has been thoroughly guaranteed."[81]

Always and everywhere, however, he was the Holy Father, exhorting his children to be strong and brave:

> You must be strong, dear brothers and sisters. You must
> be strong with the strength which comes from faith....
> I ask that you never despair, never grow weary, never
> become discouraged; that those roots from which we
> grow are never severed; that you keep your faith de-
> spite each of your weaknesses, that you always seek
> strength in Him, where so many generations of our
> mothers and fathers found it...; that you never lose
> that freedom of the spirit for which He has liberated
> man; that you never spurn that love...expressed by the
> cross, without which human life has no roots and no
> meaning. I ask this of you.[82]

The impact of these words on the Polish national psyche was incalcu-lable. It was as though a magician from a distant land had alighted in Poland and broken the evil spell that held its people in thrall. Suddenly, the 13 million Poles who turned out to pray and sing with their Pope felt empowered. Suddenly, they were aware of themselves not as passive objects of history, but as its active shapers. Suddenly cognizant of their own history, their own heritage, they wondered why they had allowed themselves to be so frightened for so long.

In the words of Adam Michnik, the Pope's visit was a great "lesson in dignity."[83]

Sent by Providence

Once the sense of apathy that had hung over Poland like a thick fog was dispersed, it was clear that a great explosion was coming. It oc-curred on July 2, 1980, when the Polish government announced a sharp increase in the price of meat and 17,000 workers from the Ursus tractor plant near Warsaw went out on strike. They were soon followed by other thousands of workers throughout Poland (which somehow did not pre-vent Gierek from going to Strasbourg later that month to receive the medal of the International Institute of Human Rights).[84] By mid-August, over 150 factories and more than 150,000 workers, including streetcar operators and garbage collectors, were on strike.[85]

The focal point of the strike was the Lenin Shipyard in Gdansk, where workers had set up an Interfactory Strike Committee (MKS) to represent all the plants in their region in negotiations with the authorities. The leader of the Gdansk MKS was Lech Walesa, and his key adviser during the first week of the strike—until more intellectuals arrived from Warsaw to help the strikers—was Bogdan Borusewicz, a KOR member hailed by Walesa as "my teacher."

Initially, Walesa had been prepared to call off the strike after the authorities agreed to his economic demands: higher wages and better working conditions. At Borusewicz's insistence, however, he added political demands as well, including Church access to the mass media, the lessening of censorship, and, most important, the right to form a free trade union and to strike.[86] Only when the regime accepted these additional political demands, on August 31, did the Gdansk workers end their strike. Two weeks later, MKS's from across Poland came together to form Solidarity, an "independent and self-governing trade union" whose membership soon numbered close to 10 million Polish citizens.

The most remarkable feature of the strikes that led to the formation of Solidarity was their religious, nonviolent character. In contrast to earlier strike waves that had swept through Poland in 1956, 1970, and 1976, when workers battled the police and the army in clashes that left many dead, workers in the summer of 1980 confined themselves to nonviolent sit-down strikes. The influence of the Church and the Pope were everywhere apparent, especially at the Gdansk shipyard. "During their memorable strike in 1980," Lech Walesa later wrote, "the first things the Gdansk workers did was to affix a cross, an image of the Virgin Mary, and a portrait of John Paul II to the gates of the shipyards."[87] Walesa himself wore a pin with a picture of Poland's most revered icon, the Black Madonna of Czestochowa, in his lapel, and the oversized pen with which he signed the August 31 Gdansk accords—a souvenir from John Paul II's trip to Poland—had the Pope's picture on it.

John Paul II, who followed events in Poland quite closely, observed privately that Walesa had been sent by Providence.[88] The movement over which he presided marked the end of Polish passivity and the beginning of Poland's liberation. "Finally," the Pope said, "something has happened in Poland which is irreversible. People will no longer remain passive. Passivity is one of the tools of authoritarianism. And now this passivity is over; and so their [the Communists'] fate is settled now. They will lose."[89]

Primate Wyszynski, however, was not so sure that the rise of Solidarity marked the beginning of the end for Communism, and some of his closest associates were even less certain. Cardinal Józef Glemp, for example—who succeeded Wyszynski as Primate after his death in 1981—considered Solidarity insufficiently Catholic, calling it "a sack into which everything had been thrown, all the opposition Marxists, all the Trotskyites."[90] ("Trotskyite" was widely understood as a code word for "Jew.")

Wyszynski did not go that far in criticizing Solidarity, but the demand for free trade unions clearly made him uneasy. "You can't demand everything at once," he said in an August 26 speech. "No one should put the nation at risk."[91] Everyone in Poland knew what the Primate meant: Demanding free trade unions might provoke a Soviet invasion; workers should stick to economic demands and leave politics to others.

But while Wyszynski was slow to grasp the significance of Solidarity (not until the early months of 1981 did he become its strong backer), Poland's bishops were far more enthusiastic. On August 27, they adopted a statement affirming "the right to independence both of organizations representing the workers and of organizations of self-government."[92] With the Church now behind the demand for free trade unions, Polish authorities felt compelled to yield. They did, however, expel Gierek from the Party, replacing him with former internal security chief Stanislaw Kania.

"What Are You Poles Doing?"

To say that Soviet officials found these events alarming would be a gross understatement. In their view, a viciously anti-Communist Pope, whose election had been engineered by the United States, was now co-operating with equally depraved counterrevolutionaries in Poland to establish an opposition movement—Solidarity—bent on toppling Communist rule in a key Soviet satellite. The fact that the Polish regime, instead of acting promptly and decisively to crush these "contras," had agreed instead to legalize free trade unions was inexcusable.

On September 3, 1980, shortly after the "Gdansk Accord" was reached, the Central Committee of the Communist Party of the Soviet Union prepared a "Top Secret, Eyes Only" document, "Theses for the Discussion with Representatives of the Polish Leadership," that clearly spelled out Soviet concerns. Addressed to the leadership of the Polish Communist Party, it explained why a lasting compromise with the opposition was impossible:

> The agreement concluded by the PPR [Polish People's Republic] government, and endorsed by the plenum of the PZPR CC [Polish United Workers Party Central Committee] exacts a high political and economic price for the "regulation" it achieves.... The agreement, in essence, signifies the legalization of the anti-socialist opposition. An organization has emerged that aims to spread its political influence through the entire country.... Because the opposition intends to continue the struggle to achieve its aims, and the healthy forces of the party and society cannot acquiesce in a regressive movement by Polish society, the compromise that has achieved will be only temporary in nature.[93]

The CPSU Central Committee document went on to explain that, having been on the defensive for too long, the Polish Communist Party must prepare a counterattack and reclaim the positions that have been lost among the working class and the people. In launching this counterattack, it would be advisable to use all the capabilities afforded by the ruling party and its strong, healthy core, by the state apparatus, and by mass social organizations, while showing political flexibility. These institutions will provide necessary support for the vanguard ranks of the working class. In the event of necessity, it would be advisable to use the contemplated administrative means.[94]

By "contemplated administrative means," the Soviets meant plans for martial law, first drawn up in deepest secrecy by Polish Defense Minister General Wojciech Jaruzelski on October 22, 1980.[95] The problem was that, far from having a "strong, healthy core," the Polish Communist Party was in total disarray, with many members openly sympathetic to Solidarity and strongly opposed to "administrative means." Moreover, even if the Party resolved its internal differences and adopted a hard line, it was far from clear that the "counterattack" advocated by Moscow could resolve Poland's worsening economic situation. Instead, chances were good that the use of force against Solidarity would ignite a national uprising, which would only compound Poland's plight.

For these reasons, while earnestly promising Brezhnev "to seize the counterrevolution by its throat,"[96] all First Secretary Kania actually did was play for time, hoping that a saving compromise might somehow be reached.

If Soviet leaders were frustrated by their Polish comrades' lack of resolve, the Communist leaders of Poland's neighbors were terrified. Firm believers in an East European version of the domino theory, they were convinced—correctly, it turned out—that a victory for Solidarity in Poland would encourage "counterrevolutionary" forces in their countries, too.

East Germany's General Secretary, Erich Honecker, was especially alarmed. Not only did he order East Germany's entire border with Poland sealed off, but on November 26, 1980, he wrote Brezhnev an extraordinary letter asking the Soviet leader to convene an emergency meeting of the leaders of the Warsaw Pact to consider the possibility of invading Poland:

> Esteemed Comrade Leonid Ilyich!
>
> In the Politburo of the SED CC [Socialist Unity Party Central Committee] we have discussed the current situation in the People's Republic of Poland, and have unanimously concluded that there is an urgent necessity to convene a meeting of the General and First Secretaries of the Communist Parties of our community of states. We believe that the situation developing in People's Republic of Poland should be discussed with Comrade S. Kania in order to work out collective measures to assist the Polish friends in overcoming the crisis, which, as you know, has been intensifying day after day.
>
> ...According to information we have received through various channels, counterrevolutionary forces in People's Republic of Poland are on the constant offensive, and any delay in acting against them would mean death—the death of socialist Poland. Yesterday our collective efforts may perhaps have been premature; today they are essential; and tomorrow they would already be too late.
>
> ...We ask you, esteemed Leonid Ilyich, to understand our extraordinary fears about the situation in Poland. We know that you also share these fears.[97]

Brezhnev did indeed share Honecker's fears, but he also faced problems of his own that severely constrained his freedom of maneuver. To begin with, there was the firm attitude of the United States. As President Carter's National Security Adviser, Zbigniew Brzezinski, has written,

> Throughout this period I was guided by the thought
> that the United States must avoid the mistake that it
> made in 1968, when it failed to communicate to the
> Soviets prior to their intervention in Czechoslovakia
> the costs of such an aggression to East–West rela-
> tions.... Accordingly, my strategy was to generate ad-
> vance understanding on the various sanctions that
> would be adopted, and to make as much of that pub-
> licly known as possible, so that the Soviets would
> know...that we were politically bound to react.[98]

Thus, when a remarkable Polish CIA agent, Colonel Ryszard
Kuklinski, informed the U.S. that Soviet forces were scheduled to enter
Poland on December 8, 1980, President Carter publicly warned the
Soviets that such a move would have dire consequences. "[T]here is no
way of knowing whether in fact the actual decision to intervene had
been reached by the Kremlin and then rescinded because of this massive
reaction," writes Brzezinski. "What we do know is that military moves
were afoot...and that initial implementing actions were on the way and
were terminated after the U.S.-led global reaction."[99]

Another, even more serious constraint on Moscow's behavior was the
Soviet Union's internal situation. Although it was not widely recognized
in the West at the time, nearly two decades of what the Soviets themselves eventually would call "Brezhnevite stagnation," coupled with an
invasion of Afghanistan whose end was nowhere in sight, had brought
the Soviet Union to the brink of economic collapse. Invading Poland
and possibly getting stuck in a second quagmire threatened to provoke
what Soviet leaders feared most of all: a crisis of revolutionary proportions in the Soviet Union itself.

Faced with this situation, even veteran Soviet hard-liners warned
against invading Poland. At a December 10, 1981, meeting of the Politburo, for example, CPSU ideologist Mikhail Suslov argued that "there
can be no consideration at all of sending in troops" because such a step
"would be a catastrophe."[100] At the same meeting, KGB Chairman Yuri
Andropov, who probably grasped the magnitude of the Soviet internal

crisis better than any other Soviet leader, went so far as to say, "We cannot risk it [an invasion].... Even if Poland were to be ruled by Solidarity, so be it."[101]

If invading Poland made no sense, however, *threatening* to invade was eminently sensible. Not only might it dissuade Solidarity's leaders from waging their counterrevolution too aggressively, but it also would distract attention from the *real* threat facing the trade union: the imposition of "administrative measures," or martial law, by the Poles themselves. For these reasons, Soviet and other Warsaw Pact forces continued to carry out massive military maneuvers along Poland's borders throughout 1981.

From the Soviet point of view, it was vital that the Polish government itself suppress Solidarity rather than rely on Warsaw Pact armies to do its dirty work. Thus, Brezhnev emphasized repeatedly that the Polish government must take the initiative. As he told General Jaruzelski in November 1981,

> It is now absolutely clear that without a vigorous struggle against the class enemy, it will be impossible to save socialism in Poland. The question is not whether there will be a confrontation, but who will start it, what means will be used to wage it, and who will gain the initiative.... The leaders of the anti-socialist forces, who long ago emerged from underground into full public view and are now openly preparing to launch a decisive onslaught, are hoping to delay their final push until they have achieved overwhelming preponderance.... This means that if you fail to take tough measures right away against the counterrevolution, you will lose the only opportunity you still have.[102]

Soviet Foreign Minister Andrei Gromyko made the same argument even more bluntly to Polish Foreign Minister Jósef Czyrek. "You're in Lenin's party, aren't you?" Gromyko asked. "Poland is crawling with counterrevolution. What do you propose to do about it? Don't you know counterrevolution has to be smashed? They'll have you hanging from the lampposts if you don't settle accounts as we did in 1917. And what are you Poles doing? Tell me, what are you doing?"[103]

In their response to the threat of a possible Soviet invasion, Solidarity's leaders were divided into three camps. The most conciliatory faction, led by Tadeusz Maziowecki, argued that the formation of a free trade union was the absolute limit of what could be achieved under present circumstances.

The moderates were opposed by a centrist faction, led by Kuron and Michnik, who subscribed to "the New Evolutionism" first outlined by Kolakowski in 1971. As Michnik explained in 1985, "For Jacek Kuron and me it was obvious that the Gdansk accord initiated changes [whereas] Tadeusz Mazowiecki and other experts treated the Gdansk agreement as the final process of change."[104] So long as they did not provoke a Soviet invasion by demanding an independent, non-Communist Poland, the centrists believed, Solidarity could force "the power" to grant "the society" ever-greater doses of autonomy and freedom.

In all probability, the moderates' views were not unlike those of Wyszynski and the Polish Episcopate, while the centrists were more in tune with papal thinking. Both groups, however, were opposed by a radical faction, many members of which belonged to a dissident organization called the Confederation of Independent Poland (KPN). Radicals believed that under no circumstances would the Soviets invade Poland—not even if Solidarity seized the reins of power. Warsaw Pact maneuvers were just a bluff designed to frighten faint-hearted people like Solidarity's leader, Lech Walesa, who kept insisting that he favored a "socialist" Poland. The radicals advocated calling Moscow's bluff by overthrowing the Communists and introducing genuine multi-party democracy.[105]

Despite their differences, all three factions agreed that the threat facing Solidarity was an external one. Internally, there was nothing to fear, since the Communist regime was too dispirited to mount an effective counterattack and, even if it tried, Solidarity would simply call a general strike and bring the government to its knees.

To a surprising extent, Soviet leaders shared Solidarity's contempt for Poland's leaders. In Politburo meetings in 1980 and 1981, Brezhnev and his colleagues complained repeatedly that First Secretary Kania and Defense Minister (later Prime Minister) Jaruzelski were "weak," "indecisive," "insufficiently bold," "untrustworthy" and "unwilling to resort to extraordinary measures despite our recommendations."[106] As late as December 10, 1981, after Jaruzelski had replaced Kania as First Secretary (while remaining Defense Minister and Prime Minister), Andropov lamented to his Politburo colleagues that there were "very disturbing signs" that Jaruzelski "is abandoning the idea of trying to carry out this step" and trying "to find some way to extricate himself."

Gromyko also believed that "Jaruzelski is now vacillating again" and that "the Polish leadership...is continuing to relinquish its positions by failing to adopt decisive measures." Another Soviet leader complained that Jaruzelski was in a "highly agitated state [and] has been transformed into a man who is extremely neurotic and diffident about his abilities."[107]

Why, then, did Jaruzelski finally impose martial law on December 13, 1981? After the fall of Polish Communism in 1989, the general claimed that he had deliberately opted for the lesser evil—martial law, which cost some 100 Polish lives—in order to avoid a greater evil—a Soviet invasion, which would have cost thousands of Polish lives. This self-serving explanation is almost certainly false.

At no time after December 1980 did Soviet leaders warn Jaruzelski that if he did not act, they would. Rather, they told him repeatedly that if he did not act, "socialism" in Poland would be destroyed and he and his colleagues would end up "hanging from lampposts." Inasmuch as Jaruzelski, for both ideological and more self-interested reasons, was deeply committed to the defense of Polish socialism, he had no choice *but* to act once it became clear that the Soviets were not about to pull his chestnuts out of the fire.

As Jaruzelski's colleague, Mieczyslaw Rakowski, admitted, Jaruzelski would have imposed martial law even in the absence of a Soviet threat. "We had chaos and the disintegration of the government apparatus," said Rakowski. "We treated Solidarity as political enemies. They wanted power, and we were not prepared to share power. That is also Jaruzelski's point of view."[108]

"I Am a Son of This Nation"

Jaruzelski's decision to impose martial law caught Solidarity entirely by surprise. Most of its leaders, including Lech Walesa, were rounded up on the night of December 12–13 in Gdansk, where the various factions had gathered to thrash out their movement's future course. Over the next few months, more than 10,000 Solidarity activists were arrested. "What a relief to be interned by men in Polish helmets rather than Russian ones," joked Tadeusz Mazowiecki, the Catholic intellectual.

To capture Solidarity leaders who had eluded the dragnet, the regime imposed a nightly curfew on the entire country, censored the mail, and instituted a requirement that purchases of typing paper and typewriter ribbons could not be made without official permission.[109] The Soviet Union was quick to applaud Jaruzelski's actions:

> Tass has been authorized to declare that the Soviet leadership and people are following attentively the Polish developments…. We greet with satisfaction the statement of W. Jaruzelski that the Polish–Soviet alliance has been and will remain the foundation of the Polish national interest and that Poland will remain an inseparable member of the Warsaw Pact and of the socialist commonwealth of nations.[110]

But while martial law succeeded in blocking Solidarity's otherwise inevitable rise to power, Jaruzelski's long-term problems remained daunting. "As Jaruzelski says," Brezhnev told his Politburo colleagues on January 14, 1982,

> the counterrevolution is now crushed. However, the tasks ahead are more complicated. After introducing relative stability in the country, the Polish comrades must now, one might say, resolve the strategic prob-

lems of what to do with the trade unions, how to revive the economy, how to change the consciousness of
the masses, etc.[111]

The problem for the Polish comrades was that, being discredited, they could not possibly "change the consciousness of the masses" by themselves. They required the help of the Catholic Church. If the Church blessed Jaruzelski's coup and urged Poles to accommodate themselves to it, the regime would acquire what it most needed: a sense of legitimacy. If the Church denounced martial law and urged Poles to resist, a major national rising almost surely would occur—and this time no one could predict whether the Polish army would side with the government or the people.

Fortunately for Jaruzelski, chances that the Church would take an outspokenly pro-Solidarity line under Cardinal Glemp's leadership were negligible. According to Weigel, Glemp "seems not to have shared John Paul II's view that Communism was essentially finished, and acted as if he expected to be negotiating with the likes of Jaruzelski for decades to come."[112] In his December 13 homily on martial law—broadcast repeatedly over Polish television—Glemp urged the Polish people to submit peacefully to the new order:

> On Sunday morning, we were astounded to find our-
> selves under martial law. By the evening we are getting
> accustomed to the idea and we are coming to see that
> it is something dangerous, and we ask ourselves: What
> next? What is going to happen tomorrow? How should
> we behave?… A representative of the Church cannot
> teach differently from what the Gospel says. In his
> teachings he has to shed light on the new reality. In our
> country the new reality is martial law. As we under-
> stand it, martial law is a new state, and a state of severe
> laws which suspend many civic achievements…. Op-
> position to the decisions of the authorities under mar-
> tial law could cause violent reprisals, including blood-
> shed, because the authorities have the armed forces at

their disposal. We can be indignant, shout about the injustice of such a state of affairs…. But this may not yield the expected results.[113]

Then, to drive home his point that Poles should obey the new government, Glemp suggested that martial law was indeed—as Jaruzelski subsequently argued—the lesser evil, chosen by the authorities to avoid the greater evil of a Soviet invasion. Submission was therefore moral as well as prudent: "The authorities consider that the exceptional nature of martial law is dictated by higher necessity, it is the choice of a lesser than a greater evil. Assuming the correctness of such reasoning, the man in the street will subordinate himself to the new situation…. There is nothing of greater value than human life."[114]

Glemp's homily deeply disappointed Solidarity members who had gone underground; they now took to calling him "Comrade Glemp." By contrast, Jaruzelski was delighted. Writing in 1983, Timothy Garton Ash suggested that Jaruzelski foresaw a

> "corporatist compromise" with the Church, conceding to it large areas of religious and cultural autonomy and perhaps even sharing power with it over some areas of social and economic life…. Between them, these two vast authoritarian corporations would guarantee Poland's stability and internal peace to Moscow…. There are ecclesiastical politicians close to Glemp who are obviously tempted by the prospect.[115]

One "ecclesiastical politician," however, was not in the least tempted by the prospect of a "corporatist compromise" with the regime: Pope John Paul II, whose views trumped even those of the Primate. On December 14, the Pope told a huge crowd praying for Poland in St. Peter's Square that "this solidarity with the Polish people serves also to bolster certain values and inalienable principles such as the rights of man and the rights of the nation…values and principles that must create, now in our times, great solidarity with a European and worldwide dimension."[116]

But if his words contrasted pointedly with Glemp's, John Paul II was as determined as the Primate to avoid bloodshed. "Too much Polish blood has already been shed, especially during the last war," he said repeatedly. "Polish blood must no longer be spilled. Everything must be done to build the future of our homeland in peace."[117] The delicate task facing the Pope was to work out an approach that, instead of either totally embracing or totally rejecting the regime, exploited all avenues for a peaceful restoration of the rights that Solidarity had won for the Polish people. Taking a leaf from the Israeli policy of "Land for Peace," the course that the Holy Father eventually adopted might be called "Legitimacy for Human Rights."

The key concept behind the Pope's approach was that the amount of legitimacy the Church would confer on Jaruzelski's government depended on how much freedom Jaruzelski granted the Polish people. An opportunity for the Pope to visit Poland again might result in some friendly meetings between the Pope and Jaruzelski, for example, or a promise to end martial law might elicit a call from the Pope to end the economic sanctions imposed on Poland by the Reagan Administration soon after Jaruzelski's crackdown. The Church would do its best to avoid an open break with the regime, but under no circumstances would it retreat from its role as *defensor hominis*: defender of the Polish people's human rights.

John Paul II's second trip to Poland, from June 16 to June 23, 1983, illustrates how this policy worked. Initially, the announcement of an impending papal visit to Poland discouraged many Solidarity activists, who thought that the mere presence of the Pope would confer legitimacy on the hated military regime. Henryk Jablonski, president of Poland's State Council, tried to reinforce this perception when he greeted the Pope by saying that "His Holiness's visit testifies to the gradual normalization of life in our country."

The Pope, however, dispelled such interpretations during his first meeting with Polish authorities by bluntly telling Jaruzelski that the starting point for any "social renewal" must be the "social accords" that ended the strikes in the summer of 1980 and gave birth to Solidarity.[118] Moreover, it seems likely that, in return for his agreeing to visit Poland, the government promised the Pope that it would end martial law, which it did on July 22, 1983, just a month after the conclusion of the Pope's visit. As Jaruzelski himself later commented, "It's significant that soon after the Pope's visit in 1983 martial law was lifted."[119]

During his trip, the Pope also issued a brief statement urging the removal of economic sanctions against Poland—obviously an important concession to the regime. Perhaps in return, he won the right to travel the length and breadth of Poland with his message to the Polish people "to call good and evil by name," "to put a firm barrier against demoralization," "to persevere in hope," and to assert "the fundamental solidarity between human beings."

Nor did the Pope's speeches neglect to make it clear, to the Episcopate as much as to the regime, that the demand for human rights—including the right of workers to form free trade unions—was not negotiable. In a homily to a crowd of over a million people in Katowice, for example, John Paul II spelled out basic workers' rights "to a just salary," "to security," and "to a day of rest." "Connected with the area of workers' rights," he emphasized, "is the question of trade unions as a mouthpiece for the struggle for social justice.... The state does not give us this right, it has only the obligation to protect and guard it. This right is given to us by the Creator who made man as a social being."[120]

Speaking at Czestochowa, site of Poland's revered Jasna Gora monastery, "which is for the Poles at once Westminster Abbey and Windsor Castle,"[121] the Pope made his commitment to Solidarity's cause unmistakably clear:

> I am a son of this nation and that is why I feel profoundly all its noble aspirations, its desire to live in truth, liberty, justice and social solidarity, its desire to live its own life. Indeed, after a thousand years of history, this nation has its own life, culture, social traditions, spiritual identity. Virgin of Jasna Gora, I want to place under your protection all that has been produced in these difficult years since August 1980, all those truths, principles, values and attitudes.[122]

Above all, in his meetings with Jaruzelski and the Polish Episcopate, John Paul stressed

> that he would not accept a solution in which the Church, in return for its independence, would cooperate with the state through officially recognized Catholic unions or an officially sanctioned Catholic "opposition" party. Some in the Polish Church favored this, and it was certainly an appealing prospect for the regime. The Pope wasn't having any of it. Solidarity had its own integrity and its right to independence. There could be no genuine dialogue, and thus no genuine social renewal, without genuinely independent workers' associations. The Church would not cut a deal behind Solidarity's back.[123]

To underscore his message, the Pope made a particular point of obtaining the regime's reluctant permission to visit the still-interred Lech Walesa. This was especially important to Walesa, given his strained relationship with Cardinal Glemp. "As the head of the Church in Poland," Walesa observed in his memoirs,

> Cardinal Glemp was responsible for preparing the Holy Father's visit; he made it known that the government's policy of normalization was more to his liking than was our ineffectual political activity. A number of his ecclesiastical advisors...shared his leanings. Others came right out and said that Walesa was finished, that he had played out his role.[124]

By meeting with Walesa, the Pope was emphasizing that, despite his diminished status, the feisty union leader was still an important force and that Cardinal Glemp and General Jaruzelski could not simply shunt him aside. The Pope's message was underscored four months later, when Walesa was awarded the Nobel Peace Prize on October 5, 1983.

In addition to all these public gestures (as well as his weekly radio broadcasts to Poland from the Vatican, which, in Walesa's words, confirmed Poles "in our belief that our resistance to communism had moral justification"[125]), the Pope used Vatican channels to provide clandestine aid to Solidarity's underground. (In the United States, the AFL–CIO and the CIA also provided much-needed assistance.) As a result, Solidarity was able to carry on its resistance activities. Throughout the period of martial law, for example, *Tygodnik Mazowsze*, Warsaw Solidarity's four-page underground weekly, never missed an issue.[126]

To be sure, it was not in John Paul II's power to undo martial law and bring about Solidarity's legalization, but he could and did help to keep Solidarity alive and "break the fever of despair that had weakened the nation since December 13, 1981."[127] It is likely that without his vigorous diplomacy, Jaruzelski and Glemp would have arranged a quiet burial for Solidarity. That they did not do so, and that Jaruzelski's regime was unable to achieve the legitimacy it craved, were largely the Pope's doing. Now all that remained was for underground Solidarity leaders like Wiktor Kulerski "to delay the Red Ones from wearing society down and hope that in the meanwhile something else happened."[128]

Eventually, of course, something *did* happen to change the equation: The Soviet system, already in a state of crisis, was brought to the point of collapse by Ronald Reagan's across-the-board economic, ideological, technological, and military offensive.[129] To save it, Mikhail Gorbachev, the new Soviet leader, decided that the costs of keeping Eastern Europe in a state of permanent subjugation outweighed the benefits.

For Poland, the turning point came in mid-1987 when Mieczyslaw Rakowski, Poland's last Communist Prime Minister, handed Jaruzelski a secret memo arguing that the Soviets were no longer prepared to buttress Communist rule in Poland. The Communists, Rakowsi maintained, would have to learn how to hold on to power in a democracy.[130]

Rakowski's analysis set off a complicated set of maneuvers culminating in the "Round Table" negotiations of 1989, in which 29 delegates from the Polish Communist Party, 26 from Solidarity, and 3 Church observers met to decide Poland's future. "I am proud to give the pope credit for coming up with the idea for the Round Table negotiations that eventually took place between the government and the democratic opposition," writes Walesa in his memoirs.[131] Within two months, an agreement was reached to hold semi-free elections on June 4.

Solidarity's landslide victory in these elections led to the formation of a new government, with Tadeusz Mazowiecki becoming, on September 12, 1989, Poland's first postwar non-Communist Prime Minister. All of a sudden, Polish Communism was finished. As John Paul put it on January 13, 1990, "The irresistible thirst for freedom broke down walls and opened doors" because "women, young people and men have overcome their fear."[132]

The Power of Words

The victory of Solidarity in 1989 marked a decisive turning point in the Cold War. It demonstrated that, far from being an irresistible historical force, Communism could be rolled back—not just in peripheral areas like Grenada, where an American invasion overthrew a Marxist dictatorship in 1983, but at its very core. This emboldened other subjects of the Soviet empire to rise up in revolt.

The result was a huge revolutionary wave that, as historian Martin Malia puts it, "soon led to the fall of the Berlin Wall, the Czech Velvet Revolution, and the end of [Romanian dictator Nicolae] Ceausescu." From Eastern Europe, the revolution touched off by Solidarity's victory

> produced a great leftward surge across the Soviet Union, which was expressed, first of all, in a series of "declarations of sovereignty," beginning with the Baltic states, among the fifteen constituent republics. This "parade of sovereignties," as the hard-line commentators called it, was accompanied by a "war of laws," in which the republics, municipalities and even districts voted measures to take economic and administrative power away from the Party and the "center," as the Gorbachev government was now called. By the end of the summer of 1990, the Soviet Union had virtually collapsed as a

cohesive structure, and Gorbachev's primary concern
came to be working out a new union treaty to salvage
state unity.[133]

It was Gorbachev's failure to work out such an arrangement that led
to the end of the Soviet Union in 1991.

How did so oppressive a structure manage to endure for nearly three-
quarters of a century? The best answer is provided by historian Richard
Pipes in his explanation of the purpose behind the campaign of terror
with which Lenin consolidated Soviet rule:

> The Red Terror gave the population to understand that
> under a regime that felt no hesitation in executing in-
> nocents, innocence was no guarantee of survival. The
> best hope of surviving lay in making oneself as incon-
> spicuous as possible, which meant abandoning any
> thought of independent public activity, indeed any
> concern with public affairs, and withdrawing into one's
> private world. Once society disintegrated into an ag-
> glomeration of human atoms, each fearful of being
> noticed and concerned exclusively with physical sur-
> vival, then it ceased to matter what society thought,
> for the government had the entire sphere of public ac-
> tivity to itself.[134]

What Karol Wojtyla accomplished was to persuade the "agglomera-
tion of human atoms" in Poland—where the process of social disintegration was not nearly so advanced as in the Soviet Union—to reconsti-
tute itself into a community of conscience that was unafraid to defy the
regime. He did so, moreover, at a time when the "center" was so preoccupied by problems of systemic breakdown that it was unable to respond effectively. This lack of response, in turn, emboldened the various other "agglomerations of human atoms," including the oppressed
nationalities of the Soviet Union, to come together and demand *their*
rights. The result was the extraordinarily rapid unraveling of a seemingly mighty empire.

It is ironic that the empire built by Joseph Stalin—who had asked mockingly at Potsdam how many divisions the Pope had—was brought down, in no small measure, by a Pope who had nothing but words at his disposal. For nearly all his life, Karol Wojtyla has been fascinated by the power of words. As an aspiring actor, and then as a priest, he sought to use this power to bring about a spiritual and cultural renewal. As Pope, he used the power of his words to inspire the Poles to overcome the fear that the "center" had instilled in them and re-establish the bonds of human solidarity that Communism had nearly severed.

For Christians, who believe that the world was created through the power of the Word (see John 1:1–3), John Paul's success may not come altogether as a surprise. For secular observers, it is astounding. In a way, though, it is only fitting that Communism, which sought to replace faith in God with faith in History, should have been defeated by someone who continued to place his trust in the Lord of History. Secularists may regard this denouement as no more than a happy coincidence. Religious observers will doubtless discern a deeper meaning in these events.

6 Ronald Reagan

Tearing Down the Wall

Ronald Reagan: Tearing Down the Wall

On June 8, 1982, in his address to members of the British Parliament, Ronald Reagan recalled the greatness of Winston Churchill. "Witty as Sir Winston was," he said, "he also had that special attribute of great statesmen—the gift of vision, the willingness to see the future based on the experience of the past." After describing the Soviet Union as a society whose Marxist–Leninist "political structure...no longer corresponds to its economic base, a society where productive forces are hampered by political ones," Reagan emulated Churchill by offering a prediction of his own: Either the Soviet ruling class would change its political structure by allowing its people greater freedom, or it would go down to sure and certain defeat.

"It has happened in the past," Reagan continued; "a small ruling elite either mistakenly attempts to ease domestic unrest through greater repression and foreign adventure, or it chooses a wiser course." If the Soviet elite chose the wiser course of domestic reform, "prospects for arms control and a world at peace" would improve significantly. But if it tried to defend the status quo, "the march of freedom and democracy...will leave Marxism–Leninism on the ash heap of history as it has left other tyrannies which stifle the freedom and muzzle the self-expression of the people."[1]

When Reagan delivered this pronouncement, wrote British political columnist Geoffrey Smith in 1991, it appeared "a bit like ritual rhetoric or meddling in the affairs of others." Now, however, it "seems prophetic."[2] Yet Reagan's words were not merely prophecy; they were also policy. The key foreign policy document of the Reagan era, National Security Decision Directive 75 (NSDD 75), echoed the Westminster speech.

United States policy toward the Soviet Union, it declared, was "to promote...the process of change in the Soviet Union toward a more pluralistic political and economic system in which the power of the privileged ruling elite is gradually reduced."[3]

Though NSDD 75 was not issued formally until half a year after the Westminster speech, at Westminster Palace Ronald Reagan in effect leaked his top-secret Soviet strategy—forcing Soviet leaders to choose between ruin and reform—to the entire world. Perhaps not surprisingly, he found that no one, apart from the Soviets, was paying much attention. Only years later would political commentators like Geoffrey Smith note the speech's prophetic character, and even then there was a widespread reluctance to credit Ronald Reagan with saying or doing anything prophetic. After all, he was only a Grade-B movie actor and hopeless right-winger. How could anyone take such a person seriously?

"Reagan's was an astonishing performance," writes Henry Kissinger, "and to academic observers, nearly incomprehensible."[4] Reagan's third National Security Adviser, Robert C. McFarlane, concurred. Shaking his head in bewilderment, he once told Secretary of State George Shultz that "[Reagan] knows so little and accomplishes so much."[5] And journalist Lou Cannon, who had covered Reagan since 1960 and written three books about him, once confessed, "I regard Reagan as a puzzle. I am still trying to understand the man."[6]

Perhaps a good way to approach the "nearly incomprehensible" enigma of Ronald Reagan's success is by recalling British philosopher Isaiah Berlin's famous division of all human beings into two basic types: "foxes" and "hedgehogs." Foxes, said Sir Isaiah, know many small things; hedgehogs know one big thing.[7]

Using Berlin's typology, Ronald Reagan stands out as a classic hedgehog. It may be, as Kissinger claims, "that he knew next to no history, and the little he did know was tailored to suit his preconceptions."[8] But Reagan subscribed passionately to one large truth that many of Kissinger's academic colleagues either never knew or had forgotten: Societies that encourage freedom and creativity tend to flourish; societies that suppress liberty tend to stagnate. This was the central truth around which

Ronald Reagan fashioned his political career. This was the crucial insight that he articulated with Churchillian eloquence and pursued with Churchillian resolve. And this was the basis of his Soviet strategy—the strategy that won the Cold War.

"A New World Suddenly Opened Up"

Ronald Wilson Reagan was born on February 6, 1911, in Tampico, Illinois—a town of about a thousand souls located some 90 miles from Chicago—into what he has called a "religiously divided family."[9] His father, John Edward Reagan, was an Irish Catholic; his mother, Nelle Wilson Reagan, was a Scots–English Protestant. Of the two, Nelle had by far the greater influence on young Ronald. Not only did her 12-year-old son join her church, the Disciples of Christ, but by encouraging him to memorize passages from poems and plays and recite them before a church audience, she played an important role in his future choice of an acting career.

Throughout his early childhood, Reagan's family moved frequently until finally settling down in Dixon, Illinois. Their unsettled life stemmed from attempts by Reagan's father, a shoe salesman, to improve his position. Possibbly because John Reagan was an alcoholic, these efforts never quite succeeded and the family's financial situation remained precarious.

Although John Reagan was the source of many of the family's problems, he also helped shape his son's profoundly egalitarian outlook. "There was no more grievous sin at our household," Reagan wrote in his autobiography, "than a racial slur or other evidence of religious or racial intolerance."[10] So intensely did John Reagan abhor bigotry that when a hotel clerk assured him, as he was checking in during one of his shoe-selling trips, that he would like this particular establishment "because we don't permit a Jew in the place," John Reagan picked up his suitcase and spent the night in his car. "If it's come to the point where you won't take Jews," he told the clerk, "then someday you won't take *me* either."[11]

When he was 13 years old, an amazing thing happened to Ronald Reagan. Putting on his mother's glasses one day as a joke, he suddenly saw the world come into focus for the first time. "By picking up my mother's glasses, I had discovered that I was extremely nearsighted. A new world suddenly opened up to me."[12] Once he was fitted for glasses, Reagan became an outstanding athlete, a fine student (he was particularly drawn to his high school drama teacher), and a genuinely popular young man. In Margaret Cleaver, his church minister's daughter, he also found young love. The two of them dated throughout high school, and when Margaret decided to go on to Eureka, a small liberal arts college run by the Disciples of Christ, Reagan naturally followed suit.

Even if the Great Depression had not rocked the United States in 1929, the Reagan family would have been hard-pressed to find $900 a year to pay for their son's college tuition. As it was, with his father out of work and his mother barely making ends meet as a seamstress, Reagan was entirely on his own financially. But with the help of a partial scholarship, various campus jobs, and some savings scraped together from summers spent as a lifeguard, he managed to get into Eureka. The next four years went by in a whirl of extracurricular activity that left him with little time for study, but he managed to maintain a C average.

Out of a vague sense that it might come in handy one day, Reagan majored in economics at Eureka, but his heart was in the Drama Society. Thanks to a gifted professor, Eureka was invited to a prestigious acting contest at Northwestern University, and placed second. Afterwards, the head of Northwestern's Speech Department called Reagan into his office and urged him to make acting his career. "I guess that was the day the acting bug really bit me," he later recalled.[13]

Reagan, however, was reluctant to admit that his goal was to get into show business. So in 1932, when Sid Altschuler, one of the regular vacationers at Lowell Park—where Reagan spent his summers as a lifeguard—asked him what he wanted to do now that he had graduated from college, Reagan replied that he wanted to be a radio sports announcer. Altschuler advised him to "start knocking on doors, tell anyone who'll listen that you believe you have a future in the business, and you'll take any kind of job, even sweeping floors, just to get in."[14]

After the beach closed, Reagan heeded Altschuler's advice. Borrowing the family Oldsmobile, he drove 75 miles to Davenport, Iowa, and made his first call at radio station WOC. It happened that the station desperately needed a sports announcer, and Reagan was the right man at the right place at the right time. The station manager tried him out on the spot, and he did brilliantly; shortly thereafter, he was hired as a staff announcer at $100 a month. Three months later, he was hired by WOC's sister station, WHO, in Des Moines. Not even breaking up with his old flame, Margaret Cleaver (who had fallen in love with a Foreign Service Officer and returned his fraternity pin and engagement ring in the mail) could dampen his enthusiasm. "At twenty-two," he later wrote, "I'd achieved my dream: I was a sports announcer. If I had stopped there, I believe I would have been happy the rest of my life."[15]

"Where's the Rest of Me?"

In 1937, Reagan found himself covering the Chicago Cubs at their spring training camp in California. Though happy as a sports announcer, he had never quite abandoned his old dream of becoming an actor and could not resist the opportunity to take a few days off to visit Los Angeles and look up an old friend, Joy Hodges, who had come to Hollywood several years earlier hoping to break into the movies herself. Over dinner, Reagan told her about his "secret yearning" to be an actor. She introduced him to her agent, Bill Meiklejohn, who arranged for him to take a screen test at Warner Brothers studios. Shortly afterwards, Warner Brothers offered Reagan a seven-year contract.

Thus it happened that Ronald Reagan became a Hollywood actor. His rise was meteoric and seemingly effortless. Years later, when he switched from acting to politics, his rise would appear almost equally meteoric. In this he resembled Winston Churchill, whose ascent to fame and fortune was similarly rapid. Churchill was born in Blenheim Palace, into one of Great Britain's most distinguished and influential families; Reagan, by contrast, was born into an obscure lower-middle-class family in the heart of America's Midwest. Nonetheless, he climbed to the top of two notoriously competitive professions and made it all seem very easy—as perhaps, for him, it really was.

By 1938, Reagan felt sufficiently well established in his new Holly-wood career as "the Errol Flynn of the B pictures"[16] to invite his parents out to California, where he bought them a home. In 1940, he married actress Jane Wyman. In 1941, he was launched on the road to stardom thanks to his role as a happy-go-lucky playboy in a movie called *King's Row*. In a memorable scene, Reagan's character wakes up after an opera-tion to find that both his legs have been amputated and cries out in horror, "Where's the rest of me?"

Reagan was now earning $3,500 a week and receiving more fan mail than any other actor at Warner Brothers except Errol Flynn. Yet he was increasingly dissatisfied. Much as he loved acting, he felt that there was more to life than constant make-believe. Like the character he played in *King's Row*, he came to believe that he was only half a man:

> I began to feel like a shut-in invalid, nursed by public-ity. I have always liked space, the feeling of freedom, a broad range of friends.... Now I had become a semi-automaton "creating" a character another had written, doing what still another person told me to do on the set. Seeing the rushes, I could barely believe that the colored shadow on the screen was myself.
>
> Possibly this was the reason I decided to find the rest of me. I loved three things: drama, politics, and sports, and I'm not sure they always came in that order. In all three of them I came out of the monastery of movies into the world.[17]

"I Thought *You* Were One of Them"

In 1942, Reagan's wish to move out of the movies and into the world came true. Three months after Japan's attack on Pearl Harbor, he was called to active duty as a lieutenant in the Army. Because his vision was so poor, he was ineligible for combat but was assigned to general duty. Eventually, he was transferred to the Army Air Corps, where he became the personnel officer for a unit composed of artists and technicians from the movie business. Located in the Hal Roach film studio in Culver

City, California, "Fort Roach" produced films narrated by Reagan that helped prepare pilots and bombardiers for their missions over Germany and Japan.

Ronald Reagan remained in the Army for nearly four years, rising to the rank of captain. (He actually received a promotion to major, but requested that it be canceled: "Who was I," he asked, "to be a major for serving in California without ever hearing a shot fired in anger?"[18]) In the course of his duties, he saw much classified footage taken by combat cameramen but never shown to the public. Some of these films, containing horrifying scenes from recently liberated Nazi death camps, made a lasting impression on him.

When World War II ended, Reagan returned to civilian life determined to help build a better world. He vowed "to work with the tools I had: my thoughts, my speaking abilities, my reputation as an actor. I would try to bring about the regeneration of the world I believed should have automatically appeared."[19] What troubled him most was what he saw as "the rise of fascism in our country, the very thing we had fought to obliterate,"[20] and he began to speak out against it:

> One day after giving one of my speeches to the men's club at the Hollywood Beverly Christian Church where I worshipped, our pastor came up to me and said he agreed with what I'd said about the rise of neofascism. But he said: "I think your speech would be even better if you also mentioned that if Communism looked like a threat, you'd be just as opposed to it as you are to fascism."

Reagan admitted that he had not thought much about the Communist threat, but agreed with the minister's suggestion. Shortly afterwards, he gave his usual speech before a local citizens' organization but added that "If I ever find evidence that Communism represents a threat to all that we believe in and stand for, I'll speak out just as harshly against Communism as I have fascism." His remarks were received with "dead silence."[21]

Reagan now began taking a closer look at some of the liberal organizations he had joined. He became especially concerned about a group called the Hollywood Independent Citizens Committee of the Arts, Sciences and Professions, popularly known as HICCASP. The group had been formed to support President Franklin Delano Roosevelt, and Reagan, considering himself "a New Dealer to the core,"[22] was proud to sit on its board of directors. One evening, however, he was astonished to hear another HICCASP official, actress Olivia de Havilland, declare that the organization was being taken over by Communists. "You know, Olivia," Reagan said, "I always thought you might be one of 'them,'" to which de Havilland replied, "That's funny. I thought *you* were one of them."[23]

Reagan and de Havilland came up with a plan. They agreed that de Havilland would present the executive board with an innocuous statement affirming HICCASP's belief "in a free enterprise system" and repudiating "Communism as desirable for the United States." When she did so, the executive board voted it down overwhelmingly. Reagan, de Havilland, and ten other prominent Hollywood figures resigned from the organization, effectively putting HICCASP out of business.

While Reagan was learning about Communism, he also was becoming increasingly involved in the Screen Actors Guild (SAG), the Hollywood actors' trade union. He had joined only reluctantly after becoming a contract player for Warner Brothers, but as he became convinced that actors were exploited by the studio bosses, he became a dedicated union man and was appointed to the board of directors in 1941.

When he returned to the board after the war, Hollywood was in the middle of a bitter dispute between two rival unions—IATSE (International Association of Theatrical and Stage Employees) and CSU (Conference of Studio Unions)—over the right to represent a third group, the Set Erectors. To enforce its jurisdictional claim, the CSU ordered its members to picket the various studios; to enforce its counterclaims, IATSE ordered its members to cross the picket lines. Soon, pitched battles were being fought in front of Hollywood's studio gates; soon, too, SAG became involved in the strike as actors demanded to know whether they should cross the picket lines.

As a member of the SAG's board of directors, Reagan suggested set-ting up a meeting between the leaders of the CSU and IATSE to sort things out. When the encounter took place, it became apparent that the CSU did not have a legitimate case, and Reagan urged SAG members to cross the picket lines. Shortly thereafter, he was visited by two FBI agents who informed him that during a recent Communist Party meeting in downtown Los Angeles, someone had asked, "What are we going to do about that son-of-a-bitching bastard Reagan?" Around this time, Reagan also became aware of a plan to end his motion picture career by throw-ing acid in his face. (For seven months, he wore a gun and shoulder holster under his arm, and his home was placed under police protec-tion.)

Several years later, a California Senate committee confirmed what Reagan strongly suspected at the time: The CSU strike was part of a Soviet-directed effort to gain control of Hollywood's film industry, and Reagan had been targeted because of his outspoken anti-Communism.[24] As Reagan later wrote:

> The strike and the efforts to gain control over
> HICCASP had a profound effect on me. More than
> anything else, it was the Communists' attempted take-
> over of Hollywood and its worldwide weekly audience
> of more than five hundred million people that led me
> to accept a nomination to serve as president of the
> Screen Actors Guild and, indirectly at least, set me on
> the road that would lead me into politics.[25]

"Beating the Bushes for Private Enterprise"

If Reagan's decision to accept the presidency of the SAG in 1947 led ultimately to a remarkable political career, its immediate consequences were disastrous. In 1948, finding that the man she had married was more preoccupied with politics than with acting, Jane Wyman filed for divorce. Reagan was devastated.

Reagan's movie career also suffered as a result of his union activities. "I think I became too identified with the serious side of Hollywood's off-screen life," Reagan later said. "There were too many people who saw me as only a committee member."[26] Yet being president of the Screen Actors Guild fulfilled a need for public service that he had felt before World War II and that the war strongly reinforced. Since he was so good at what he did, his fellow actors re-elected him four times, and then brought him back for a sixth term in 1959.

Reagan's personal fortunes took a major turn for the better in 1952, when he married a 28-year-old actress named Nancy Davis. Unlike Wyman, Davis had no great career ambitions. She gladly gave up acting to devote herself to her husband and children, and from all reports, they enjoyed a near-perfect marriage. "Sometimes," Reagan later confessed, "I think my life really began when I met Nancy."[27]

In 1954, with his movie career languishing and a new family to support, Reagan accepted an offer from the General Electric Company to serve as host for its new television series, *GE Theater*. He also agreed to make personal appearances at GE plants and in selected communities across the country as part of the company's Employee and Community Relations Program.[28] Reagan has estimated that during his eight-year association with the company, he visited all of its 139 plants and met every one of its 250,000 employees.

It was the community relations aspect of his job that proved decisive. Addressing groups like the local United Fund or chamber of commerce, he began by talking about what he knew best, focusing on Hollywood's achievements (for example, in beating back an attempted Communist takeover) and the challenges facing the motion picture industry. The principal challenge, in Reagan's view, stemmed from a Justice Department decision, made in response to an antitrust suit brought by an independent chain of theater owners, to force studios to sell the theaters they controlled. To Reagan, "the government's decision to break up the studio system was wrong. It destroyed the stability of the industry under the justification that the studios monopolized the picture business."[29]

This argument was one that Reagan had made many times as president of the SAG, but "an interesting thing happened" when he began making it during his GE appearances. "No matter where I was, I'd find people from the audience waiting to talk to me after a speech and they'd all say, 'Hey, if you think things are bad in your business, let me tell you what is happening in my business....'"[30]

These GE tours eventually became "almost a postgraduate course in political science" for Reagan. Although a staunch anti-Communist, when he began speaking for GE he was still a liberal who believed that the federal government, despite occasional lapses, was basically a force for good in American life. Listening to one complaint after another "about how the ever-expanding federal government was encroaching on liberties we'd always taken for granted" changed his mind. It gradually dawned on him that, nearly always, big government was part of the problem, not the solution. This was most evident in Communist countries, where the government brutally oppressed the very people it claimed to be serving; but even in the United States "a federal bureaucracy...was becoming so powerful [that] it was able to set policy and thwart the desires not only of ordinary citizens, but their elected representatives in Congress."[31]

As Reagan jettisoned his old-fashioned liberalism in favor of his newly discovered libertarian conservatism, he acquired a mission in life: to remind Americans about the virtues of limited government and alert them to the dangers of expansive government. "As time went on," he later recalled, "the portion of my speech about government began to grow longer and I began to shorten the Hollywood part. Pretty soon, it became basically a warning to people about the threat of government. Finally, the Hollywood part just got lost and I was out there beating the bushes for private enterprise."[32]

Thanks to General Electric, the liberal Ronald Reagan vanished forever and the crusading, conservative Ronald Reagan entered the political arena. His message—to which he subscribed with the zeal of a recent convert—boiled down to five words: Freedom works; big government doesn't.

"A Rendezvous With Destiny"

Ronald Reagan's rise to the top of American politics was almost as rapid as his ascent to Hollywood stardom. As a political figure, he first came to prominence on October 27, 1964, the night he spoke on national television on behalf of Republican presidential candidate Barry Goldwater. (He had been approached to give the speech by some wealthy Goldwater backers, who happened to hear Reagan deliver it one evening at the Ambassador Hotel in Los Angeles and were sufficiently impressed to persuade the campaign to run it on national television.)

The October speech did not save Goldwater's sagging political fortunes, but it made Ronald Reagan—who had registered as a Republican only two years earlier—the most prominent conservative in America. The message was vintage Reagan:

> The idea that government is beholden to the people, that it has no other source of power except the sovereign people, is still the newest and most unique idea in all the long history of man's relation to man. This is the issue of this election: whether we believe in our capacity for self-government or whether we abandon the American Revolution and confess that a little intellectual elite in a far-distant capital can plan our lives for us better than we can plan them ourselves....
>
> You and I have a rendezvous with destiny. We will preserve for our children this, the last best hope of man on earth, or we will sentence them to take the last step into a thousand years of darkness....[33]

The next stage of Ronald Reagan's rise to power might have been scripted by a Hollywood screenwriter. A group of conservative California millionaires, recognizing that in Reagan they had a potential political superstar, approached him to run as the Republican candidate for governor in 1966. The 54-year-old Reagan turned them down, arguing that he was too old to embark upon a second career. Eventually, however, he agreed to go on an extensive exploratory tour to discover for himself whether the people of California were responsive to his message—limiting and reforming state government—and to him personally. After canvassing the state for six months, Reagan agreed to run for governor.

Reagan went on to win the governorship of California by a million votes and 15 percentage points and served for two successful terms, reforming California's welfare system and saving the state's government from bankruptcy. On the eve of the 1968 Republican presidential convention, Reagan made a bid for the nomination but was soundly defeated by Richard Nixon. Yet he did not lose hope, and when he left the governor's office in 1974 his sights were clearly set on higher things.

In 1975, convinced that the Republican presidential incumbent, Gerald Ford, was not trying hard enough to reduce the size and power of big government and that the Ford–Kissinger policy of détente was little more than a futile attempt to appease the Soviets, Reagan challenged Ford in the primaries. He failed to wrest the nomination from Ford in 1976, but his margin of defeat was so narrow that he decided to take another stab at the presidency in 1979. This time, he easily captured the Republican nomination and went on to win the presidential election by over 8 million votes against a lackluster Jimmy Carter.

Reagan's 1980 campaign was dominated by two great themes: "that government had grown too big and should be reduced, and America's military had grown too weak and ought to be strengthened."[34] On January 20, 1981, he became the 40th President of the United States.

"Communism Was Doomed"

The conventional wisdom has it that no matter what a politician may say in his quest for the White House, the realities of power invariably force him to moderate his views once he becomes President. This was not true of Ronald Reagan. On the contrary, where the Soviet Union was concerned, his experiences as President strongly reinforced the unconventional opinions he had long held. As a Goldwater supporter in the early 1960s, Reagan subscribed to the hard-line anti-Soviet policy laid out in the Arizona Senator's 1962 book, *Why Not Victory?* As President, what Reagan learned about the Soviet Union's internal crisis made Goldwater's question seem more relevant—and sensible—than ever.

On March 26, 1982, President Ronald Reagan made the following entry in his diary: "Briefing on Soviet economy. They are in very bad shape and if we can cut off their credit they'll have to yell 'Uncle' or starve."[35] Reagan did not explain what he meant by forcing the Soviets to yell "Uncle." Did he believe that if the U.S. pressed them hard enough, they would finally concede NATO's right to deploy Pershing and cruise missiles in Western Europe to counter the menacing Soviet SS–20s? Was he thinking of an even more far-reaching Soviet concession—say, Soviet willingness to conclude a major strategic arms reduction agreement? Or did the President have something *really* radical in mind—a Soviet withdrawal from Afghanistan, for example?

To answer these questions, it is useful to look at another situation in which Reagan used the same phrase and explained exactly what he meant. In a news conference on February 25, 1985, he argued that the goal of the American-backed Contras in Nicaragua was to make the regime "say Uncle"—which, he elaborated, meant to "remove" the Sandinista regime "in the sense of its present structure, in which it is a communist totalitarian state."[36]

In 1982, Ronald Reagan had exactly the same fate in mind for the Soviet Union. Like previous Presidents, he wanted to get the Soviets out of Afghanistan and persuade them to reduce the size of their strategic arsenal. Unlike any other President before him, however, he recognized that the Soviet Union's economic vulnerability gave the U.S. the opportunity to secure a vastly more significant victory: to "remove" the Soviet regime "in the sense of its present structure, in which it is a communist totalitarian state." As Reagan put it in his memoirs:

> I had always believed that, as an economic system, Communism was doomed. Not only was it lacking in the free market incentives that motivated people to work hard and excel—the economic propulsion that had brought such prosperity to America—but history was full of examples showing that any totalitarian state that deprived its people of liberty and freedom of choice was ultimately doomed. The Bolshevik revolution had simply replaced an inherited aristocracy with a self-appointed one, the Soviet leadership, and it, like its predecessor, could not survive against the inherent drive of all men and women to be free.

Now, the economic statistics and intelligence reports I was getting during my daily National Security Council briefings were revealing tangible evidence that Communism as we knew it was approaching the brink of collapse not only in the Soviet Union but throughout the Eastern bloc. The Soviet economy was being held together with baling wire; it was a basket case, partly because of massive spending on armaments. In Poland and other Eastern-bloc countries, the economies were also a mess, and there were rumblings of nationalistic fervor within the captive Soviet empire.

You had to wonder how long the Soviets could keep their empire intact. If they didn't make some changes, it seemed clear to me that in time Communism would collapse of its own weight, and I wondered how we as a nation could use these cracks in the Soviet system to accelerate the process of collapse.[37]

"We Win and They Lose"

According to Richard V. Allen, Reagan's first National Security Adviser, the President had been wondering about how to promote the Soviet Union's collapse for some time:

> In January 1977, I visited Ronald Reagan in his Los Angeles home to ask of him a personal favor.... He agreed to do the favor, and then asked if I had some time to talk. During the next four hours he said many memorable things, but none more significant than this: "My idea of American policy toward the Soviet Union is simple, and some would say simplistic. It is this: 'we win and they lose.' What do you think of that?"
>
> This enormously appealing formula was something I had never heard from the mouth of a leading political figure. Until then, we had thought only in terms of "managing" the relationship with the Soviet Union.

> This man had gotten to the heart of the matter: utiliz-
> ing American values, strength and creativity, we could
> outdistance the Soviets and cause them to withdraw
> from the Cold War, or perhaps even collapse. I needed
> no additional information, and resolved to help him,
> in some way, elevate that thought to the status of na-
> tional policy.
>
> Herein lay the great difference, back in 1977, between
> Ronald Reagan and every other politician: he literally
> believed that we could win, and was prepared to carry
> this message to the nation as the intellectual founda-
> tion of a presidency.[38]

The reason Reagan differed from virtually every other American political figure was that he had boundless faith in the strength of the free
enterprise system and boundless contempt for Soviet collectivism.
Whereas other politicians viewed the Cold War as a complex struggle
between two more or less evenly matched superpowers, Reagan saw it as
a totally uneven contest between two *systems*, one of which (capitalism)
was infinitely superior, both morally and economically, to the other. It
seemed self-evident to him that the United States would win the Cold
War, provided that its economy was freed from the shackles of big government and allowed to reach its full potential. Hence, promoting
America's economic recovery through tax cuts and deregulation became,
for Reagan, the basis for any winning Cold War strategy. As Allen writes,
Reagan believed that victory in the Cold War depended "upon a revival
of the American economy."[39]

Reagan's literal belief in the possibility of an American victory in the
Cold War is confirmed by Robert Gates, the Central Intelligence Agency's
top Soviet analyst during most of the Reagan Administration and later
its director under George Bush:

> While Reagan's view of the economic failings of the
> Soviet Union may have been rudimentary, even primi-
> tive, it also happened generally to conform to Soviet
> reality. Thus he was highly receptive to the content of

the briefings he received on the Soviet economy....
Reagan, nearly alone, truly believed in 1981 that the
Soviet system was vulnerable, not in some vague, long-
range historical sense, but right then. And he was determined to move the United States and the West from
defense to offense.[40]

These briefings on the Soviet economy, which served to reinforce
Reagan's strongly held conviction that Communism was a doomed system, resulted from some highly unorthodox procedures developed by
the President's new CIA director, William Casey. A veteran of the clandestine Office of Strategic Services (OSS) during World War II, Casey
had been intrigued by a series of articles that appeared in *Fortune* magazine during the late 1970s documenting the Soviet Union's economic
and social decline. The articles mirrored Casey's own sense of the Soviet
Union's growing vulnerability, but were sharply at odds with the conventional wisdom at the CIA, where analysts continued to argue well
into the mid-1980s that the Soviet Union enjoyed robust economic
health and that only "right wing kooks" seriously entertained the notion
that the Soviet Union could be brought to its knees through sustained
economic and social pressure.[41]

Casey therefore made Herbert Meyer, the author of the *Fortune* series
and a Soviet affairs specialist, his special assistant with a broadly defined
mandate: Question the conventional wisdom at CIA headquarters and
bring alternative views to Casey's attention. In effect, Meyer became the
head of an informal "Team B" that challenged the conclusions of the
Agency's official "Team A."

Both as Casey's special assistant and, from 1982 to 1985, as vice chairman of the National Intelligence Council, Meyer was able to produce a
stream of assessments that underscored the Soviet Union's economic
plight and predicted its imminent collapse. Casey, in turn, made sure
that this material, ranging from lengthy analytical papers to little more
than bits and pieces of economic data, was brought to the President's
attention on a regular basis.[42] Reagan was especially interested in raw
intelligence data. "The president loved seeing the raw intelligence on
the Soviet economy," according to John Poindexter, Reagan's fourth

National Security Adviser. "The anecdotal intelligence especially—factories that were shutting down for a lack of spare parts, hard currency shortages, food lines—interested him greatly and helped determine his belief that the Soviet economy was in monumental trouble."[43]

Reagan's belief that Soviet Communism was on its last legs, and that this gave the United States the opportunity to administer the *coup de grace* by sharply ratcheting up the pressure on the Soviet system, went completely against the established view at the time. In 1982, for example, former President Richard Nixon told *Time* magazine's Strobe Talbott that

> We've got to make [the Soviets] understand that we're not out to get them. I know there's a school of thought that if we can fence them in with sanctions, their whole rotten system will come tumbling down. There's a school of thought that hard-line policies on our part will induce change for the better on their part. I wish that were the case, but it's just not going to happen.[44]

Nixon's criticisms of Reagan's foreign policy were shared not only by such liberal commentators as historian Arthur Schlesinger, Jr. (who wrote in 1982 that "Those in the U.S. who think the Soviet Union is on the verge of economic and social collapse, ready with one small push to go over the brink, are...only kidding themselves"[45]), but even by Vice President George Bush. According to the former Soviet ambassador to the United States, Anatoly Dobrynin,

> The vice president felt that the most important thing was to make Reagan revise his notions, the almost unimaginable ideas and prejudices he brought to the White House from his past. When Bush got closer to him in the initial months of his presidency, he was simply amazed to see to what extent Reagan was dominated by Hollywood clichés and the ideas of his wealthy but conservative and poorly educated friends from California. Unfortunately, many deep-seated stereo-

types remained in the president's head, and they were reinforced by the conservatives in Reagan's White House entourage.

"Well, he's hard, very hard indeed," Bush repeated of Reagan. "But I think he wouldn't be altogether hopeless if Soviet–American relations came to be the focus of the election campaign."[46]

Bush was wrong about Reagan's lack of sophistication, but right about one thing: With his unusual background and peculiar intellectual evolution, Ronald Reagan was a most unconventional politician.

"By Every Available Means"

Of course, *believing* that the U.S. could win the Cold War by exploiting the Soviet Union's internal crisis was one thing; translating that belief into a coherent strategy was something else again. The former required faith, vision, and courage—qualities that Reagan had in abundance; the latter demanded a detailed knowledge of Soviet conditions, which he lacked.

Fortunately, there were many gifted policy intellectuals on Reagan's National Security Council staff. One of the most brilliant was Harvard historian Richard Pipes, who served for over two years as the NSC's leading Soviet specialist. During this time, aided by other NSC staffers, Pipes drafted National Security Decision Directive 75, which transformed and codified Reagan's vision into a series of policy guidelines. "In the early 1980's," Pipes later wrote, "the U.S. government occasionally received intelligence reports that depicted in stark terms the internal crisis afflicting the Soviet Union.... The grand strategy of the Reagan administration with respect to the USSR was to exploit this crisis by every available means in order to push Moscow toward reform."[47] By "reform," the Reagan Administration meant a situation whereby "the [Soviet] elite is prepared to sacrifice some of its authority and bring society into partnership, if only of a limited kind."[48]

Issued on January 17, 1983, NSDD 75 bore the relatively innocuous title "U.S. Relations With The USSR." A more accurate title might have been "How to Demoralize the *Nomenklatura*," for that was NSDD

75's basic thrust: to launch an extraordinarily broad array of economic, military, and political initiatives which, in combination with the economic and social meltdown already underway within the USSR, would convince the Soviet ruling elite that the "correlation of forces" was moving sharply and inexorably against it, and that unless it was willing to share *some* of its power with the Soviet people—to move, in other words, from a totalitarian to an authoritarian system—it would soon lose *all* of its power.

Through relentless pressure on the Soviet system, the Reagan Administration sought to engender a kind of "grand compromise" between the *nomenklatura* and its subjects in which the former, to avoid falling hopelessly behind the United States, would permit greater freedom and private initiative in the economic sphere while the latter would endorse a system in which the *nomenklatura* continued to rule. In such a system, the *nomenklatura*'s legitimacy would derive increasingly from a general sense that, under its guidance, living standards were gradually improving, and not from the fact that Communism was gaining ground internationally. Hence, the Soviet Union would be far less likely to engage in foreign adventurism and far more prone to concentrate on internal development.

NSDD 75 called on the United States to seize the offensive in the Cold War through military strategy, economic policy, and political action. Militarily, it declared,

> The U.S. must modernize its military forces—both nuclear and conventional—so that Soviet leaders perceive that the U.S. is determined never to accept a second place or a deteriorating military posture. Soviet calculations of possible war outcomes under any contingency must always result in outcomes so unfavorable to the USSR that there would be no incentive for Soviet leaders to initiate an attack. U.S. military technology advances must be exploited, while controls over transfer of military related dual/use technology, products and services must be tightened.[49]

This was the rationale for the vast Reagan military buildup, which was already well underway when NSDD 75 was issued. It had three great objectives:

- To demoralize the *nomenklatura* by demonstrating that, apart from virtually bankrupting the country, the Soviet effort to attain military supremacy, pursued at great cost and with single-minded tenacity over the past two decades, had failed;

- To underscore to the *nomenklatura* that, absent major systemic reform, there was no way it could compete militarily with the United States; and

- To discourage an increasingly alarmed *nomenklatura* from trying to escape from the Soviet Union's growing internal crisis through external aggression.

To achieve these goals, says Lawrence Korb, "In his first six years in office, Reagan purchased nearly 3,000 combat aircraft, 3,700 strategic missiles and about 10,000 tanks."[50] As one of Reagan's key advisers, his second Attorney General, Edwin Meese III, has pointed out,

> These procurement levels were nearly double those of the 1970s; and, of course, the weapons being brought on line in the 1980s were much more sophisticated than their predecessors.... It was from the Reagan buildup that we achieved "smart" bombs and radar suppression, Tomahawk cruise missiles and Patriot defenses, Aegis cruisers and Abrams tanks, Apache helicopters, night-fighting capability, and other military advances that were exhibited in the Persian Gulf.[51]

In addition to modernizing both conventional and strategic forces, the Reagan Administration "hardened" U.S. command and control capacities to enable them to survive a Soviet surprise attack.

Economically, NSDD 75 made it U.S. policy "to seek to minimize the potential for Soviet exercise of reverse leverage on Western trade, energy supply, and financial relationships"; "to avoid subsidizing the Soviet economy or unduly easing the burden of Soviet resource allocation decisions, so as not to dilute pressures for structural change in the

Soviet system"; and "above all, to ensure that East–West economic relations do not facilitate the Soviet military buildup. This requires prevention of the transfer of technology and equipment that would make a substantial contribution directly or indirectly to Soviet military power."[52]

To understand the reason for this unusually heavy stress on economic measures, it should be remembered that the Reagan Administration was convinced, as Pipes wrote shortly after leaving the National Security Council, that

> Western economic involvement in the Soviet Union
> and Eastern Europe since the 1960s has been deep and
> consequential. Once again, as happened in the 1890s
> and 1930s, the USSR has received from the West essential help modernizing those industries that advances
> in technology had rendered obsolete and familiarizing
> it with technologies that it has not been able to master
> on its own.[53]

Pipes singled out one particularly egregious example of Western technology transfer:

> The most shocking instance of the contribution that
> Western technology has made to Soviet military capabilities was the sale by the United States in the early
> 1970s of equipment to manufacture miniature ball
> bearings.... [T]he Soviet leadership decided in 1959–
> 60 to proceed with the mass production of nuclear
> weapons. German technology, acquired after World
> War II, combined with native science and industry,
> provided nearly all the components required. Among
> the equipment that could not be produced domestically, however, was machinery to manufacture large
> quantities of miniature ball bearings for missile guidance systems. At the time Soviet representatives approached the only firm that made such machinery, the
> Bryant Chucking Grinder Company, of Springfield,
> Vermont. In 1961, with Soviet orders pending, Bryant

applied for a license to sell this equipment to the Soviet Union, but Defense Department objections moved President Kennedy to deny the application. In 1972, in the more favorable climate of détente, Bryant applied once again for a license to ship to the USSR its Centalgin grinders. This time, permission came through. The bearings produced by this United States equipment are almost certainly integrated into the guidance system of Soviet missiles. In the opinion of some experts, they have materially contributed to the enhancement of accuracies of Soviet missiles, to the extent of putting at risk the United States force of Minuteman ICBMs and requiring the development of a new land-based missile, the MX.[54]

It was to prevent disasters of this sort from recurring, and also to block the Soviet Union from acquiring the hard currency it needed to purchase vital Western technology by selling its plentiful oil and gas resources to the West, that the Reagan Administration adopted the economic policies outlined in NSDD 75. The expectation was that by curtailing Soviet access to Western credit and technology, these measures would further demoralize the *nomenklatura*, impede its attempts to compete militarily, and eventually force it to succumb to "pressures for structural change in the Soviet system." As Reagan puts it in his autobiography, the Soviet economy was in such bad shape "that if the Western countries got together and cut off credits to it, we could bring it to its knees."[55]

"This was the principal motive behind the battle over the so-called Siberian pipeline" writes Meese,

> and also behind the systematic effort of the Pentagon's office on technology transfer, to impede the flow of Western computers, precision machinery, microelectronics, and other militarily useful systems to the East. The coordinated effort at the Department of Defense (headed up by Stephen Bryen) to curtail such trans-

fers, both from the United States and from third countries receiving our technology, was one of the great
unsung successes of the Reagan era.[56]

" A Major Ideological/Political Offensive"

On the political front, NSDD 75 called for nothing less than "Building and sustaining a major ideological/political offensive which, together
with other efforts, will be designed to bring about evolutionary change
of the Soviet system...." Specifically, "U.S. policy must have an ideological thrust which clearly affirms the superiority of U.S. and Western
values of individual dignity and freedom, a free press, free trade unions,
free enterprise, and political democracy over the repressive features of
Soviet Communism."[58]

Potentially, this was the most demoralizing initiative of all. If it ever
became clear to the *nomenklatura* and its subjects that democracy, not
Communism, was the wave of the future, then the former would lose
heart while the latter would gain it, thereby subjecting the Soviet system
to pressure from both above and below.

To implement this directive, the Reagan Administration upgraded
the personnel and increased the budgets of the United States Information Agency, the Voice of America, the Board for International Broadcasting, Radio Liberty, and Radio Free Europe. The President also established Radio Martí to broadcast into Cuba.[59]

"When I had entered office," Reagan later wrote, "I'd been struck by
something that didn't seem right: The democracies were up against an
expansionist powerhouse that was trying all over the world to peddle its
system, yet we who had the system of government that *worked* were
doing nothing to sell our vision of freedom...."[60] To correct this anomaly,
Reagan used his 1982 address to members of the British Parliament to
launch his "Democracy Initiative," pledging "to foster the infrastructure of democracy, the system of a free press, unions, political parties,
universities, which allows a people to choose their own way, to develop
their own culture, to reconcile their own differences through peaceful

means."[61] In 1983, the Reagan Administration helped to establish the National Endowment for Democracy, charged with strengthening indigenous democratic institutions around the world.

In addition to establishing broad objectives for American economic, political, and military policy, NSDD 75 targeted "the Soviet empire" for special attention. "There are a number of important weaknesses and vulnerabilities in the Soviet empire which the U.S. should exploit," it declared. In the Third World, for example,

> U.S. policy will seek to limit the destabilizing activities of Third World allies and clients. It is a further objective to weaken and, where possible, undermine the existing links between them and the Soviet Union. U.S. policy will include active efforts to encourage democratic movements and forces to bring about political change inside these countries.[62]

This is the earliest formulation of what later became known as the Reagan Doctrine, enunciated publicly by the President in his State of the Union Address on February 6, 1985:

> We must stand by all our democratic allies. And we must not break faith with those who are risking their lives—on every continent, from Afghanistan to Nicaragua—to defy Soviet-supported aggression and secure rights which have been ours from birth…. Support for freedom fighters is self-defense and totally consistent with the OAS and UN Charters.[63]

This forthright support for anti-Communist insurgencies around the world was dubbed the "Reagan Doctrine" by columnist Charles Krauthammer. In an essay in *Time* magazine, Krauthammer pointed out that, whereas the Truman Doctrine set out simply to contain Soviet expansion, the Reagan Doctrine sought to reverse it: "This is a challenge to the peripheral acquisitions of [the Soviet] empire…. It supports not the status quo but revolution."[64]

Critics of the Reagan Doctrine charged that there was no strategic conception behind it beyond "bleeding" the Soviets, and even Robert McFarlane, who succeeded Judge William Clark as Reagan's National Security Adviser in October 1983, has argued that there was no well-thought-out policy behind the Reagan Doctrine. In fact, the Reagan Doctrine (like all the other Reagan initiatives) did have an overriding strategic purpose: to demoralize the *nomenklatura* and force it to undertake internal reform. The Reagan Doctrine's great insight was that a defeat on the Soviet empire's periphery could help destabilize the "Center" itself. As Richard Pipes explained in *Foreign Affairs*,

> Russian history...strongly suggests, and informed Russian opinion corroborates, that such *changes for the better that one can expect in the nature of the Soviet government and in its conduct of foreign relations will come about only from failures, instabilities and fears of collapse and not from growing confidence and sense of security.*[65]

The consequences of the Soviet Union's defeat in Afghanistan bear out the accuracy of this analysis. Soviet forces had been dispatched to Afghanistan in December 1979 to shore up a pro-Soviet government and help put down a guerrilla rebellion. Although Soviet military progress against the *mujahedin* fighters proved much slower than anticipated, by 1984–1985 the tide of battle appeared to be turning in Moscow's favor. But President Reagan's April 1986 decision to arm the *mujahedin* with Stinger missiles led to a sharp increase in Soviet losses and a growing recognition that the war could not possibly be won. When the Soviet Union finally acknowledged defeat and withdrew its forces in 1989, it was not merely a few Politburo members who were discredited for initiating a disastrous war. Rather, as Peter Rodman has pointed out, "the very core of the system was held to blame—the arbitrariness of dictatorial rule, the party's monopoly of power, and the complete absence of accountability.... Many an autocracy has been discredited and undermined by failure in war. This one should be added to the list."[66]

The Reagan Doctrine in Latin America

If Afghanistan was a strategic opportunity for the United States, the coming to power in 1979 of the Leninist Sandinista National Liberation Front (FSLN) in Nicaragua constituted a strategic windfall for Moscow—and a major test of the Reagan Doctrine. As Reagan explained in his memoirs,

> Once they were in power, the Sandinistas began trying to export their Marxist revolution to neighboring El Salvador and other countries in Central America.... If the Soviet Union and its [Cuban and Nicaraguan] allies were allowed to continue subverting democracy with terrorism and fomenting so-called "wars of national liberation" in Central America, it wouldn't stop there: It would spread into the continent of South America and north to Mexico. Then, as I was told that Lenin once said, "Once we have Latin America, we won't have to take the United States, the last bastion of capitalism, because it will fall into our outstretched hands like overripe fruit...."[67]

Although Reagan and some of his advisers—particularly Secretary of State Alexander Haig, CIA Director William Casey, and Ambassador to the United Nations Jeane Kirkpatrick—believed that the Sandinista regime posed a strategic threat to the United States, the Administration was unwilling to sanction the use of American troops to overthrow the Sandinistas. Instead, Reagan turned to the CIA to organize anti-Sandinista Nicaraguans into the Contras, "a military fighting force that, with our aid and support, undertook the task of bringing democracy to Nicaragua in the same way that the freedom fighters who led the American Revolution brought democracy to our people."[68]

The CIA's involvement enraged many congressional Democrats, who felt, as Senator Christopher Dodd of Connecticut said in a 1983 speech, that the U.S. was standing against "the tide of history" in Central America. The result was a bitter conflict between the executive and legislative branches that exploded into a political firestorm once it became known that two members of the National Security Council staff, John Poindexter and Oliver North, had used profits from the sale of arms to Iran to aid the Contras.

In the end, for all its difficulties with Congress, the fact remains that the Reagan Administration succeeded in keeping a 16,000-man Contra army in place long enough to extract a crucial concession from the Sandinistas: a free election in February 1990. The victory of the democratic United Nicaraguan Opposition (UNO) in that election marked the end of the FSLN's grip on Nicaragua—and a belated victory for the Reagan Doctrine.

"To Make a Stand on Poland"

The Reagan Administration did not confine its efforts to overthrow pro-Soviet regimes to the periphery of the Soviet empire. On the contrary, in Poland it exploited an opportunity to destabilize a Communist government in the very heart of the Soviet bloc.[69] From the outset of his presidency, Reagan understood that the rise of the free Polish trade union, Solidarity, represented a major threat to Moscow and a major opportunity for the West. "This is what we had been waiting for since World War II," Reagan wrote in his autobiography. "What was happening in Poland might spread like a contagion throughout Eastern Europe."[70]

On January 30, 1981—only ten days after his inauguration—Reagan met with senior members of his national security team: Vice President George Bush, National Security Adviser Richard Allen, CIA chief William Casey, Secretary of State Alexander Haig and Secretary of Defense Caspar Weinberger. "It was there," Weinberger later recalled, "that we decided on the need to make a stand on Poland—not only to prevent an invasion, but to seek ways to undermine [Communist] power in Poland."[71] Thus, when Poland's military government arrested Solidarity's leaders and imposed martial law on December 13, 1981, Reagan was furious. "We can't let this revolution against Communism fail without our offering a hand," he wrote in his diary. "We may never have an opportunity like this in our lifetime."[72]

To demonstrate America's anger over the violation of human rights in Poland, Reagan imposed a host of sanctions against both Poland and the Soviet Union:

> We suspended negotiations [with Moscow] on a new long-term grain-sale agreement; banned flights to the United States by the Soviet airline, Aeroflot; canceled several exchange programs; and imposed an embargo on shipment to the Soviet Union of critical American-made products, including pipe-laying equipment that was to be used in the construction of a trans-Siberian [Yamal] gas pipeline.[73]

Although U.S. efforts to derail the Yamal pipeline (which was supposed to bring Siberian natural gas to Western Europe) led to a nasty dispute within the Western alliance, a compromise eventually was reached whereby one of the pipeline's two strands was canceled.

But the Reagan Administration did more than impose sanctions. It also initiated a covert effort to provide aid to Solidarity despite martial law. The meeting in which this crucial decision was taken is described by Peter Schweitzer in his book, *Victory*:

> Shortly after the declaration of martial law, the president spoke with his closest advisers about the situation in Poland and U.S. options. Much of the NSC was not included. "National Security Council meetings were not considered leak proof, he [the President] didn't want to risk anything," recalls Pipes. At the meeting were Vice President Bush, [National Security Adviser] William Clark, Secretaries Haig and Weinberger, Ed Meese, Richard Pipes and William Casey.
>
> There was a general consensus that the United States had to send a strong message to Warsaw and Moscow. Economic sanctions were universally supported as a way of demonstrating American anger. But then Pipes raised the stakes: what about doing something proactive? What about covertly funding Solidarity to ensure

that the first anti-Communist organization aboveground in the Soviet bloc survived this harsh political winter? The specter of such a risky operation haunted the room. After a few moments, Al Haig cut through the silence with his explosive voice. "That's crazy, it just won't work," he said. "The Soviets would never tolerate it. Solidarity is lost." Bush agreed, expressed concerns about inflaming Moscow, and counseled against any operation.

Pipes, the only NSC staffer at the meeting (and a Pole himself), tried to contain his anger. "What worries the Soviets is the survival of Solidarity," he retorted. "They are afraid of an infection, that it will spread to the rest of the Soviet bloc—even Lithuania and Russia itself. You don't know the Poles, Mr. Secretary. Solidarity will survive." Weinberger, Casey and Bill Clark voiced enthusiastic support for the operation. But the president "didn't need any encouragement," according to Pipes. He immediately asked Casey to draw up a covert operation plan. "He not only wanted to free Poland but shatter the myth of Soviet invincibility," recalls Clark.

A premium was placed on secrecy. In the end, the operation was funded and executed outside traditional government requirements. "No formal intelligence action was taken," recalls Pipes. "It was feared it would leak. This was a highly secret operation, handled 'off the books.'"[74]

Journalists Carl Bernstein and Marco Politi have claimed that the U.S. covertly spent over $50 million to keep Solidarity alive.[75] In any event, it seems clear that covert U.S. assistance played an important role in Solidarity's survival and eventual triumph. And since the emergence of a non-Communist government in Poland in 1989 set the stage for the unraveling of Communism, first in Eastern Europe and then in the

Soviet Union itself, it is equally clear that Reagan's willingness to "offer a hand" to Solidarity after the imposition of martial law was one of the turning points in the history of the Cold War.[76]

"An Idea Worth Exploring"

Given the Soviet Union's severe internal crisis, it is quite possible that the Reagan initiatives discussed thus far—the military buildup, the economic and technological sanctions, the ideological offensive, the Reagan Doctrine, and the covert support for Solidarity—would have been enough to demoralize the *nomenklatura*. But on March 23, 1983, the President announced what was perhaps his most dramatic departure from conventional wisdom: the Strategic Defense Initiative (SDI).

According to former Secretary of State George Shultz, "SDI was entirely the president's idea."[77] Reagan was profoundly convinced that it was immoral to leave the American people undefended against a Soviet attack, yet that was precisely what the official U.S. policy of Mutual Assured Destruction (MAD) required. Therefore, as he writes in his memoirs,

> Early in my first term, I called a meeting of the Joint Chiefs of Staff—our military leaders—and said to them: Every offensive weapon ever invented by man has resulted in the creation of a defense against it; isn't it possible in this age of technology that we could invent a defensive weapon that could intercept nuclear weapons and destroy them as they emerged from their silos?
>
> They looked at each other, then asked if they could huddle for a few moments. Very shortly, they came out of their huddle and said, "Yes, it's an idea worth exploring." My answer was, "Let's do it."
>
> So the SDI was born, and very shortly some in Congress and the press named it "Star Wars."[78]

Reagan announced his intention to develop a strategic defense against Soviet missiles in a nationally televised speech on March 23, 1983: "I call upon the scientific community in our country, those who gave us nuclear weapons, to turn their great talents now to the cause of mankind and world peace: to give us the means of rendering these nuclear weapons impotent and obsolete."[79] As Henry Kissinger has observed,

> Those last words, "impotent and obsolete," must have had a chilling ring in the Kremlin. The Soviet nuclear arsenal was the keystone of the Soviet Union's entire superpower status. For the twenty years of [Leonid] Brezhnev's tenure, achieving strategic parity with the United States had been the principal Soviet objective. Now, with a single technological stroke, Reagan was proposing to erase everything that the Soviet Union had propelled itself into bankruptcy trying to accomplish.[80]

But would SDI work? Outside of conservative circles, there was a great deal of skepticism. The conventional view was that, like his belief in the Soviet Union's imminent demise, what some mischaracterized patronizingly as "Star Wars" was yet another example of the President's alarming susceptibility to bizarre ideas. Former Defense Secretary Robert McNamara, for example, called SDI "pie in the sky." Strobe Talbott, then with *Time*, wrote that it was "more like an arcade video game" than a strategy. And the *New York Times* dismissed it as a "pipe dream, a projection of fantasy into policy."[81]

In retrospect, however, it is clear that SDI was one of the most important reasons for America's victory in the Cold War—because of its demoralizing psychological impact on the *nomenklatura*. As former CIA Director Robert Gates has written:

> It wasn't SDI per se that frightened the Soviet leaders; after all, at best it would take many years to develop and deploy as an effective system. I think it was the *idea* of SDI and all it represented that frightened them. As they looked at the United States, they saw an America that apparently had the resources to increase defense spending dramatically and then add this program on top, and all of it while seeming hardly to break a sweat.

Meanwhile, an enfeebled Soviet leadership, presiding over a country confronting serious economic and social problems, knew they could not compete—at least not without some major changes. In my view, it was the broad resurgence of the West—symbolized by SDI—that convinced even some of the conservative members of the Soviet leadership that major internal changes were needed in the USSR. That decision, once made, set the stage for the dramatic events inside the Soviet Union over the next several years.[82]

"A Formidable Adversary"

Before Ronald Reagan became President, observed Soviet ambassador Anatoly Dobrynin,

the Soviet leadership had hoped that Reagan would abandon his anti-Soviet attitudes of the election campaign and take a more sober approach when confronted with power, but these hopes proved groundless. The White House sought to damage the Soviet Union at every opportunity and obsessively viewed all international events in terms of confrontation with the Soviet Union, restricting American foreign policy to a gross and even primitive anti-Sovietism. In any case, that was the impression in Moscow.[83]

Former KGB general Oleg Kalugin put the matter even more starkly: "Reagan and his views disturbed the Soviet government so much they bordered on hysteria. There were cables about an imminent crisis. He was seen as a very serious threat."[84]

The new American challenge clearly demanded a vigorous response; but to Politburo member (and former KGB chief) Yuri Andropov, the aging Leonid Brezhnev, now approaching the end of his 20-year rule, seemed incapable of vigorous action. Thus, even before Brezhnev's death on November 10, 1982, Andropov set out to discredit the decrepit leader. As Robert Gates observes, the contest for power was worthy of a Mel Brooks plot:

> In early 1982…the KGB went after several of Brezhnev's closest associates and even his family for corruption. Stories reached CIA, and journalists as well, that the KGB had investigated Brezhnev's daughter Galina, who had been having an affair with a Moscow singer and playboy…nicknamed "Boris the Gypsy." The scandal involved a sizable diamond-smuggling ring including members of the Moscow Circus, and Boris the Gypsy was apparently part of it. In the course of the investigation, the first deputy chairman of the KGB (and Brezhnev's brother-in-law), General Semion Tsvigun, apparently committed suicide…. Other Brezhnev associates soon found themselves under investigation, and there were rumors of other suicides.[85]

When Yuri Andropov succeeded Leonid Brezhnev as head of the Soviet Union, it seemed that Moscow at last had a leader capable of taking on Ronald Reagan. As Secretary of State George Shultz, who met Andropov during Brezhnev's funeral, later recalled,

> He looked more like a cadaver than did the just-interred Brezhnev, but his mental powers filled the room. He reminded me of Sherlock Holmes's deadly enemy, Professor Moriarty…. He projected immense intelligence and energy. This was a powerhouse, I thought. I knew that Andropov, as head of the KGB for so long, must have a capacity for brutality as well as for skill in propaganda. I put him down as a formidable adversary.[86]

Despite his formidable abilities, however, as well as his awareness of the growing Soviet internal crisis, Andropov was at heart a policeman who believed that by tightening labor discipline and rooting out corruption, he could pull the Soviet Union out of its tailspin. In Sovietologist Seweryn Bialer's apt formulation, Andropov saw only a "crisis of performance, not a crisis of the system."[87] And since it was the Soviet system that was in crisis, Andropov's police methods "produced short-term success without affecting fundamental causes."[88]

It was in foreign policy that Andropov thought he saw an opportunity to overcome growing American pressure and secure a fundamental breakthrough. By exploiting the anti-American nuclear freeze movement that was gaining ground throughout Western Europe, and especially in West Germany, Andropov hoped to detach the Federal Republic from NATO—a long-standing Soviet goal which, had it been successful, would have altered the European balance of power dramatically in Moscow's favor.

Andropov's opportunity came about as a result of Brezhnev's decision in 1977 to begin deploying the SS–20, a three-warhead intermediate-range Soviet missile capable of hitting any city or military target in Western Europe. ("Intermediate" meant that the SS–20 could not reach the U.S. and therefore was not considered a "strategic" weapon.) By the end of 1979, 140 SS–20s with 420 warheads had been deployed by the Soviets. It seemed obvious that NATO had to restore the balance by deploying Pershing II and cruise intermediate-range missiles.

But public opinion in Western Europe—again, especially in West Germany—balked at the prospect of such a response, which it was feared would heighten the possibility of a nuclear war fought on European soil. In 1979, therefore, NATO adopted a "dual-track" policy. The alliance would deploy some 500 American missiles in Britain, Italy, Belgium, the Netherlands, and West Germany by late 1983 (with the Federal Republic stationing Pershing II and cruise missiles on its territory and the other NATO members deploying cruise missiles alone). At the same time, it would pursue arms control negotiations with the Soviet Union in Geneva.

Preserving NATO

When the Reagan Administration came into office, however, the dual-track policy seemed to be falling apart. Encouraged by Soviet propaganda and massive covert funding, the nuclear freeze movement, encompassing thousands of people, took to the streets of Europe to protest NATO's planned deployment of American missiles. The movement was especially strong in West Germany, as Reagan found out when he spoke to Helmut Kohl in Washington in 1981:

> Helmut Kohl, leader of the opposition [Christian Democratic] party in Germany, told me during a White House visit that the [Soviet] propaganda offensive was becoming highly sophisticated and effective in convincing Europeans that the United States was a bloodthirsty, militaristic nation. This view of America shocked me: We were the most moral and generous people on earth, we'd spent thirty-five years since World War II helping to rebuild the economies of our former allies and enemies, we had gone to the corners of the world in the defense of freedom and democracy, and now we were being cast—effectively, Kohl said—as villains. It was clear we'd have to do a better job of conveying to the world our sense of morality and our commitment to the creation of a peaceful, nuclear-free world.[89]

It was in this growing perception of the United States as a "bloodthirsty, militaristic nation" that Yuri Andropov saw his opportunity. Hoping that German neutralism would lead to NATO's unraveling, Andropov "made opposition to the deployment of intermediate-range missiles the linchpin of Soviet foreign policy."[90] When German Chancellor Kohl visited the Kremlin in July 1983, Andropov all but threatened war if Germany accepted the Pershing II missiles:

> The military threat for West Germany will grow manifold. Relations between our two countries will be bound to suffer certain complications as well. As for the Germans in the Federal Republic of Germany and the German Democratic Republic, they would have, as someone [*Pravda*] recently put it, to look at one another through thick palisades of missiles.[91]

To blunt Andropov's propaganda offensive, the Reagan Administration came up with a ploy of its own. In a speech before the National Press Club on November 19, 1981, President Reagan called for the elimination of all intermediate-range nuclear missiles by both sides—the Soviet Union and NATO. This became known as the "zero–zero" option.

Like so many other Reagan initiatives, the zero–zero option was widely derided by the foreign policy establishment as totally unrealistic, since the Soviets would never agree to eliminate all their INF (Intermediate Nuclear Forces) missiles in exchange for an American pledge not to deploy missiles that European public opinion would never accept in any case. (As it turned out, in December of 1987 the Soviets accepted the zero–zero option that Reagan had advanced in 1981). But Reagan's proposal was not directed at the Soviets; rather, he was making a bid to counter Soviet propaganda by reaching out to West Europeans and re-assuring them that America was not bent on nuclear war. As Reagan put it in his memoirs,

> I thought our goal should be the total elimination of
> all INF weapons from Europe, and stating this before
> the world would be a vivid gesture demonstrating to
> the Soviets, our allies, the people storming the streets
> of West Germany, and others that we meant business
> about wanting to reduce nuclear weapons.[92]

Reagan's zero–zero proposal was strongly supported by British Conservative Prime Minister Margaret Thatcher. Reagan and Thatcher had enjoyed a special relationship ever since April 1975, when the recently retired governor of California visited the recently elected leader of the British Opposition at her room in the House of Commons. "We found," he later recalled, "that we were really akin with regard to our views of government and economics and government's place in people's lives and all that sort of thing."[93] When Mrs. Thatcher was elected Prime Minister on May 3, 1979, Reagan was the first foreign politician to congratulate her; and when Reagan was elected President on November 4, 1980, Mrs. Thatcher was among the first to congratulate him.

In her memoirs, Thatcher explained both the significance of Ronald Reagan's election and what she understood Britain's role in the Anglo–American alliance to be:

> The election of Ronald Reagan as President of the United States in November 1980 was as much of a watershed in American affairs as my own election victory in May 1979 was in those of the United Kingdom, and, of course, a greater one in world politics. As the years went by, the British example steadily influenced other countries in different continents, particularly in economic policy. But Ronald Reagan's election was of immediate and fundamental importance because it demonstrated that the United States, the greatest force for liberty that the world has known, was about to reassert a self-confident leadership in world affairs. I never had any doubt of the importance of this change and from the first I regarded it as my duty to do everything I could to reinforce and further President Reagan's bold strategy to win the Cold War which the West had been slowly but surely losing.[94]

Given these views, it comes as no surprise that Thatcher strongly supported the stationing of cruise and Pershing missiles in Europe:

> If [the deployment] went ahead as planned, the Soviet Union would suffer a real defeat; if it was abandoned in response to the Soviet-sponsored "peace offensive", there was a real danger of a decoupling of Europe and America. My meetings with President Reagan had persuaded me that the new Administration was apprised of these dangers and determined to combat them. But a combination of exaggerated American rhetoric and the perennial nervousness of European opinion threatened to undermine the good transatlantic relationship that would be needed to guarantee that deployment went ahead. I saw it as Britain's task to put the Ameri-

can case in Europe since we shared their analysis but tended to put it in less ideological language. And this we did in the next few years.[95]

A more surprising Reagan supporter was France's Socialist President, François Mitterrand. As Henry Kissinger has written,

In 1983, Mitterrand emerged unexpectedly as the chief European supporter of the American plan to deploy intermediate range missiles. Mitterrand campaigned for the missiles in Germany. "Anyone gambling on uncoupling the European continent from the American would, in our view, jeopardize the balance of forces and therefore the maintenance of peace," Mitterrand told the German Bundestag.[96]

The European leader who faced the most determined opposition to the deployment of the American missiles was West Germany's Christian Democratic leader, Helmut Kohl, who replaced Socialist Helmut Schmidt as Chancellor in October 1982. As Kohl later recalled,

In the area of foreign policy the situation was enormously complicated. In 1982–1983, the debate over the deployment of the American medium-range missiles on German soil was at its high point. It was one of the most dramatic situations in German postwar history. The majority of the Social Democrats fought the deployment of Pershing II and cruise missiles, which Helmut Schmidt had recommended.[97]

Kohl believed that rejecting the missiles would have had "devastating consequences." Specifically, "The Soviet leadership would have been successful in their attempt to decouple American and European security with their SS–20s. With that, an important pillar of the Atlantic Alliance would have been seen as fragile, and as a consequence, it could have resulted in the breakdown of NATO."[98] Kohl therefore strongly supported both the zero–zero option and deployment.

On March 6, 1983, Kohl's pro-NATO policy was vindicated resoundingly when he won a major victory in West Germany's national elections. On November 23, the day after the Bundestag voted to accept the Pershing and cruise missile deployments, the Soviet Union withdrew from the INF negotiations in Geneva, promising military countermeasures.[99] But whether because Andropov died shortly afterwards (February 9, 1984) or because his threat had simply been a bluff, no Soviet countermeasures ensued, and 15 months later Moscow returned to the negotiating table. Andropov's desperate bid to seize victory from the jaws of defeat by detaching Germany from NATO had failed.

Though no one could confuse Ronald Reagan with Sherlock Holmes, the former Hollywood movie star—with help from Margaret Thatcher, François Mitterrand, and Helmut Kohl—had bested the Soviet Moriarty.

Gorbachev and the "New Thinking"

After Andropov's death, the Politburo appointed Brezhnev's crony, Konstantin Chernenko, as his successor. Chernenko was in poor health, however, and died on March 10, 1985, after little more than a year in power. The next day the Politburo appointed Mikhail Gorbachev General Secretary of the Communist Party.

The mood among the party's ruling elite was one of growing anxiety. In the words of Yevgenny Novikov, a former senior staff member of the International Department of the Central Committee, "We very firmly believed that the correlation of forces was shifting against us. In the military–technology sphere, in the ideological sphere, and in the economic sphere. Something had to be done to arrest these developments, to correct the American challenge."[100]

Mikhail Gorbachev was the CPSU's chosen instrument to repel the Reagan offensive. Born in 1931, in the midst of Stalin's collectivization campaign and subsequent famine in the grain-rich Stavropol region, he pursued a conventional career in the party apparatus until he was spotted by Yuri Andropov, who brought him into the Politburo in 1981. Gorbachev, then only 49 years old, became the youngest member of the party's ruling body. A dynamic, talented, and loyal member of the *nomenklatura*, he was just the sort of person Andropov hoped could help breathe new life into the empire.

Gorbachev, who was deeply committed to Soviet-style "socialism," shared Andropov's goals. Just before becoming General Secretary, he stated publicly that "radical" measures were needed "if the Soviet Union were to enter the next century in a manner worthy of a great power."[101] But never, before becoming leader of the Soviet Union, did Gorbachev suggest that this required what NSDD 75 demanded: "A more pluralistic political system in which the power of the privileged elite is gradually reduced."

It is important to keep Gorbachev's background and early statements in mind, because since his fall he has claimed that he had intended, all along, to replace "totalitarianism" with "democracy" and to "liberate" Eastern Europe. As historian Martin Malia has observed, to accept Gorbachev's assertions at face value is to believe "that he had been a secret conspirator against the Party and the state of which he was in charge"—an obviously absurd proposition.[102] Rather, Gorbachev sought to prevent a further deterioration in the "correlation of forces" through foreign policy initiatives designed to blunt the American onslaught, and through domestic initiatives designed to revive—not replace—the Soviet system.

In foreign policy, Gorbachev's approach went under the name of "New Thinking," and it differed markedly from Andropov's confrontational style. Andropov had sought to exploit what seemed like a golden opportunity—growing German neutralism. Once it was clear that Germany would remain a loyal NATO member and would deploy American missiles despite Soviet threats, the failure of Andropov's strategy became apparent. "New Thinking" was necessary.

The basic point made by the New Thinkers was that Brezhnev's "old thinking" not only had failed, but also had provoked the extraordinary American military buildup. One of the most prominent New Thinkers,

Vyacheslav Dashishev, a German expert at the Moscow Institute for East European and Foreign Policy Studies, made the case for the new approach in the Soviet newspaper *Literaturnaya Gazeta* in May 1988:

> [A]s the West saw it, the Soviet leadership was actively exploiting détente to build up its own military forces, seeking military parity with the United States and in general with all the opposing powers—a fact without historical precedent. The United States, paralyzed by the Vietnam catastrophe, reacted sensitively to the expansion of Soviet influence in Africa, the Near East, and other regions.
>
> All this was interpreted in the West as a further increase in the Soviet threat. The extreme right-wing political circles that came to power in the United States and other NATO countries [the reference here is to Prime Minister Thatcher of Great Britain and Chancellor Kohl of West Germany] turned sharply away from détente toward confrontation. The Soviet Union found itself faced with unprecedented new pressure from imperialism....
>
> It is our conviction that the crisis was caused chiefly by the miscalculations and incompetent approach of the Brezhnev leadership toward the resolution of foreign policy tasks.... Though we were politically, militarily (via weapons supplies and advisers), and diplomatically involved in regional conflicts, we disregarded their influence on the relaxation of tension between the USSR and the West and on their entire system of relationships.

Dashishev expanded his critique of "old thinking" in a June 1988 interview. Brezhnev's attempt to extend "socialism" to the Third World, he argued, provoked the United States into major military expenditures and SDI, and Soviet efforts to compete threatened to bankrupt the system:

[W]e launched an offensive against imperialism's positions in the mid-seventies. We attempted to expand
the sphere of socialism's influence to various develop-
ing countries which, I believe, were totally unprepared
to adopt socialism. And what came of all this? A sharp
clash of political contradictions with the Western powers (and that was not all—even China opposed our
actions in the Third World). Détente was derailed, and
we came up against a new and unprecedented explosion of the arms race.

The United States wanted to use it to push us back
against a wall, to corner us, to create economic, social,
and political difficulties. It adopted the form of the
SDI and the inflation of military budgets beyond belief, and we naturally tried to follow suit. This proved
that our foreign policy was not cost-effective. In other
words, our foreign policy actions made us shoulder
the steadily growing burden of military expenditures
and moral costs.[103]

The conclusion to which the New Thinking led was obvious: The
Soviet Union had to abandon its relentlessly confrontational, "class-
based" approach to foreign policy and seek instead a kinder, gentler,
friendlier relationship with Washington—in short, a return to détente.
Moscow sought to achieve this through sweeping arms control proposals designed, as Soviet spokesmen put it, to deprive the West of an enemy. In such a new atmosphere, the more "peace-loving" members of
the American political class gradually would regain the upper hand over
such primitive anti-Soviet ideologues as Ronald Reagan. The result would
be a curtailed military buildup, an end to the economic and technological sanctions, and, most important, the abandonment of SDI. The Soviet Union would avoid a ruinous arms race with the United States, and
its great power status would be preserved.

Perestroika and Glasnost

If New Thinking was Gorbachev's foreign policy response to the Reagan challenge, perestroika (restructuring) was his domestic response: As Soviet member of parliament Ilya Zaslavsky accurately put it, "Ronald Reagan was the father of perestroika."[104] Perestroika went through three phases, each more radical than its predecessor. Gorbachev actually referred to the first phase as *uskorenie* (acceleration) rather than perestroika, and it was basically a continuation of Andropov's emphasis on greater discipline and efficiency. In the words of historian Michael Mandelbaum,

> At first Gorbachev continued the approach that Yuri Andropov had begun in 1982: he tried to impose greater discipline on the work force. The centerpiece of his initial set of economic measures was a highly publicized and intrusive public campaign against the consumption of alcohol. It earned Gorbachev the title of "Mineral Water General Secretary," but did not noticeably reduce Russian drinking. Instead, by forcing people to make their own liquor rather than buying it from the state, the campaign caused shortages of sugar and deprived the government of a large chunk of its income.[105]

It is likely that, when he commenced with *uskorenie*, Gorbachev, like Andropov before him, saw a "crisis of performance, not a crisis of the system." This was the CIA's view. On June 27, 1985, William Casey forwarded the Agency's first assessment of Gorbachev to Reagan: "While some Soviet officials have indicated [that Gorbachev] is sympathetic to the use of pragmatic methods, including tapping private initiative, his statements and actions underscore his overall commitment to the current economic system and his determination to make it work better."[106]

It appears, however, that something happened to Gorbachev early in his tenure to make him realize that what the Soviet Union faced was a profound systemic crisis, not just a performance crisis. In his autobiography, Reagan speculates that "the tragedy of [the nuclear accident at]

Chernobyl a year after Gorbachev took office" affected him profoundly.[107] In his own memoirs, Gorbachev appears to concur with
Reagan's assessment:

> Chernobyl made me and my colleagues rethink a great
> many things. We saw the need to strengthen discipline
> and order, first of all in the nuclear power industry.
> But as I pondered these matters I became ever more
> convinced that the problem could not be solved merely
> by administrative pressure, punishment, stringent mea-
> sures, Party penalties and reprimands. We had to move
> perestroika forward.[108]

Moving perestroika forward meant changing the system by limiting
the *nomenklatura*'s power and giving the empire's subjects greater (but
not total) freedom. This, at any rate, is how the distinguished
Sovietologist Adam Ulam understands the onset of genuine perestroika
as opposed to *uskorenie*:

> German jurists in the nineteenth century developed
> the concept of the *Rechtsstaat*, the state in which, though
> it is not a democracy, its rulers abide by legal norms
> and constraints. Gorbachev's notion of perestroika en-
> visaged what he called a "state under the law," a kind
> of Communist *Rechtsstaat*. The last vestiges of Stalinism
> would be removed, there would be much greater (but
> not complete) freedom of speech and of the press,
> though the latter of course would continue to be run
> by the party. Rules on emigration would be relaxed,
> and Soviet citizens would be freer to travel abroad. The
> constitution would have to be revamped in a way that
> allowed for free elections and yet guaranteed the party's
> continued predominance.[109]

If this truly was Gorbachev's understanding of perestroika, it would
seem that, in effect, by 1987 or so he had come to accept the principal
goal of Reagan's NSDD 75: systemic change designed to "restructure"
the Soviet Union from a totalitarian to an authoritarian state in which

the *nomenklatura*, in the interest of economic recovery, surrenders some of its stifling control over society. Had the *nomenklatura* been willing to go along with this version of perestroika, a nominally Communist Soviet Union in all likelihood would still exist today. Such a Soviet Union, however, would have had far more in common, both politically and economically, with Franco's Spain of the 1950s than with Brezhnev's Russia of the 1960s and 1970s.

From today's post-Soviet perspective, this clearly would have been an unsatisfactory outcome: Why settle for an authoritarian Soviet Union when you can get a democratic Russia? From the perspective of the early 1980s, however, it would have amounted to a stunning victory for Ronald Reagan and his policy of massive and sustained pressure on the Soviet Union.

Unfortunately for Gorbachev, the *nomenklatura*—or at least a significant portion of it—was unwilling to go along with this version of perestroika. During this second phase of perestroika, Gorbachev increasingly turned against his enemies in the party who, he believed, were blocking his efforts to create a Communist *Rechtsstaat*. His principal weapon was the policy of glasnost (transparency or openness), which he hoped to use as a weapon to expose and embarrass his opponents, but matters quickly got out of hand. As Mandelbaum writes:

> The policy of glasnost relaxed bureaucratic controls on information, broadened the parameters of permitted discussion and thereby enabled the people of the Soviet Union to say more, hear more and learn more about the past and present. Gorbachev's purpose had been to enlist the intelligentsia in his campaign to revitalize the country and to generate popular pressure on the party apparatus, which had resisted the changes he was trying to make.... Glasnost, however, did not stop there. The sainted Lenin, and even Gorbachev himself, came in for critical attention. Gorbachev wanted to foster a reassessment of some selected features of

Soviet life. Instead glasnost called all of it into question, including, ultimately, the role of the General Secretary of the Communist Party.[110]

The "Real Turning-Point"

Glasnost had another unexpected—and, to Gorbachev, unwelcome—consequence: the rise of "informal" associations dedicated to profound systemic reform. As Martin Malia writes:

> The years 1987–1988 saw a proliferation of self-organized "informal" associations, the *neformalny*. Independent of the Party, they were created to address one or another social problem...in areas where the Party had been remiss or actively at fault. Very often their origin was in threats to the ecology, such as the pollution of Lake Baikal or the nuclear power plants of the Baltic states.... But since these groups had to pressure the Party, they soon moved on to politics. By early 1987 clubs in support of *perestroika* had appeared, and many of these put the term "democratic *perestroika*" in their name to emphasize that, though they wished to work within the system, they would also push reform farther than the regime intended.[111]

Confronted with widespread intellectual dissent and the rise of informal associations that soon (especially in the Baltic states) began taking on a nationalist, anti-Soviet tinge, a prudent Soviet leader would have reconsidered his commitment to perestroika. But Mikhail Sergeyevich Gorbachev was not a prudent man. Eugene Rostow has compared him to Marshal Foch, who sent a famous message to headquarters during the battle of the Marne in 1914: "My center is ceding ground, my right is recoiling. Situation excellent. I attack."[112]

It is an apt comparison. Instead of regrouping and biding his time, Gorbachev launched an all-out offensive against the recalcitrant *nomenklatura*. The "real turning-point," as he puts it in his memoirs, "when perestroika became irreversible, was the XIXth All-Union Party Conference" in June 1988. At this conference, Gorbachev proposed transferring power from the Communist Party to a new system based on a president (himself) and an elected parliament, to be called the Congress of People's Deputies. In March 1989, for the first time in Russia since 1917, a relatively free election to the Congress was held, and the result was a massive repudiation of Communist candidates.

The new Congress of People's Deputies met from May 25 through June 9, 1989, and its sessions were televised. The impact was shattering. "For the first time," writes Gates,

> real politics came to the Soviet Union. A spellbound national audience saw Gorbachev, the party, even the KGB, subjected to direct, withering criticism. They saw the arguing and the debates. They saw the leadership in the flesh—angry, scornful, disputatious, egotistical, rude, and divided. The communists who had run the country from behind Oz's curtain for so long were exposed to the entire country—and the world— as venal, petty, squabbling bureaucrats.[113]

In the course of this third, "democratic" phase of perestroika, Gorbachev succeeded in breaking the back of the *nomenklatura*. He failed, however, to establish a new political structure by which to govern the Soviet Union. Moreover, by 1989, reform-minded Communists had lost faith in Gorbachev and began resigning from the Communist Party to pursue radical change in the Soviet Union's 15 constituent republics.[114] For Gorbachev—and the Soviet Union—it was the beginning of the end.

"Time to Speak the Truth"

As the Soviets wrestled with their response to the dual threat posed by stagnation at home and a renewed American challenge abroad, Ronald Reagan made no secret of the fact that he thought Communism was in its death throes. Even before he became President, Reagan had believed that "Communism was near collapse, dying from a terminal disease called tyranny."[115] Now that the CIA's briefings had confirmed his deepest intuitions, "I felt it was time to speak the truth, not platitudes, even though a lot of liberals and some members of the State Department's

Striped Pants Set sometimes didn't like my choice of words. Some congressmen and columnists claimed that I was determined to get us into a nuclear war with the Soviets."[116]

Reagan first predicted the Soviet Union's forthcoming demise publicly on May 17, 1981, in a speech at the University of Notre Dame. "The West won't contain Communism," he said. "It will transcend Communism. It will dismiss it as some bizarre chapter in human history whose last pages are even now being written."[117]

Almost exactly a year later, on May 9, 1982, in a commencement address at his alma mater, Eureka College, Reagan once again prophesied Communism's imminent demise:

> The Soviet empire is faltering because rigid centralized control has destroyed incentives for innovation, efficiency and individual achievement. But in the midst of social and economic problems, the Soviet dictatorship has forged the largest armed force in the world. It has done so by preempting the human needs of its people and, in the end, this course will undermine the foundations of the Soviet system.[118]

The next month, on June 8, 1982, speaking to British parliamentarians at Westminster Palace, Reagan brought similar glad tidings:

> The decay of the Soviet experiment should come as no surprise to us. Wherever the comparisons have been made between free and closed societies—West Germany and East Germany, Austria and Czechoslovakia, Malaysia and Vietnam—it is the democratic countries that are prosperous and responsive to their people. And one of the simple but overwhelming facts of our time is this: Of all the millions of refugees we've seen in the modern world, their flight is always away from, not towards the Communist world.[119]

Finally, speaking to the National Association of Evangelicals on March 8, 1983, Reagan not only called the Soviet Union "the focus of evil in the modern world," but also returned to the formulation he had used nearly two years earlier at Notre Dame:

> I believe that communism is another sad, bizarre chapter in human history whose last pages even now are being written. I believe this because the source of our strength in the quest for human freedom is not material, but spiritual. And because it knows no limitation, it must terrify and ultimately triumph over those who would enslave their fellow man.[120]

This language, as harsh as any ever spoken by an American President during the Cold War, was meant to demoralize the *nomenklatura*—and it succeeded. Based on three visits to the Soviet Union in 1983–1984, Seweryn Bialer reported that

> President Reagan's rhetoric has badly shaken the self-esteem and patriotic pride of the Soviet political elites. The administration's self-righteous moralistic tone, its reduction of Soviet achievements to crimes by international outlaws from an "evil empire"—stunned and humiliated the Soviet leaders...[who] who believe that President Reagan is determined to deny the Soviet Union nothing less than its legitimacy and status as a global power...status...they thought had been conceded once and for all by Reagan's predecessors.[121]

Unfortunately, Reagan's rhetoric, combined with the military buildup and the other measures contained in NSDD 75, may have done more than humiliate the *nomenklatura*. It is possible (though far from certain) that it strengthened Yuri Andropov's fear that the United States was seriously contemplating a nuclear first strike against the Soviet Union.

According to CIA Director Gates, in May 1981, only four months into Reagan's presidency, Andropov told a KGB conference that the United States was "actively preparing for nuclear war." Although it is unclear whether KGB chief Andropov, who had not yet succeeded

Brezhnev as leader of the Soviet Union, actually believed this or was seeking merely to manufacture a war scare to enhance the KGB's power, directives were issued to KGB residencies abroad calling for "close observation of all political, military and intelligence activities that might indicate preparations for mobilization." The program was called RYAN—a Russian acronym for "Nuclear Missile Attack."

Soviet fears reportedly reached their height during a NATO command exercise held from November 2–11, 1983. Called "Able Archer," its purpose was to practice nuclear release procedures. According to Gates, KGB defector Oleg Gordievsky disclosed subsequently that "the KGB concluded that American forces had been placed on alert—and might even have begun the countdown to nuclear war." Gates believes that "there is a good chance…that [the Soviets] really felt that a NATO attack was at least possible and that they took a number of measures to enhance their military readiness short of mobilization."[122]

Reagan was first briefed by Casey about the dangerous Soviet reaction to Able Archer on December 22, 1983,[123] and it may be that Reagan's remarkably conciliatory speech of January 16, 1984, in which he speculated about how a typical Soviet couple, Ivan and Anya, might find that they had much in common with an American couple, Jim and Sally, was an attempt to calm Soviet fears. ("They might even have decided that they were all going to get together for dinner some evening soon," said Reagan.[124])

Be that as it may, it is clear that this episode, which starkly revealed the depth of Soviet paranoia, had a profound impact on Reagan. Although he never mentions "Able Archer" in his autobiography, he obviously is alluding to it when he writes that

> During my first years in Washington, I think many of
> us in the administration took it for granted that the
> Russians, like ourselves, considered it unthinkable that
> the United States would launch a first strike against
> them. But the more experience I had with Soviet leaders and other heads of state who knew them, the more
> I began to realize that many Soviet officials feared us

not only as adversaries but as potential aggressors who might hurl nuclear weapons at them in a first strike.... Well, if that was the case, I was even more anxious to get a top Soviet leader in a room alone and try to con- vince him we had no designs on the Soviet Union and Russians had nothing to fear from us.[125]

The Geneva Summit

Reagan's desire to "get a top Soviet leader in a room alone" led him to try to arrange a summit meeting with Andropov's successor, Konstantin Chernenko. Perhaps America's policies have been misinterpreted in Moscow, Reagan wrote the Soviet leader in March 1984. The United States "has no desire to threaten the security of the Soviet Union and its allies, nor are we seeking military superiority or to impose our will on others."[126] Because Chernenko demanded the removal of American Pershing and cruise missiles from Europe as the precondition for a sum- mit, however, nothing came of Reagan's initiative.

After Chernenko's death, Reagan lost no time in trying to arrange a meeting with his successor, Mikhail Gorbachev—an eagerness to meet the new Russian leader that no doubt was reinforced by Prime Minister Thatcher's comment after meeting Gorbachev in 1984: "I like Mr. Gorbachev. We can do business together."[127] When Vice President Bush arrived in Moscow for Chernenko's funeral, he handed Gorbachev an invitation for a summit conference in the United States. After the usual diplomatic fencing, it was agreed that a two-day U.S.–Soviet summit would be held in Geneva in November 1985.

Within the Administration, Reagan's decision to meet with Gorbachev in Geneva provoked a good deal of controversy. Secretary of Defense Weinberger in particular was concerned that Secretary of State Shultz might persuade Reagan to agree to what Shultz's arms control adviser, the venerable Paul Nitze, called a "grand compromise": trading SDI for extensive Soviet strategic arms reductions. But as Reagan noted in his diary on September 11, 1985, "One thing I do know is, I won't trade our SDI off for some offer of weapon reductions...."[128] What Reagan was looking forward to, rather, was the opportunity to meet with Gorbachev alone and convince him "that we wanted peace and they had nothing to fear from us."[129]

When Reagan and Gorbachev did meet in Geneva, that is precisely what Reagan tried to do. He suggested that the Soviet leader accompany him to a cozy summer cottage on the bank of Lake Geneva and discuss their disagreements privately:

> As our conversation continued beside the blazing fire, he convinced me that I had been right to suspect there was a deep-seated fear of the United States and its nuclear arsenal among Soviet leaders. I tried to dispel this vision. After World War II, I pointed out, we had a monopoly on nuclear weapons, but had not used them for aggression or to exert our influence because America was not an expansionist country. We had no designs on any people or any nation; we had built our force of nuclear missiles only to deter a Soviet attack. Then we began debating the Strategic Defense initiative; he was adamant and so was I.[130]

Even though Reagan and Gorbachev did not reach agreement on SDI, Reagan judged the summit a success, and not just because it gave him the opportunity to dispel Soviet paranoia. Immediately after their private tête-à-tête, Reagan had proposed and Gorbachev had accepted two more summits—one in Washington, the other in Moscow. The idea of getting the Soviet leader to visit the United States, where he could see for himself how false all his anti-American views were, appealed deeply to Ronald Reagan. As his biographer, Lou Cannon, has written:

> One of Ronald Reagan's fantasies as president was that he would take Mikhail Gorbachev on a tour of the United States so the Soviet leader could see how ordinary Americans lived. Reagan often talked about it. He imagined that he and Gorbachev would fly by helicopter over a working-class community, viewing a factory and its parking lot filled with cars and then

circling over the pleasant neighborhood where the factory workers lived in homes "with lawns and backyards, perhaps with a second car or a boat in the driveway, not the concrete rabbit warrens I'd seen in Moscow." The helicopter would descend, and Reagan would invite Gorbachev to knock on doors and ask the residents "what they think of our system." The workers would tell him how wonderful it was to live in America.[131]

Although there was more than a touch of naiveté in Reagan's belief that a private talk with Gorbachev beside a crackling fireplace, or a presidentially conducted tour of a working-class neighborhood, could change the viewpoint of the hard-bitten General Secretary of the Soviet Communist Party, But Reagan's overall policy in dealing with Gorbachev was anything but naive. The key NSC meeting at which Reagan's basic approach to Gorbachev was determined occurred on June 25, 1985, three months after Gorbachev came to power. There was a great deal of discussion as to whether Gorbachev really was a new type of Soviet leader; but after listening closely for about 20 minutes, Reagan ended it: "Mr. Gorbachev may or may not be a new type of Soviet leader," he said. "Time will only tell, and it may not be for a decade. But I want to keep the heat on the Soviets. I don't want to let up on anything we're doing."[132]

Throughout the remainder of Reagan's presidency, the Administration did indeed "keep the heat on the Soviets." Reagan's military buildup actually increased after Gorbachev came to power, with the percentage of defense as a share of the federal budget going from 26.7 percent in 1985 to 27.6 percent in 1986, 28.1 percent in 1987, 27.3 percent in 1988, and 26.5 percent in 1989.[133] Similarly, covert assistance to anti-Communist resistance forces in the Third World increased after 1985, with both the *mujahedin* in Afghanistan and UNITA forces in Angola receiving the deadly Stinger antiaircraft missile in 1986. Meanwhile, the various anti-Soviet economic and technological sanctions that Reagan had imposed during his first term remained in place during his second term, and aid to the Solidarity underground continued. And, of course, research on SDI not only continued, but expanded as Great Britain signed an agreement in December 1985 to participate in the American SDI program—the first of several close allies to do so.[134]

"Mr. Gorbachev, Tear Down This Wall!"

Only in one respect did his new relationship with Gorbachev change Reagan's approach to Soviet–American relations: His harsh denunciations of the Soviet Union came to an end by 1985. As Reagan writes in his autobiography, "Once we'd agreed to hold a summit, I made a conscious decision to tone down my rhetoric and avoid goading Gorbachev with remarks about the 'evil empire.'" He asked Defense Secretary Weinberger "to mute his most critical comments about the Soviets" as well.[135]

But Reagan's decision to tone down his rhetoric did not mean that his anti-Soviet ideological offensive was over. He would not, in the interest of improved Soviet–American relations, stop contrasting the failures of socialism with the successes of democratic capitalism. "Just because our relationship with the Soviet Union is improving," he said," doesn't mean we have to begin denying the truth. That is what got us into such a weak position with the Soviet Union in the first place."[136]

Reagan's new, less strident style of ideological warfare proved highly effective, since Soviet leaders like Gorbachev and his new foreign minister, Eduard Shevardnadze, agreed privately with much of what Reagan was saying. In 1984, shortly before Gorbachev became the Soviet Union's new leader, Shevardnadze (who was then the party boss of his native republic of Georgia) told him that everything was "rotten" in the Soviet Union. "We cannot go on living like this," he said. "We must think what we can do to salvage the country."[137]

Especially during the brief reign of Gorbachev's predecessor, Konstantin Chernenko, many Soviet citizens shared Shevardnadze's feelings of shame and disgust at the state of their country. "Chernenko's absolute grayness and incompetence," writes Seweryn Bialer, "engendered in the Communist intelligentsia, parts of the elite and, of course, the Soviet people themselves a particular feeling not only of hopelessness but also deep embarrassment and shame."[138]

Reagan's post-1985 speeches played brilliantly on these feelings of shame and linked them to the absence of freedom in the Soviet Union. As he said in his speech before the Berlin Wall in 1987,

> In the 1950s, [Nikita] Khrushchev predicted: "We will bury you." But in the West today, we see a free world that has achieved a level of prosperity and well-being unprecedented in all human history. In the Communist world, we see failure, technological backwardness, declining standards of health, even want of the most basic kind—too little food. Even today, the Soviet Union still cannot feed itself. After these four decades, then, there stands before the entire world one great and inescapable conclusion: Freedom leads to prosperity. Freedom replaces the ancient hatreds among the nations with comity and peace. Freedom is the victor.[139]

Reagan did not follow up these observations (as he might well have done during his first term in office) by pronouncing a death sentence on socialism and all its works. Instead, he called on the Soviet Union's new leader to demonstrate the courage of his convictions. Gorbachev claimed to be committed to the reform of his moribund system. Very well, then: Let him prove his sincerity by dismantling the repressive apparatus of totalitarian rule. As Reagan dramatically declared in his remarks at the Berlin Wall, "General Secretary Gorbachev, if you seek peace, if you seek prosperity for the Soviet Union, if you seek liberalization: Come here to this gate! Mr. Gorbachev, open this gate! Mr. Gorbachev, tear down this wall!"[140]

In this way, Reagan subtly transformed his relationship with Gorbachev. He became more than Gorbachev's determined adversary and outspoken opponent. He positioned himself as Gorbachev's conscience and prodded the Soviet leader to live up to his best instincts. He adopted the rhetorical pose of the Soviet Union's solicitous friend, eager to help that nation attain the prosperity and dignity that come with freedom.

That enacting the fundamental changes he proposed most probably would lead to the Soviet empire's demise was not something Reagan chose to emphasize. Instead, as Stephen Sestanovich has pointed out, Reagan in effect handed Gorbachev a gun and suggested that he do the honorable thing:

> As is so often true in such situations, the victim-to-be is more likely to accept the advice if it is offered in the gentlest possible way and if he concludes that his friends, family and colleagues will in the end think better of him for going through with it. For Soviet communism, the international environment of the late 1980s was a relaxed setting in which, after much anguished reflection, to turn the gun on itself.[141]

"The Meeting Is Over"

No doubt Gorbachev and his Politburo colleagues interpreted Reagan's friendlier tone as a significant victory for New Thinking, but from their point of view, it was far from enough. In particular, Reagan's SDI program was proceeding full blast, and this deeply alarmed them. "When we were talking about SDI," former Soviet Foreign Minister Aleksandr Bessmertnykh told a Princeton Conference on the Cold War in 1993, "just the feeling that if we get involved in this SDI arms race, trying to do something like what the U.S. was going to do, to do space programs, space-based weapons, et cetera, looked like a horror to Gorbachev."[142]

Whenever it was confronted with potentially dangerous American technological advances, the Soviet Union typically sought to derail them through arms control negotiations. As Richard Pipes has explained, "Evidence from SALT I, SALT II and START negotiations suggests that the Soviet side first determines what weapons it requires to meet its strategic objectives and then concentrates on constraining, through negotiation, America's ability to respond."[143] In this respect, Gorbachev's new thinking was remarkably similar to Brezhnev's old thinking. Having determined that SDI posed a mortal threat to the Soviet system, he set out to eliminate it through arms control negotiations and high-level summits.

Disappointingly for Gorbachev, the 1985 Geneva Summit turned out to be little more than a get-acquainted session with the American President. (Gorbachev probably found Reagan's little ploy of a heart-to-heart chat in a cozy cottage utterly pathetic, but "he was a very good actor" and played along.[144]) He therefore jumped at Reagan's offer to hold two additional summits. Amazingly, State Department officials thought Gorbachev had made a major concession: "Our people couldn't believe it when I told them what had happened," Reagan later recalled. "Everything was settled for two more summits. They hadn't dreamed it was possible."[145]

In fact, this was exactly what Gorbachev wanted, for it meant two additional opportunities to block SDI. As Anatoly Dobrynin notes in his memoirs, "[Soviet Foreign Minister Andrei] Gromyko was the first to congratulate Gorbachev on the skillful accomplishment of a difficult mission in Geneva."[146]

But Gorbachev's mission was not completed at Geneva. He tried to use the negotiations for the forthcoming Washington summit to get Reagan to abandon SDI—refusing to set a date until the Administration acceded to his terms. Then, when this ploy failed, he launched one of his typical initiatives: audacious, original, and totally unexpected. In effect, he decided to set a trap for the seemingly naive American President.

Thus, on September 19, 1986, the Soviets proposed, and the Americans agreed, to hold a "preparatory summit" between Reagan and Gorbachev in Reykjavik, Iceland, on October 10. The Americans were given the impression that this meeting would focus on the stalled INF negotiations—Reagan's zero–zero option—and, acting on that assumption, did not prepare for a broader agenda. Not so the Soviets. "The basic Soviet strategy at Reykjavik," according to one account, "was to advance a disarmament package of historic importance with one big string attached; the cuts would happen only if Reagan reined in the SDI program. The curbing of SDI was an essential part of the plan."[147] If Reagan agreed to Gorbachev's proposals, SDI would be finished. If he did not agree, American public opinion, recognizing that only SDI stood in the way of a historic arms control agreement, would force Reagan to abandon it. Either way, the Soviets would win.

Just as he had bested Andropov, however, at Reykjavik Ronald Reagan outmaneuvered Gorbachev. At first, Reagan recalls in his memoirs, "George [Shultz] and I couldn't believe what was happening. We were getting amazing agreements"—including an agreement to reduce all strategic forces by 50 percent within five years and destroy all ballistic missiles within ten years.

> Then, after everything had been decided, or so I thought, Gorbachev threw us a curve. With a smile on his face he said: "This all depends, of course, on you giving up SDI."
>
> I couldn't believe it and blew my top. "I've said again and again the SDI wasn't a bargaining chip. I've told you, if we find out that the SDI is practical and feasible, we'll make that information known to you and everyone else so that nuclear weapons can be made obsolete. Now, with all we have accomplished here, you do this and throw in this roadblock and everything is out the window...."
>
> Gorbachev heard the translation of my remarks, but he wasn't listening. He wouldn't budge from his position.... I was getting angrier and angrier. I realized that he had brought me to Iceland with one purpose: to kill the Strategic Defense Initiative. He must have known from the beginning that he was going to bring it up at the last minute.
>
> "The meeting is over," I said. "Let's go, George, we're leaving."[148]

Then, according to Henry Kissinger, "Reagan responded in a way no foreign policy professional would have advised: he simply got up and left the room. Years later, when I asked a senior Gorbachev adviser why the Soviets had not settled for what the United States had already accepted, he replied: 'We had thought of everything except that Reagan might leave the room.'"[149]

The failure at Reykjavik, as former British Prime Minister Margaret Thatcher has written,

> was widely portrayed as the result of the foolish intransigence of an elderly American president, obsessed with an unrealizable dream. In fact, President Reagan's refusal to trade away SDI for the apparent near fulfillment of his dream of a nuclear-free world was crucial to the victory over communism. He called the Soviets' bluff. The Russians may have scored an immediate propaganda victory when the talks broke down. But they had lost the game and I have no doubt that they knew it.[150]

Mrs. Thatcher is almost surely correct. Faced with Reagan's refusal to trade away SDI, Gorbachev and his fellow reformers had no choice but to press forward with perestroika to the bitter end—a process which led eventually to the Soviet Union's collapse. As for American public opinion, the fact that the Soviets were so eager to scuttle SDI convinced many otherwise skeptical observers that there must be something to it after all. Once again, and not for the last time, Gorbachev had miscalculated.

"The First Breath of Freedom"

During the final two years of the Reagan Administration, a President more and more distracted by the Iran–Contra scandal that greeted him shortly after his return from Iceland and eager to demonstrate diplomatic progress despite what was widely (though wrongly) perceived as the Reykjavik fiasco, increasingly allowed the State Department to set the pace and tone of Soviet–American relations. Two more summits were held, and an agreement eliminating all INF weapons was signed. This alarmed conservatives, who deeply distrusted Shultz's State Department and doubted whether any agreements it negotiated truly served the American national interest.[151]

In their anger, some conservatives turned on Ronald Reagan, whom they blamed, in George Will's words, for accelerating "the moral disarmament of the West—actual disarmament will follow—by elevating wishful thinking to the status of political philosophy."[152] In this view, Reagan's willingness to treat Gorbachev as a genuine reformer and not as a cunning Leninist still bent, despite all the Soviet Union's problems, on the West's subjugation was fostering dangerous illusions about the benign character of Soviet power that Moscow was bound to exploit to America's disadvantage.

What Reagan's conservative critics failed to recognize was that by 1988, the Soviet Union was an empire on the verge of meltdown. Reagan's policies had succeeded in demoralizing at least some members of the *nomenklatura* to the point where they were willing to share a portion of their power with the Soviet people—but the people had become increasingly unwilling to defer to the *nomenklatura*. "By 1988," as David Satter has pointed out, "a crisis of faith began to seize the Soviet Union. The reason was the policy of glasnost, which, by permitting for the first time an increasing flow of truthful information, undermined the core of the Soviet system, the Soviet ideology."[153] In the absence of ideology, only brute force could hold the Soviet empire together, but neither Gorbachev nor his critics quite had the stomach—or the self-confidence—to resort to repression on a massive scale.

It was in the midst of this "crisis of faith" in the Soviet Union that Reagan delivered one of the most stirring addresses of his presidency. Speaking to students at Moscow State University on May 31, 1988, the President eloquently defended the philosophy that had inspired him throughout his political career, and that he hoped one day would guide the Russian people as well—faith in freedom:

> We Americans make no secret of our belief in freedom. In fact, it's something of a national pastime.... Freedom is the right to question and change the established way of doing things. It is the continuing revolution of the marketplace. It is the understanding that allows us to recognize shortcomings and seek solutions. It is the right to put forth an idea, scoffed at by the

experts, and watch it catch fire among the people. It is the right to dream—to follow your dream or stick to your conscience, even if you're the only one in a sea of doubters.

Freedom is the recognition that no single person, no single authority or government has a monopoly on the truth, but that every individual life is infinitely precious, that everyone of us put on this world has been put there for a reason and has something to offer....

Your generation is living in one of the most exciting, hopeful times in Soviet history. It is a time when the first breath of freedom stirs the air and the heart beats to the accelerated rhythm of hope, when the accumulated spiritual energies of a long silence yearn to breathe free....

We do not know what the conclusion will be of this journey, but we're hopeful that the promise of reform will be fulfilled. In this Moscow spring, this May 1988, we may be allowed that hope: that freedom, like the fresh green sapling planted over Tolstoy's grave, will blossom forth at last in the rich fertile soil of your people and culture. We may be allowed to hope that the marvelous sound of a new openness will keep rising through, ringing through, leading to a new world of reconciliation, friendship, and peace.[154]

Judging by their enthusiastic response to his words, Reagan had succeeded in impressing his audience. Far more impressive, however, was the burst of freedom that surged through Eastern Europe in 1989. First in Poland, then in Hungary, East Germany, Czechoslovakia, Romania, and (in 1990) Bulgaria, Communist governments relinquished their hold on power and political dissidents who had been persecuted only a short while before were catapulted to positions of national authority.[155]

These extraordinary developments inspired nationalist leaders in the Soviet republics to accelerate their efforts to break away from the "Center." The process began in Lithuania, which declared its independence from the Soviet Union on March 11, 1990. The other 14 republics soon followed suit, and by the end of 1990, "signs of the union's disintegration were increasingly apparent.... To try to preserve the vestiges of a unified system, Gorbachev drafted a new Union Treaty."[156] The failure of the republics to endorse this treaty marked the end of the Soviet Union. On December 26, 1991 it ceased to exist.

A Legacy of Courage

Although the Soviet Union's official demise occurred during George Bush's presidency, the fall of Soviet Communism was Ronald Reagan's doing. One can cite all sorts of secondary reasons—the strength of the American economy, the weakness of the Soviet system, the astuteness of Reagan's foreign policy advisers, the blunders of Gorbachev and his team—to explain Reagan's achievement; but the primary reason was that Ronald Reagan had a profound (his critics would say childlike or simplistic) faith in freedom.

Years before he became President, Ronald Reagan decided that America *would* win the Cold War. He simply *knew* that there was no way a closed society could defeat an open society once the open society made up its mind to prevail. The rest, as the saying goes, is commentary.

It was because of this implacable desire to win that Reagan's presidency merits the adjective "Churchillian." Also Churchillian was Reagan's determination to seize the offensive, notably in the series of policy directives embodied in NSDD 75. These directives, with their call for economic warfare, technological warfare, and a vast military buildup, recall Churchill's determination, first enunciated at Fulton, Missouri, in 1946, to confront Stalin with such an overwhelming preponderance of Anglo–American power that the Soviet dictator would be forced, in effect, to yell "Uncle."

That is precisely what Reagan did, and the Soviet Politburo finally did yell "Uncle" when it agreed to try to implement Gorbachev's plans to "restructure" the Soviet Union in a way that would begin to empower ordinary citizens. This was unprecedented.

Reagan's foreign policy was equally unprecedented. The traditional American approach was to seek to "contain" Soviet power and hope that, at some unspecified point in the future, containment would convince the *nomenklatura* to abandon its expansionist course. By contrast, Reagan sought not to contain the Soviets but to overwhelm them with demonstrations of American power and resolve that left them with no alternative but to undertake massive systemic reforms. "His strength," said Richard Pipes, "lay in understanding the crisis and vulnerability of the [whole] system, which all the academics were telling him was stable and solid and popular. And he would buy none of this. And that took a lot of courage."[157]

The great question facing the world today is whether post-Soviet Russia will evolve along the peaceful, democratic capitalist lines outlined by Reagan in his Moscow State University speech, or whether continuing economic and social turmoil presages the rise of a new dictatorship. But whatever the future holds for Russia and the world, Americans have reason to be grateful to Ronald Reagan for ridding us, finally, of the Evil Empire. Reagan's historic success demonstrates that great leadership does not depend on intellectual brilliance or wide-ranging knowledge. What is needed, above all, is the right set of convictions and the courage to stand by those convictions.

Ronald Reagan's convictions about freedom and tyranny were rooted in the bedrock of American experience, and his courage reflected the quiet self-confidence of the American heartland. His was truly an American presidency that changed the world.

Notes

Introduction

[1]See Joseph Shattan, "How Anti-Americanism Won the Cold War," *The American Spectator*, January 1999, pp. 71–74.

[2]Henry Kissinger, *Diplomacy* (New York: Simon and Schuster, 1994), p. 767.

[3]Norman A. Bailey, *The Strategic Plan That Won the Cold War* (McLean, Va.: The Potomac Foundation, 1998), p. 29.

[4]Stephen Sestanovich, "Did the West Undo the East?" *The National Interest*, Spring 1993, p. 30.

Chapter 1
Harry S. Truman: Setting the Course

[1]Alonzo Hamby, *Man of the People: A Life of Harry S. Truman* (New York: Oxford University Press, 1995), pp. 571–572.

[2]Cabell Phillips, *The Truman Presidency: The History of a Triumphant Succession* (New York: The Macmillan Company, 1966), p. 10.

[3]Alonzo Hamby, "An American Democrat: A Reevaluation of the Personality of Harry S. Truman," *Political Science Quarterly*, Vol. 106, No. 1 (1991), p. 37.

[4]Hamby, *Man of the People*, p. 8.

[5]*Ibid.*, p. 14.

[6]*Ibid.*, pp. 12–13.

[7]Hugh Thomas, *Armed Truce: The Beginnings of the Cold War 1945–46* (New York: Atheneum, 1986), p. 117.

[8]Phillips, *The Truman Presidency*, pp. 13–14.

[9]Robert H. Ferrell, *Harry S. Truman: A Life* (Columbia and London: University of Missouri Press, 1994), p. 92.

[10]Thomas, *Armed Truce*, p. 117.

[11]William E. Leuchtenberg, *In the Shadow of FDR: From Harry Truman to Ronald Reagan* (Ithaca and London: Cornell University Press, 1983), p. 4.

[12]Phillips, *The Truman Presidency*, p. 27.

[13]Leuchtenburg, *In the Shadow of FDR*, p. 6.

[14]Henry Kissinger, *Diplomacy* (New York: Simon and Schuster, 1994), p. 423.

[15]Leuchtenburg, *In the Shadow of FDR*, p. 6.

[16]David McCullough, *Truman* (New York: Simon and Schuster, 1992), p. 353.

[17]Leuchtenburg, *In the Shadow of FDR*, p. 7.

[18]Thomas, *Armed Truce*, p. 121.

[19]*Ibid.*, p. 171.

[20]Kissinger, *Diplomacy*, p. 395.

[21]George F. Kennan and John Lukacs, *George F. Kennan and the Origins of Containment, 1944–1946* (Columbia: University of Missouri Press, 1997), p. 33.

[22]John Lewis Gaddis, *We Now Know* (Oxford: Clarendon Press, 1997), p. 21.

[23]Arthur Schlesinger, Jr., "Origins of the Cold War," in Hamilton Fish Armstrong, ed., *Fifty Years of Foreign Affairs* (New York: Praeger Publishers, 1972), p. 403.
[24]Kissinger, *Diplomacy*, p. 384.
[25]*Ibid.*, p. 427.
[26]Hamby, *Man of the People*, p. 270.
[27]*Ibid.*, pp. 313–314.
[28]Deborah Welch Larson, *Origins of Containment: A Psychological Approach* (Princeton, N.J.: Princeton University Press, 1985), p. 150.
[29]Hamby, *Man of the People*, p. 316.
[30]Thomas, *Armed Truce*, p. 120.
[31]*Ibid.*, p. 121.
[32]Larson, *Origins of Containment*, p. 157.
[33]*Ibid.*
[34]*Ibid.*, p. 174.
[35]Thomas, *Armed Truce*, p. 122.
[36]Larson, *Origins of Containment*, p. 175.
[37]*Ibid.*
[38]*Ibid.*, p. 176.
[39]Hamby, *Man of the People*, p. 320.
[40]Thomas, *Armed Truce*, p. 124.
[41]Larson, *Origins of Containment*, p. 181.
[42]*Ibid.*, p. 183.
[43]*Ibid.*, p. 186.
[44]Kissinger, *Diplomacy*, p. 433.
[45]Robert H. Ferrell, ed., *Off the Record: The Private Papers of Harry Truman* (Columbia and London: University of Missouri Press, 1980), p. 53.
[46]George F. Kennan, *Memoirs: 1925–1950* (Boston: Little, Brown, 1967), p. 279.
[47]Ferrell, *Harry S. Truman: A Life*, p. 206.
[48]Hamby, *Man of the People*, p. 328.
[49]Larson, *Origins of Containment*, p. 201.
[50]Ferrell, *Harry S. Truman: A Life*, p. 265.
[51]*Ibid.*, p. 331.
[52]Winston S. Churchill, *Triumph and Tragedy* (Boston: Houghton Mifflin, 1953), pp. 669–670.
[53]Gaddis, *We Now Know*, p. 94.
[54]Kennan, *Memoirs: 1925–1950*, p. 279.
[55]Gaddis, *We Now Know*, p. 95.
[56]*Ibid.*, p. 90.
[57]See Chapter 2, *infra.*
[58]Hamby, *Man of the People*, p. 340.
[59]*Ibid.*
[60]Kennan, *Memoirs: 1925–1950*, p. 287.
[61]Larson, *Origins of Containment*, p. 246.
[62]*Ibid.*, p. 249.
[63]Thomas, *Armed Truce*, p. 121.
[64]*Ibid.*, p. 229.
[65]*Ibid.*, p. 224.
[66]*Ibid.*, p. 481.
[67]Kennan, *Memoirs: 1925–1950*, p. 293.

[68]Clark Clifford, *Counsel to the President* (New York: Random House, 1991), p. 102.

[69]Kissinger, *Diplomacy*, p. 447.

[70]Don Cook, *Forging the Alliance: NATO, 1945–50* (New York: Arbor House, 1989), p. 62.

[71]Kissinger, *Diplomacy*, p. 448.

[72]Gaddis, *We Now Know*, p. 21.

[73]Kennan, *Memoirs: 1925–1950*, p. 295.

[74]Ferrell, *Harry S. Truman: A Life*, p. 248.

[75]*Ibid.*

[76]Hamby, *Man of the People*, p. 346.

[77]McCullough, *Truman*, p. 491.

[78]Robert L. Beisner, "Patterns of Peril: Dean Acheson Joins the Cold Warriors, 1945–46," *Diplomatic History*, Vol. 20, No. 3 (Summer 1996), p. 338.

[79]Thomas, *Armed Truce*, p. 491.

[80]Spencer Warren, "Churchill's Realism: Reflections on the Fulton Speech," *The National Interest*, Winter 1995/96, p. 43.

[81]Clifford, *Counsel to the President*, p. 108.

[82]*Ibid.*

[83]Beisner, "Patterns of Peril," p. 339.

[84]Adam B. Ulam, *The Rivals: America and Russia Since World War II* (New York: Viking Press, 1971), p. 119.

[85]Walter Bedell Smith, *My Three Years in Moscow* (Philadelphia and New York: J. B. Lippincott, 1950), pp. 26–27.

[86]*Ibid.*, p. 53.

[87]Bruce R. Kuniholm, "Loy Henderson, Dean Acheson, and the Origins of the Truman Doctrine," in Douglas Brinkley, ed., *Dean Acheson and the Making of U.S. Foreign Policy* (New York: St. Martin's Press, 1953), pp. 91–92.

[88]Beisner, "Patterns of Peril," pp. 343–344.

[89]Walter Isaacson and Evan Thomas, *The Wise Men: Six Friends and the World They Made* (New York: Simon and Schuster, 1986), p. 371.

[90]See *ibid* and Dean Acheson, *Present at the Creation: My Years in the State Department* (New York: W. W. Norton, 1969), pp. 195–196. In Acheson's account, it was General Eisenhower, then Army chief of staff, who asked Acheson whether Truman understood that the U.S. risked war with the Soviets.

[91]Kuniholm, "Loy Henderson, Dean Acheson, and the Origins of the Truman Doctrine," p. 92.

[92]"It was good we backed down in time," Molotov later recalled, "otherwise it would have led to joint aggression against us." Vyacheslav Molotov, *Molotov Remembers: Inside Kremlin Politics, Conversations with Felix Chuev*, ed. Albert Reiss (Chicago: Ivan R. Dee, 1993), p. 74.

[93]Hamby, *Man of the People*, p. 355.

[94]Clifford, *Counsel to the President*, p. 110.

[95]*Ibid.*, p. 111.

[96]Arthur Krock, *Memoirs: Sixty Years on the Firing Line* (New York: Funk and Wagnall's, 1968), pp. 431, 476.

[97]"X" (George F. Kennan), "The Sources of Soviet Conduct," *Foreign Affairs*, July 1947.

[98]Clifford, *Counsel to the President*, p. 125.

[99]Krock, *Memoirs*, p. 482.

[100]*Ibid.*, pp. 123–124. In 1966, Clifford showed a draft of the report to *New York Times* columnist Arthur Krock. In 1968, the entire 63-page report appeared in the Appendix to Krock's *Memoirs.*

[101]Krock, *Memoirs*, p. 478.

[102]Joseph M. Jones, *The Fifteen Weeks* (New York: The Viking Press, 1955), p. 176.

[103]Hamby, *Man of the People*, p. 360.

[104]Clifford, *Counsel to the President*, p. 129.

[105]Krock, *Memoirs*, p. 482.

[106]Larson, *Origins of Containment*, p. 299.

[107]Hamby, *Man of the People*, p. 386.

[108]Clifford, *Counsel to the President*, p. 131.

[109]*Ibid.*, p. 132.

[110]Harry S. Truman, "The Truman Doctrine," in *The Annals of America* (Chicago: Encyclopaedia Britannica, Inc., 1968), Vol. 16, pp. 434–437.

[111]Larson, *Origins of Containment*, p. 311.

[112]Clifford, *Counsel to the President*, p. 138.

[113]Hamby, *Man of the People*, pp. 392–393.

[114]*The Annals of America*, Vol. 16, p. 439.

[115]Gaddis, *We Now Know*, p. 42.

[116]Walter McDougall, *Promised Land, Crusader State: The American Encounter with the World Since 1776* (Boston: Houghton Mifflin, 1997), p. 164.

[117]Paul Johnson, *A History of the American People* (New York: HarperCollins, 1997), p. 813.

[118]Kissinger, *Diplomacy*, p. 457.

[119]For a detailed discussion of the Berlin blockade and the creation of West Germany, see Chapter 3, *infra.*

[120]Hamby, *Man of the People*, p. 444.

[121]McDougall, *Promised Land, Crusader State*, p. 169.

[122]*Ibid.*, p. 165.

[123]*Ibid.*, p. 36.

[124]Hamby, *Man of the People*, p. 318.

[125]*Ibid.*, p. 641.

Chapter 2
Winston Churchill: Seizing the Initiative

[1]Winston S. Churchill, *Triumph and Tragedy* (Boston: Houghton Mifflin, 1953), pp. 456, 549–550.

[2]Winston S. Churchill, *His Father's Son: The Life of Randolph Churchill* (London: Phoenix Giant, 1997), pp. 293–294.

[3]Martin Gilbert, *Churchill: A Life* (New York: Henry Holt, 1991), p. 395.

[4]Norman Rose, *Churchill: The Unruly Giant* (New York: The Free Press, 1995), p. 179.

[5]Winston Churchill, Weekly Dispatch, June 22, 1919, cited in Martin Gilbert, *Churchill's Political Philosophy* (London: Oxford University Press, 1981), p. 75.

[6]Rose, *Churchill: The Unruly Giant*, p. 179.

[7]Winston Churchill, Cabinet Memorandum, May 1, 1920, cited in Gilbert, *Churchill's Political Philosophy*, p. 76.

[8]Rose, *Churchill: The Unruly Giant*, p. 439.

[9]A. L. Rowse, *The Later Churchills* (Harmondsworth: Penguin Books, 1971), p. 439.

[10]Gilbert, *Churchill's Political Philosophy*, p. 74.

[11]Gilbert, *Churchill: A Life*, p. 420, and Rose, *Churchill: The Unruly Giant*, p. 126.

[12]Rose, *Churchill: The Unruly Giant*, p. 174.

[13]Winston Churchill, letter of December 10, 1901, cited in Gilbert, *Churchill's Political Philosophy*, p. 27.

[14]Rowse, *The Later Churchills*, p. 393 (emphasis in original).

[15]Gilbert, *Churchill: A Life*, p. 460.

[16]*Ibid.*, p. 462.

[17]Winston S. Churchill, *The Gathering Storm* (Boston: Houghton Mifflin,1948), p. 274.

[18]Robert Blake and William Roger Louis, *Churchill* (New York: W. W. Norton, 1993), p. 311.

[19]*Ibid.*, p. 312.

[20]Churchill, *The Gathering Storm*, p. 393.

[21]John Colville, *The Fringes of Power: 10 Downing Street Diaries 1939–1955* (New York and London: W. W. Norton, 1985), p. 404.

[22]Adam B. Ulam, *Stalin: The Man and His Era* (Boston: Beacon Press, 1973), p. 529.

[23]Colville, *The Fringes of Power*, p. 405.

[24]Gilbert, *Churchill: A Life*, p. 701.

[25]Winston Churchill, broadcast of June 22, 1941, cited in Gilbert, *Churchill's Political Philosophy*, p. 79.

[26]Winston S. Churchill, *The Hinge of Fate* (Boston: Houghton Mifflin, 1950), p. 337.

[27]Colville, *The Fringes of Power*, p. 624.

[28]Lead editorial, *The Economist*, January 1, 1945, cited in Robin Edmonds, *The Big Three* (New York: W. W. Norton, 1991), p. 411.

[29]Memorandum by Charles Taussig, March 15, 1944, cited in William Roger Louis, *Imperialism at Bay: The United States and the Decolonization of the British Empire, 1941–1945* (New York: Oxford University Press, 1978) p. 486.

[30]Warren F. Kimball, *The Juggler: Franklin Roosevelt as Wartime Statesman* (Princeton, N.J.: Princeton University Press, 1991), p. 85.

[31]*Ibid.*, p. 159.

[32]Francois Kersaudy, *Churchill and De Gaulle* (New York: Atheneum, 1982), p. 386.

[33]Cable from Eden to Churchill, January 5, 1942, and cable from Churchill to Eden, January 8, 1942, cited in Steven M. Miner, *Between Churchill and Stalin: The Soviet Union, Great Britain, and the Origins of the Grand Alliance* (Chapel Hill: University of North Carolina Press, 1988), p. 219.

[34]Cable from Roosevelt to Churchill, March 18, 1942, cited in *ibid.*, p. 219.

[35]For a description of Davies, see Chapter 1, *supra.*

[36]Herbert Feis, *Churchill, Roosevelt, Stalin: The War They Waged and the Peace They Sought* (Princeton, N.J.: Princeton University Press, 1957), pp. 131–132.

[37]Edmonds, *The Big Three*, p. 329.

[38]Sir John Wheeler-Bennett and Anthony Nichols, *The Semblance of Peace: The Political Settlement After the Second World War* (New York: St. Martin's Press, 1972), p. 290 (emphasis in original). In *His Father's Son: The Life of Randolph Churchill*, Winston Churchill places this same conversation immediately after, rather than immediately before, the Teheran Conference.

[39]Lord Moran (Charles Wilson), *Churchill: Taken from the Diaries of Lord Moran* (Boston: Houghton Mifflin, 1966), p. 142.

[40]Edmonds, *The Big Three*, p. 455.

[41]Franklin Roosevelt to Frances Perkins, cited in Henry Kissinger, *Diplomacy* (New York: Simon and Schuster, 1994), p. 412.

[42]Rose, *The Unruly Giant*, p. 379.

[43]Warren F. Kimball, "Churchill and Roosevelt," in Blake and Louis, *Churchill*, p. 302.

[44]Wheeler-Bennett and Nichols, *The Semblance of Peace*, pp. 560–561.

[45]Colville, *The Fringes of Power*, p. 562, 565, 566.

[46]Gilbert, *Churchill: A Life*, p. 830.

[47]Kimball, *The Juggler*, p. 177.

[48]W. Averell Harriman and Elie Abel, *Special Envoy to Churchill and Stalin: 1941–1946* (New York: Random House, 1975), p. 236.

[49]Kimball, *The Juggler*, p. 180.

[50]Churchill, *Triumph and Tragedy*, pp. 572–574.

[51]Martin Gilbert, *Never Despair: Winston S. Churchill, 1945–1965* (London: Minerva, 1990), p. 26.

[52]*Ibid.*, p. 87.

[53]*Ibid.*, p. 89.

[54]Winston Churchill, broadcast of June 4, 1945, cited in *ibid.*, p. 32.

[55]Gilbert, *Churchill: A Life*, p. 857.

[56]*The Annals of America* (Chicago: Encyclopaedia Britannica, Inc., 1968), Vol. 16, pp. 365–369.

[57]David McCullough, *Truman* (New York: Touchstone, 1993), p. 490.

[58]Gilbert, *Never Despair*, pp. 265–266.

[59]*Ibid.*, p. 266.

[60]*Ibid.*

[61]*Ibid.*, p. 337.

[62]For a more detailed discussion of the Marshall Plan and NATO, see Chapter 1, *supra*.

[63]Gilbert, *Churchill: A Life*, p. 879.

[64]Kissinger, *Diplomacy*, p. 466.

[65]*Ibid.*, pp. 466–467.

[66]Colville, *The Fringes of Power*, p. 654.

[67]For more on the theory of containment, see Chapter 1, *supra*.

Chapter 3
Konrad Adenauer: Opting for the West

[1]Paul Weymar, *Adenauer: His Authorized Biography* (New York: E. P. Dutton, 1957), p. 146.

[2]Hans-Peter Schwarz, *Konrad Adenauer: A German Politician and Statesman in a Period of War, Revolution and Reconstruction* (Providence: Berghahn Books, 1995), Vol. 1, p. 283.

[3]Konrad Adenauer, *Memoirs 1945–53* (London: Weidenfeld and Nicolson, 1965), p. 78.

[4]Schwarz, *Konrad Adenauer*, Vol. 1, p. 47.

[5]See especially Charles Wighton, *Adenauer: A Critical Biography* (New York: Coward–McCann, 1963).

[6]Noel Annan, *Changing Enemies: The Defeat and Regeneration of Germany* (New York: W. W. Norton, 1995), p. 172.

[7]Schwarz, *Konrad Adenauer*, Vol. 1, p. 41.

[8]Weymar, *Adenauer*, p. 16.

[9]Schwarz, *Konrad Adenauer*, Vol. 1, p. 48.

[10]Weymar, *Adenauer*, p. 28.

[11]Schwarz, *Konrad Adenauer*, Vol. 1, p. 85.

[12]Weymar, *Adenauer*, p. 31.

[13]*Ibid.*, p. 36.

[14]Terence Prittie, *Konrad Adenauer* (Chicago: Cowles Book Company, 1971), p. 40.

[15]Schwarz, *Konrad Adenauer*, Vol. 1, p. 126.

[16]Weymar, *Adenauer*, p. 68.

[17]*Ibid.*, pp. 44–47.

[18]Schwarz, *Konrad Adenauer*, Vol. 1, p. 155.

[19]Adenauer, *Memoirs 1945–53*, p. 44.

[20]*Ibid.*, p. 162.

[21]*Ibid.*, p. 221.

[22]*Ibid.*, p. 233.

[23]Weymar, *Adenauer*, p. 92.

[24]*Ibid.*, pp. 99–100.

[25]Schwarz, *Konrad Adenauer*, Vol. 1, p. 133.

[26]*Ibid.*, p. 260.

[27]*Ibid.*, p. 284.

[28]Sir William Strang, cited in Hugh Thomas, *Armed Truce* (New York: Atheneum, 1987), p. 324.

[29]Adenauer, *Memoirs 1945–53*, p. 38.

[30]*Ibid.*, p. 39.

[31]*Ibid.*, p. 40.

[32]*Ibid.*, p. 36.

[33]*Ibid.*, p. 36.

[34]*Ibid.*, p. 45.

[35]Schwarz, *Konrad Adenauer*, Vol. 1, p. 300.

[36]*Ibid.*, p. 303.

[37]Adenauer, *Memoirs 1945–53*, p. 33.

[38]*Ibid.*, p. 34.

[39]Schwarz, *Konrad Adenauer*, Vol. 1, p. 319.

[40]Adenauer, *Memoirs 1945–53*, p. 153.

[41]Weymar, *Adenauer*, pp. 176–177.

[42]Adenauer, *Memoirs 1945–53*, p. 169.

[43]Frank Ninkovich, *Germany and the United States* (New York: Twayne Publishers, 1995), p. 66.

[44]*Ibid.*, p. 67.

[45]John Lewis Gaddis, *We Now Know* (Oxford: Clarendon Press, 1997), p. 123.

[46]Ninkovich, *Germany and the United States*, p. 68.

[47]Gaddis, *We Now Know*, p. 116.

[48]Thomas Alan Schwartz, *America's Germany: John J. McCloy and the Federal Republic of Germany* (Cambridge, Mass.: Harvard University Press, 1991), p. 54.

[49]Gavriel Ra'anan, *International Policy Formation in the USSR* (Hamden, Conn.: Archon Books, 1983), p. 94.

[50]Martin Malia, *The Soviet Tragedy* (New York: The Free Press, 1994), p. 300.

[51]Schwarz, *Konrad Adenauer*, Vol. 1, p. 55.

[52]Wolfram F. Hanrieder, *Germany, America, Europe: Forty Years of German Foreign Policy* (New Haven: Yale University Press, 1989), p. 156.

[53]John Maynard Keynes, *The Economic Consequences of the Peace* (New York: Harcourt, Brace and Howe, 1920).

[54]Dean Acheson, *Present at the Creation: My Years in the State Department* (New York: W. W. Norton, 1969), p. 341.

[55]Schwarz, *Konrad Adenauer*, Vol. 1, pp. 509–510.

[56]Don Cook, *Ten Men and History* (Garden City, N.Y.: Doubleday, 1981), p. 131.

[57]Schwarz, *Konrad Adenauer*, Vol. 1, p. 511.

[58]Adenauer, *Memoirs 1945–53*, p. 257.

[59]Schwarz, *Konrad Adenauer*, Vol. 1, p. 514.

[60]Adenauer, *Memoirs 1945–53*, p. 354.

[61]Dennis L. Bark and David R. Gress, *From Shadow to Substance 1945–1963* (Cambridge: Blackwell Publishers, 1989), p. 270.

[62]Adenauer, *Memoirs 1945–53*, p. 331.

[63]Alan S. Milward, *The Reconstruction of Western Europe, 1945–1951* (Berkeley: University of California Press, 1984), p. 420.

[64]Charles W. Thayer, *The Unquiet Germans* (New York: Harper & Brothers, 1957), p. 210.

[65]Ninkovich, *Germany and the United States*, p. 80.

[66]Schwarz, *Konrad Adenauer*, Vol. 1, p. 623.

[67]*Ibid.*, p. 552.

[68]Bark and Gress, *From Shadow to Substance*, p. 286.

[69]Schwarz, *Konrad Adenauer*, Vol. 1, pp. 552–553.

[70]Adenauer, *Memoirs 1945–53*, p. 302.

[71]Acheson, *Present at the Creation*, p. 341.

[72]Schwartz, *America's Germany*, p. 262.

[73]*Ibid.*, pp. 265–266.

[74]Schwarz, *Konrad Adenauer*, Vol. 1, p. 624.

[75]*Ibid.*, pp. 655–656.

[76]Andrei Gromyko, *Memoirs* (New York: Doubleday, 1989), p.196.

[77]Gaddis, *We Now Know*, p. 127.

[78]William G. Hyland, *The Cold War Is Over* (New York: Random House, 1990), p. 78.

[79]Schwarz, *Konrad Adenauer*, Vol. 2, p. 120.

[80]Gaddis, *We Now Know*, p. 143.

[81]Nikita Khrushchev, *Khrushchev Remembers: The Last Testament*, trans. and ed. Strobe Talbott (Boston: Little, Brown, 1974), p. 358.

[82]Hope M. Harrison, *Ulbricht and the Concrete "Rose"* (Washington, D.C.: Cold War International History Project, The Woodrow Wilson Center, May 1993), p. 35.

[83]Gaddis, *We Now Know*, p. 139.

[84]Charles de Gaulle, *Memoirs of Hope: Renewal and Endeavor* (New York: Simon and Schuster, 1970), pp. 223–224.

[85]*Ibid.*, p. 223.

[86]*Ibid.*

[87]William R. Smyser, *From Yalta to Berlin: The Cold War Struggle Over Germany* (New York: St. Martin's Press, 1999), p. 151.

[88]*Ibid.*, p. 161.

[89]*Ibid.*, p. 182.

[90]It may well be that the October 1962 Cuban missile crisis was another Soviet effort to force the U.S. to withdraw from West Berlin by placing intermediate-range missiles into Cuba. President Kennedy told Prime Minister Macmillan during the crisis that "Khrushchev's main intention may be to increase his chances at Berlin," and U.S. Secretary of State Dean Rusk later said that Khrushchev's main purpose in deploying the missiles had been "to liquidate the occupation regime in West Berlin." If so, Khrushchev's humiliating defeat in the Caribbean marks the real end of the second Berlin crisis. See Smyser, *From Yalta to Berlin*, p. 187.

[91]Schwarz, *Konrad Adenauer*, Vol. 2, p. 617.

[92]Ghita Ionescu, *Leadership in an Interdependent World* (Boulder and San Francisco: Westview Press, 1991), p. 70.

[93]Schwarz, *Konrad Adenauer*, Vol. 2, p. 753.

[94]Henrik Bering, *Helmut Kohl* (Washington, D.C.: Regnery Publishing, Inc., 1999), p. 43.

[95]George Bush and Brent Scowcroft, *A World Transformed* (New York: Knopf, 1998), p. 231.

[96]*Ibid.*, p. 250.

[97]Smyser, *From Yalta to Berlin*, p. 395. As Smyser notes, "Bonn literally bought East Germany's liberation from Soviet forces."

Chapter 4
Alexander Solzhenitsyn: Re-Moralizing the Struggle

[1]Alexander Solzhenitsyn, *Warning to the West* (New York: Farrar, Straus and Giroux, 1976), pp. 13–14.

[2]*Ibid.*, p. 46.

[3]Carl Bernstein and Marco Politi, *His Holiness: John Paul II and the Hidden History of Our Time*, (New York: Doubleday, 1996), p. 358.

[4]Alexander Solzhenitsyn, "Autobiography," cited in John B. Dunlop, Richard Haugh, and Alexis Klimoff, eds., *Aleksandr Solzhenitsyn: Critical Essays and Documentary Materials* (Belmont, Mass.: Nordland Publishing Company, 1973), p. 459.

[5]Michael Scammell, *Solzhenitsyn: A Biography* (New York: W. W. Norton, 1984), pp. 84–85.

[6]*Ibid.*, p. 73.

[7]Dunlop *et al.*, *Aleksandr Solzhenitsyn*, p. 460.

[8]Scammell, *Solzhenitsyn: A Biography*, p. 88.

[9]Aleksandr I. Solzhenitsyn, *The Gulag Archipelago 1918–1956: An Experiment in Literary Investigation*, trans. Thomas P. Whitney and Harry Willetts, abr. Edward E. Ericson, Jr. (New York: Harper and Row, 1985), pp. 73–75 (emphasis in original).

[10]Natalya Reshetovskaya, *Sanya: My Life with Aleksandr Solzhenitsyn* (Indianapolis: Bobbs-Merrill, 1974), p. 23.

[11]Scammell, *Solzhenitsyn: A Biography*, p. 133.

[12]D. M. Thomas, *Alexander Solzhenitsyn* (New York: St. Martin's Press, 1998), p. 105.

[13]Reshetovskaya, *Sanya*, pp. 56, 64.

[14]Abraham Rothberg, *Aleksandr Solzhenitsyn: The Major Novels* (Ithaca: Cornell University Press, 1971), pp. 4–5.

[15]Thomas, *Alexander Solzhenitsyn*, p. 129.

[16]*Ibid.*, p. 140.

[17]Alexander Solzhenitsyn, *The Gulag Archipelago*, trans. Thomas Whitney (New York: Harper and Row, 1974), p. 293.

[18]Solzhenitsyn, *The Gulag Archipelago*, Ericson abridgment, p. 39.

[19]*Ibid.*, p. 89.

[20]*Ibid.*, p. 313.

[21]*Ibid.*, p. 299.

[22]Dunlop *et al.*, *Aleksandr Solzhenitsyn*, p. 259.

[23]*Ibid.*, p. 258.

[24]Scammell, *Solzhenitsyn: A Biography*, p. 95.

[25]Dunlop *et al.*, *Aleksandr Solzhenitsyn*, p. 251.

[26]David Aikman, *Great Souls: Six Who Changed the Century* (Nashville: Word Publishing, 1998), p. 151.

[27]Dunlop *et al.*, *Aleksandr Solzhenitsyn*, p. 461.

[28]Solzhenitsyn, *The Gulag Archipelago*, Ericson abridgment, pp. 309–310.

[29]*Ibid.*, pp. 311–312.

[30]*Ibid.*, p. 355.

[31]*Ibid.*, p. 442.

[32]Thomas, *Alexander Solzhenitsyn*, p. 218.

[33]Scammell, *Solzhenitsyn: A Biography*, p. 344.

[34]Thomas, *Alexander Solzhenitsyn*, p. 224.

[35]Alexander Solzhenitsyn, *The Oak and the Calf: A Memoir* (New York: Harper and Row, 1979), p. 4.

[36]Alexis Klimoff, ed., *One Day in the Life of Ivan Denisovich: A Critical Companion* (Evanston, Ill: Northwestern University Press, 1997), p. 4.

[37]*Ibid.*, p. 5.

[38]*Ibid.*

[39]*Ibid.*, p. 7.

[40]Solzhenitsyn, *The Oak and the Calf*, pp. 10–11.

[41]*Ibid.*, p. 14.

[42]Klimoff, *One Day in the Life of Ivan Denisovich: A Critical Companion*, p. 99.

[43]*Ibid.*, p. 103.

[44]Thomas, *Alexander Solzhenitsyn*, p. 292.

[45]Solzhenitsyn, *The Oak and the Calf*, pp. 103–104.

[46]Michael Scammell, ed., *The Solzhenitsyn Files: Secret Soviet Documents Reveal One Man's Fight Against the Monolith* (Chicago: Edition Q, 1995), p. 8.

[47]*Ibid.*, p. 9.

[48]*Ibid.*, p. 10.

[49]*Ibid.*, pp. 12–13.

[50]*Ibid.*, p. 23.

[51]*Ibid.*, p. xxv.

[52]Solzhenitsyn, *The Oak and the Calf*, p. 118.

[53]*Ibid.*, p. 144 (emphasis in original). Solzhenitsyn's reference to excerpts from "records taken out of context" is rather less than candid; the excerpts from *The Feast of the Victors* circulated by the KGB clearly reflected his views accurately.

[54]*Ibid.*, p. 146.

[55]Edward E. Ericson, Jr., *Solzhenitsyn and the Modern World* (Washington, D.C.: Regnery Gateway, 1993), p. 54.

[56]Solzhenitsyn, *The Oak and the Calf*, p. 462.

[57]Scammell, *The Solzhenitsyn Files*, p. 41.

[58]Thomas, *Alexander Solzhenitsyn*, p. 339.

[59]Scammell, *The Solzhenitsyn Files*, pp. 138–139.

[60]Solzhenitsyn, *The Oak and the Calf*, p. 370.

[61]Andrei Sakharov, *Memoirs* (New York: Knopf, 1990), pp. 292–293.

[62]Alexander Solzhenitsyn, "Repentance and Self-Limitation," in Alexander Solzhenitsyn *et al.*, *From Under the Rubble* (Boston: Little, Brown, 1975), pp. 136–137 (emphasis in original).

[63]Alexander Solzhenitsyn, "The Smatterers," in *From Under the Rubble*, p. 273.

[64]Solzhenitsyn and Alya were married in 1973 after Natalya finally granted Solzhenitsyn a divorce and after two of Solzhenitsyn's three sons had been born out of wedlock.

[65]Solzhenitsyn, *The Oak and the Calf*, p. 360.

[66]Ericson, *Solzhenitsyn and the Modern World*, p. 247.

[67]Scammell, *The Solzhenitsyn Files*, pp. 200–210.

[68]Solzhenitsyn, *The Oak and the Calf*, p. 348.

[69]*Ibid.*, p. 534.

[70]Ericson, *Solzhenitsyn and the Modern World*, p. 370.

[71]Ludmilla Alexeyeva, *Soviet Dissent: Contemporary Movements for National, Religious and Human Rights* (Middletown, Conn.: Wesleyan University Press, 1985), p. 320.

[72]*Ibid.*

[73]*Ibid.*

[74]For a more detailed discussion of the effects of Gorbachev's *glasnost* policy, see Chapter 6, *infra*.

[75]Scammell, *Solzhenitsyn: A Biography*, pp. 829–831.

[76]Scammell, *The Solzhenitsyn Files*, pp. 283–285.

[77]Solzhenitsyn, *The Oak and the Calf*, p. 408.

[78]Aikman, *Great Souls*, p. 182.

[79]Solzhenitsyn, *Warning to the West*, p. 47.

[80]John B. Dunlop, Richard Haugh, and Michael Nicholson, eds., *Solzhenitsyn in Exile* (Stanford: Hoover Institution Press, 1985), pp. 27–28.

[81]*Ibid.*, pp. 28–29 (emphasis in original).

[82]*Ibid.*, p. 26.

[83]Gabriel Schoenfeld, "Was Kissinger Right?" *Commentary*, May 1999, p. 60.

[84]Lee Edwards, *The Conservative Revolution: The Movement That Remade America* (New York: The Free Press, 1999), p. 201.

[85]Dunlop *et al.*, *Solzhenitsyn in Exile*, p. 35.

[86]Dinesh D'Souza, *Ronald Reagan: How an Ordinary Man Became an Extraordinary Leader* (New York: The Free Press, 1997), pp. 77–78.

[87]*Ibid.*, p. 36.

[88]Ronald Berman, ed., *Solzhenitsyn at Harvard* (Washington, D.C.: Ethics and Public Policy Center, 1980), pp. 5–6.

[89]Scammell, *Solzhenitsyn: A Biography*, p. 972.

[90]Ericson, *Solzhenitsyn and the Modern World*, p. 143.

[91]Thomas, *Solzhenitsyn*, pp. 501–502.

[92]Alexander Solzhenitsyn, *"The Russian Question" at the End of the Twentieth Century* (New York: Farrar, Straus and Giroux, 1995), p. 108.

[93]Thomas, *Alexander Solzhenitsyn*, p. 534.

[94]Ronald Reagan, *Speaking My Mind* (New York: Simon and Schuster, 1989), p. 178.

Chapter 5
Pope John Paul II: Inspiring the Hopeless

[1]Lech Walesa, *The Struggle and the Triumph* (New York: Arcade Publishing, 1992), p. 190.

[2]Tad Szulc, *Pope John Paul II: The Biography* (New York: Scribner, 1995), p. 415.

[3]Carl Bernstein and Marco Politi, *His Holiness: John Paul II and the Hidden History of Our Time* (New York: Doubleday, 1996), pp. 121–122.

[4]Szulc, *Pope John Paul II*, p. 244.

[5]Jonathan Kwitny, *Man of the Century* (New York: Henry Holt, 1997), p. 223.

[6]André Frossard and Pope John Paul II, *"Be Not Afraid!"* (New York: St. Martin's Press, 1982), p. 14.

[7]Darcy O'Brien, *The Hidden Pope* (New York: Daybreak Books, 1998), p. 209.

[8]Szulc, *Pope John Paul II*, p. 69.

[9]Bernstein and Politi, *His Holiness*, p. 35.

[10]O'Brien, *The Hidden Pope*, p. 85.

[11]Rocco Buttiglione, *Karol Wojtyla: The Thought of the Man Who Became Pope John Paul II* (Grand Rapids, Mich.: William B. Eerdmans, 1997), p. 18.

[12]*Ibid.*, pp. 19–20.

[13]Szulc, *Pope John Paul II*, p. 48.

[14]Robert Zuzowski, *Political Dissent and Opposition in Poland* (Westport, Conn.: Praeger, 1992), p. 121.

[15]O'Brien, *The Hidden Pope*, p. 41.

[16]Bernstein and Politi, *His Holiness*, p. 85.

[17]Frossard and John Paul II, *"Be Not Afraid!"* p. 15.

[18]Bernstein and Politi, *His Holiness*, pp. 48–49.

[19]Kwitny, *Man of the Century*, p. 57.

[20]Frossard and John Paul II, *"Be Not Afraid!"* p. 18.

[21]*Ibid.*, p. 15. One biographer suggests that "the priesthood began to loom larger [for Wojtyla] as a way to live in resistance to the degradation of human dignity by a brutal ideology." George Weigel, *Witness to Hope: The Biography of John Paul II* (New York: CliffStreet Books/HarperCollins, 1999), p. 52.

[22]O'Brien, *The Hidden Pope*, p. 215.

[23]Kwitny, *Man of the Century*, p. 59.

[24]Buttiglione, *Karol Wojtyla*, p. 30.

[25]Mieczyslaw Malinski, *Pope John Paul II: The Life of Karol Wojtyla* (New York: Seabury Press, 1979), p. 51.

[26]Frossard and John Paul II, *"Be Not Afraid!"* p. 17.

[27]Malinski, *Pope John Paul II*, p. 94.

[28]*Encyclopedia of Philosophy*, ed. Paul Edwards (New York: Macmillan, 1967), Vol. 7, p. 302.

[29]Szulc, *Pope John Paul II*, p. 182.

[30]Buttiglione, *Karol Wojtyla*, p. 38.

[31]Pope John Paul II, *Centesimus Annus*, *http:listserv.anerican.edu/catholic/church/papal/jp.ii/jp2hundr.txt*, p. 8.

[32]Bernstein and Politi, *His Holiness*, p. 141.

[33]John Paul II, *Centesimus Annus*, p. 9.

[34]Weigel, *Witness to Hope*, p. 155.

[35]Bernstein and Politi, *His Holiness*, p. 78.

[36]Szulc, *Pope John Paul II*, p. 194.

[37]Bernstein and Politi, *His Holiness*, p. 108.

[38]Weigel, *Witness to Hope*, p. 148.

[39]George Weigel, *The Final Revolution* (New York: Oxford University Press, 1992), p. 72.

[40]Weigel, *Witness to Hope*, p. 148.

[41]Kwitny, *Man of the Century*, p. 201.

[42]Weigel, *The Final Revolution*, pp. 73–74.

[43]Zuzowski, *Political Dissent and Opposition in Poland*, p. 129.

[44]O'Brien, *The Hidden Pope*, pp. 345–346.

[45]Bernstein and Politi, *His Holiness*, p. 128.

[46]Kwitny, *Man of the Century*, p. 233.

[47]Zuzowski, *Political Dissent and Opposition in Poland*, p. 130.

[48]Weigel, *The Final Revolution*, p. 128. Michnik's book was banned in Poland but published in France.

[49]Timothy Garton Ash, *The Polish Revolution: Solidarity 1980–82* (London: Jonathan Cape, 1983), p. 20.

[50]Weigel, *Witness to Hope*, p. 211.

[51]*Ibid.*, p. 167.

[52]Bernstein and Politi, *His Holiness*, p. 100.

[53]Weigel, *Witness to Hope*, p. 200.

[54]Adam Ulam, *The Communists* (New York: Scribner's, 1992), p. 343.

[55]*Ibid.*, p. 349.

[56]*Ibid.*, p. 352.

[57]Tina Rosenberg, *The Haunted Land: Facing Europe's Ghosts After Communism* (New York: Random House, 1995), p. 159.

[58]Ulam, *The Communists*, p. 371; Garton Ash, *The Polish Revolution*, p. 16.

[59]Garton Ash, *The Polish Revolution*, p. 16.

[60]*Ibid.*, pp. 16–17.

[61]Zuzowski, *Political Dissent and Opposition in Poland*, pp. 84, 97.

[62]Ulam, *The Communists*, p. 356.

[63]Garton Ash, *The Polish Revolution*, p. 23.

[64]Zuzowski, *Political Dissent and Opposition in Poland*, p. 100.

[65]Garton Ash, *The Polish Revolution*, p. 19.

[66]Weigel, *Witness to Hope*, pp. 210–211.

[67]*Ibid.*, pp. 212–213.

[68]Bernstein and Politi, *His Holiness*, p. 273.

[69]*Ibid.*, pp. 189–190.

[70]Weigel, *The Final Revolution*, p. 93.

[71]*Centesimus Annus*, p. 12.

[72]Weigel, *Witness to Hope*, p. 261.

[73]Szulc, *Pope John Paul II*, p. 311.

[74]Bernstein and Politi, *His Holiness*, p. 306.

[75]Weigel, *Witness to Hope*, p. 400.

[76]Bernstein and Politi, *His Holiness*, p. 191.

[77]Weigel, *Witness to Hope*, p. 283.

[78]Kwitny, *Man of the Century*, p. 324.

[79]Garton Ash, *The Polish Revolution*, p. 29.

[80]Bernstein and Politi, *His Holiness*, p. 228.

[81]Kwitny, *Man of the Century*, p. 326.

[82]*Ibid.*, pp. 329–330.

[83]Weigel, *Witness to Hope*, p. 301.

[84]Ulam, *The Communists*, p. 364.

[85]Abraham Brumberg, "Poland—The 'Bloodless Revolution' and Its Aftermath," in George Schopflin, ed., *The Soviet Union and Eastern Europe* (New York: Facts on File, 1986), p. 313.

[86]Zuzowski, *Political Dissent and Opposition in Poland*, pp. 101, 170–176.

[87]Walesa, *The Struggle and the Triumph*, p. 10.

[88]Bernstein and Politi, *His Holiness*, p. 241.

[89]*Ibid.*, p. 316.

[90]Brumberg, "Poland—The 'Bloodless Revolution' and Its Aftermath," p. 315.

[91]Bernstein and Politi, *His Holiness*, p. 245.

[92]*Ibid.*, p. 246.

[93]Mark Kramer, "Poland, 1980–81: Soviet Policy During the Polish Crisis," in Cold War International History Project *Bulletin*, Issue 5 (Spring 1995), Woodrow Wilson International Center for Scholars, Washington, D.C., pp. 117, 126.

[94]*Ibid.*, p. 126.

[95]Vojtech Mastny, "The Soviet Non-Invasion of Poland in 1980/81 and the End of the Cold War," *Working Paper* No. 23, Cold War International History Project, Woodrow Wilson International Center for Scholars, Washington, D.C., September 1998, p. 9.

[96]*Ibid.*, p. 23.

[97]Kramer, "Poland, 1980–81," p. 124.

[98]Zbigniew Brzezinski, *Power and Principle: Memoirs of the National Security Adviser 1977–1981* (New York: Farrar, Straus and Giroux, 1985), p. 465.

[99]*Ibid.*, p. 468.

[100]Kramer, "Poland, 1980–81," p. 121.

[101]Mastny, "The Soviet Non-Invasion of Poland in 1980/81 and the End of the Cold War," p. 29.

[102]Kramer, "Poland, 1980–81," p. 119.

[103]Bernstein and Politi, *His Holiness*, p. 314.

[104]Zuzowski, *Political Dissent and Opposition in Poland*, p. 187.

[105]*Ibid.*, pp. 187–188.

[106]Kramer, "Poland, 1980–81," p. 119.

[107]*Ibid.*, p. 122.

[108]Rosenberg, *The Haunted Land*, p. 217.

[109]*Ibid.*, pp. 223–224.

[110]Ulam, *The Communists*, p. 378.

[111]Kramer, "Poland, 1980–81," p. 138.

[112]Weigel, *Witness to Hope*, p. 436.

[113]Bernstein and Politi, *His Holiness*, pp. 337–338.

[114]*Ibid.*, p. 338.

[115]Timothy Garton Ash, "The Pope in Poland," in *The Uses of Adversity: Essays on the Fate of Central Europe* (New York: Random House, 1989), pp. 57–58.

[116]Bernstein and Politi, *His Holiness*, pp. 341–342.

[117]*Ibid.*, p. 341.

[118]Garton Ash, "The Pope in Poland," p. 53.

[119]Bernstein and Politi, *His Holiness*, p. 383.

[120]*Ibid.*, pp. 380–381.

[121]Garton Ash, "The Pope in Poland," p. 47.

[122]Walesa, *The Struggle and the Triumph*, pp. 116–117.

[123]Weigel, *Witness to Hope*, p. 439.

[124]Walesa, *The Struggle and the Triumph*, pp. 113–114.

[125]*Ibid.*, p. 100.

[126]Michael T. Kaufman, *Mad Dreams, Saving Graces* (New York: Random House, 1989), p. 80.

[127]Weigel, *Witness to Hope*, p. 437.

[128]Kaufman, *Mad Dreams, Saving Graces*, p. 100.

[129]For a detailed discussion of the Reagan onslaught, see Chapter 6, *infra*.

[130]Rosenberg, *The Haunted Land*, p. 231.

[131]Walesa, *The Struggle and the Triumph*, p. 111.

[132]Weigel, *Witness to Hope*, pp. 583–584.

[133]Martin Malia, "Popular Elections for the Russian Parliament," in Paul A. Winters, ed., *The Collapse of the Soviet Union* (San Diego: Greenhaven Press, 1999), pp. 150, 155.

[134]*Ibid.*, p. 175.

Chapter 6
Ronald Reagan: Tearing Down the Wall

[1]Ronald Reagan, *Speaking My Mind* (New York: Simon and Schuster, 1989), pp. 110–119.

[2]Geoffrey Smith, *Reagan and Thatcher* (New York: W. W. Norton, 1991), p. 98.

[3]Norman A. Bailey, *The Strategic Plan That Won the Cold War* (McLean, Va.: The Potomac Foundation, 1998), p. 29.

[4]Henry Kissinger, *Diplomacy* (New York: Simon and Schuster, 1994), p. 764.

[5]George P. Shultz, *Turmoil and Triumph: My Years as Secretary of State* (New York: Charles Scribner's Sons, 1993), p. 1134.

[6]Dinesh D'Souza, *Ronald Reagan: How an Ordinary Man Became an Extraordinary Leader* (New York: The Free Press, 1997), p. 7.

[7]Berlin's typology was based on a line from the Greek poet Archilochus: "The fox knows many things, but the hedgehog knows one big thing." See Isaiah Berlin, *The Hedgehog and the Fox: An Essay on Tolstoy's View of History* (New York: Simon and Schuster, 1966), p. 1.

[8]Kissinger, *Diplomacy*, p. 764.

[9]Ronald Reagan, *An American Life* (New York: Simon and Schuster, 1990), p. 31.

[10]*Ibid.*, p. 30.

[11]*Ibid.*

[12]*Ibid.*, p. 36.

[13]*Ibid.*, p. 58.

[14]Ronald Reagan and Richard Hubler, *Where's the Rest of Me?* (New York: Duell, Sloan and Pearce, 1965), pp. 44–45.

[15]Reagan, *An American Life*, p. 71.

[16]*Ibid.*, p. 89.

[17]Reagan and Hubler, *Where's The Rest of Me?* pp. 6–7.

[18]Lee Edwards, *Ronald Reagan: A Political Biography* (Houston: Nordland Publishing International, 1981), p. 46.

[19]Reagan and Hubler, *Where's the Rest of Me?* pp. 139–140.

[20]Reagan, *An American Life*, p. 106.

[21]*Ibid.*, pp. 106–107.

[22]*Ibid.*, p. 105.

[23]*Ibid.*, p. 112.

[24]*Ibid.*, pp. 107–114.

[25]*Ibid.*, p. 114.

[26]Edwards, *Ronald Reagan: A Political Biography*, p. 57.

[27]Reagan, *An American Life*, p. 123.

[28]Edwards, *Ronald Reagan: A Political Biography*, p. 61.

[29]Reagan, *An American Life*, p. 117.

[30]*Ibid.*, p. 129.

[31]*Ibid.*

[32]*Ibid.*

[33]*Ibid.*, pp. 141–142.

[34]Lee Edwards, *The Conservative Revolution: The Movement That Remade America* (New York: The Free Press, 1999), p. 224.

[35]*Ibid.*, p. 316.

[36]Peter Rodman, *More Precious Than Peace: The Cold War and the Struggle for the Third World* (New York: Charles Scribner's Sons, 1994), p. 407.

[37]Reagan, *An American Life*, pp. 237–238.

[38]Richard V. Allen, "An Extraordinary Man in Extraordinary Times: Ronald Reagan's Leadership and the Decision to End the Cold War," remarks to the Hoover Institution and the William J. Casey Institute, Center for Security Policy, Washington, D.C., February 22, 1999, p. 6.

[39]*Ibid.*, p. 12.

[40]Robert M. Gates, *From the Shadows* (New York: Touchstone, 1996), pp. 194–197.

[41]*Ibid.*, p. 195.

[42]Herbert E. Meyer, interview with the author, April 19, 1999.

[43]Peter Schweizer, *Victory: The Reagan Administration's Secret Strategy That Hastened the Collapse of the Soviet Union* (New York: Atlantic Monthly Press, 1994), pp. 5–6.

[44]Stephen F. Knott, "Reagan's Critics," *The National Interest*, Summer 1996, p. 67.

[45]Lee Edwards, *The Conservative Revolution*, p. 243.

[46]Anatoly Dobrynin, *In Confidence: Moscow's Ambassador to America's Six Cold War Presidents* (New York: Times Books, 1995), p. 530.

[47]Richard Pipes, "Misinterpreting the Cold War," *Foreign Affairs*, January/February 1995, p. 157.

[48]Richard Pipes, "Can the Soviet Union Reform?" *Foreign Affairs*, Fall 1984, cited in James F. Hoge, Jr., and Fareed Zakaria, *The American Encounter: Essays from 75 Years of Foreign Affairs* (New York: Basic Books, 1997), p. 461.

[49]Bailey, *The Strategic Plan That Won the Cold War*, p. 30.

[50]Edwin Meese III, *With Reagan: The Inside Story* (Washington, D.C.: Regnery Gateway, 1992), p. 180.

[51]*Ibid.*

[52]Bailey, *The Strategic Plan That Won the Cold War*, p. 30.

[53]Richard Pipes, *Survival Is Not Enough* (New York: Simon and Schuster, 1984), p. 262.

[54]*Ibid.*, p. 264.

[55]Reagan, *An American Life*, p. 552.

[56]Meese, *With Reagan: The Inside Story*, p. 168.

[57]See Gus W. Weiss, "The Farewell Dossier," *Studies in Intelligence*, United States Central Intelligence Agency, Washington, D.C., Vol. 39, No. 5 (1996).

[58]Bailey, *The Strategic Plan That Won the Cold War*, pp. 31, 36.

[59]*Ibid.*, p. 15.

[60]Reagan, *An American Life*, p. 555.

[61]Reagan, *Speaking My Mind*, p. 116.

[62]Bailey, *The Strategic Plan That Won the Cold War*, p. 33.

[63]Rodman, *More Precious than Peace*, pp. 271–272.

[64]Charles Krauthammer, "The Reagan Doctrine," *Time*, April 1, 1985, pp. 54–55.

[65]Pipes, "Can the Soviet Union Reform?" in Hoge and Zakaria, *The American Encounter*, p. 460 (emphasis in original).

[66]Rodman, *More Precious than Peace*, p. 317.

[67]Reagan, *An American Life*, pp. 300, 474. The quote attributed to Lenin is, in fact, apocryphal.

[68]*Ibid.*, p. 477.

[69]For a detailed discussion of Polish events, see Chapter 5, *supra*.

[70]Reagan, *An American Life*, p. 301.

[71]Carl Bernstein and Marco Politi, *His Holiness: John Paul II and the Hidden History of Our Time* (New York: Doubleday, 1996), p. 262.

[72]Reagan, *An American Life*, p. 304.

[73]*Ibid.*, p. 306.

[74]Schweitzer, *Victory*, pp. 68–69.

[75]Bernstein and Politi, *His Holiness*, p. 357.

[76]Reagan's willingness to help Solidarity no doubt explains why Pope John Paul II told his biographer, George Weigel, that Reagan was "a good president." See George Weigel, *Witness to Hope: The Biography of Pope John Paul II* (New York: CliffStreet Books/HarperCollins, 1999), p. 417.

[77]D'Souza, *Ronald Reagan*, p. 175.

[78]Reagan, *An American Life*, pp. 547–548.

[79]Kissinger, *Diplomacy*, p. 778.

[80]*Ibid.*

[81]D'Souza, *Ronald Reagan*, p. 176.

[82]Gates, *From the Shadows*, p. 266.

[83]Dobrynin, *In Confidence*, p. 481.

[84]Schweitzer, *Victory*, p. 17.

[85]Gates, *From the Shadows*, p. 186.

[86]Shultz, *Turmoil and Triumph*, p. 126.

[87]Seweryn Bialer, ed., *Politics, Society and Nationality Inside Gorbachev's Russia* (Boulder, Colo.: Westview Press, 1988), p. 18.

[88]Martin Malia, *The Soviet Tragedy: A History of Socialism in Russia, 1917–1991* (New York: The Free Press, 1994), p. 408.

[89]Reagan, *An American Life*, pp. 295–296.

[90]Kissinger, *Diplomacy*, p. 776.

[91]*Ibid.*, p. 777.

[92]Reagan, *An American Life*, p. 297.

[93]Smith, *Reagan and Thatcher*, p. 1.

[94]Margaret Thatcher, *The Downing Street Years* (New York: HarperCollins, 1993), p. 157.

[95]*Ibid.*, p. 171.

[96]Kissinger, *Diplomacy*, p. 777.

[97]Henrik Bering, *Helmut Kohl* (Washington, D.C.: Regnery Publishing, 1999), p. 14.

[98]*Ibid.*

[99]Gates, *From the Shadows*, p. 262.

[100]Schweitzer, *Victory*, p. 238.

[101]Malia, *The Soviet Tragedy*, p. 411.

[102]*Ibid.*

[103]Rodman, *More Precious Than Peace*, pp. 309–311.

[104]Schweitzer, *Victory*, p. 198.

[105]Paul A. Winters, ed., *The Collapse of the Soviet Union* (San Diego: Greenhaven Press, 1999), p. 177.

[106]Gates, *From the Shadows*, p. 331.

[107]Reagan, *An American Life*, p. 708.

[108]Mikhail Gorbachev, *Memoirs* (New York: Doubleday, 1996), p. 193.

[109]Adam Ulam, *The Communists: The Story of Power and Lost Illusions* (New York: Charles Scribner's Sons, 1992), p. 409.

[110]Winters, *The Collapse of the Soviet Union*, p. 175.

[111]Malia, *The Soviet Tragedy*, pp. 436–437.

[112]Eugene V. Rostow, *A Breakfast for Bonaparte* (Washington, D.C.: National Defense University Press, 1993), p. 431.

[113]Gates, *From the Shadows*, p. 439.

[114]Winters, *The Collapse of the Soviet Union*, p. 26.

[115]Reagan, *An American Life*, p. 555.

[116]*Ibid.*, p. 552.

[117]D'Souza, *Ronald Reagan*, p. 4.

[118]*Ibid.*, p. 140.

[119]Reagan, *Speaking My Mind*, p. 113.

[120]*Ibid.*, p. 180.

[121]Stephen F. Knott, "Reagan's Critics," *The National Interest*, Summer 1996, p. 70.

[122]Gates, *From the Shadows*, pp. 270–273.

[123]*Ibid.*, p. 271.

[124]John Lewis Gaddis, *The United States and the End of the Cold War* (New York: Oxford University Press, 1992), p. 126.

[125]Reagan, *An American Life*, pp. 588–589.

[126]*Ibid.*, p. 596.

[127]Shultz, *Turmoil and Triumph*, p. 507.

[128]Reagan, *An American Life*, p. 628.

[129]*Ibid.*, p. 12.

[130]*Ibid.*, p. 636.

[131]Lou Cannon, *President Reagan: The Role of A Lifetime* (New York: Simon and Schuster, 1991), p. 792.

[132]Schweitzer, *Victory*, p. 236.

[133]Meese, *With Reagan: The Inside Story*, p. 177.

[134]Smith, *Reagan and Thatcher*, p. 175.

[135]Reagan, *An American Life*, p. 628.

[136]Reagan, *Speaking My Mind*, p. 348. Reagan was referring to the Nixon–Ford policy of détente, whereby the U.S., in order not to offend Soviet sensibilities, refused to engage in such provocations as inviting Alexander Solzhenitsyn to the White House. For a detailed discussion of the Solzhenitsyn incident, see Chapter 4, *supra.*

[137]Michael Dobbs, *Down with Big Brother: The Fall of the Soviet Empire* (New York: Alfred A. Knopf, 1997), p. 28.

[138]Seweryn Bialer, "The Death of the 'Old Guard'," in Winters, *The Collapse of the Soviet Union*, p. 42.

[139]Reagan, *Speaking My Mind*, p. 351.

[140]*Ibid.*, p. 352.

[141]Stephen Sestanovich, "Did the West Undo the East," *The National Interest*, No. 31 (Spring 1993), p. 30.
[142]Schweitzer, *Victory*, p. 239.
[143]Pipes, *Survival Is Not Enough*, p. 234.
[144]Dobrynin, *In Confidence*, p. 588.
[145]Reagan, *An American Life*, p. 15.
[146]Dobrynin, *In Confidence*, p. 592.
[147]Don Oberdorfer, *From the Cold War to a New Era: The United States and the Soviet Union, 1983–1991* (Baltimore: Johns Hopkins University Press, 1998), p. 186.
[148]Reagan, *An American Life*, pp. 677–679.
[149]Kissinger, *Diplomacy*, p. 783.
[150]Thatcher, *The Downing Street Years*, p. 471.
[151]In particular, conservatives feared that a "denuclearized" Western Europe would be vulnerable to pressure from Soviet conventional forces.
[152]George F. Will, "How Reagan Changed America," *Newsweek*, January 9, 1969, p. 16.
[153]David Satter, *Age of Delirium: The Decline and Fall of the Soviet Union* (New York: Alfred A. Knopf, 1996), p. 31.
[154]Reagan, *An American Life*, p. 714.
[155]For a discussion of how the anti-Communist revolution began in Poland, see Chapter 5, *supra*.
[156]Winters, *The Collapse of the Soviet Union*, p. 33.
[157]Bernstein and Politi, *His Holiness*, p. 359.

Index

About the Author

Joseph Shattan served for three years during the Bush Administration as speechwriter for Vice President Dan Quayle. During the Reagan Administration, he was a speechwriter for U.S. Ambassador to the United Nations Jeane Kirkpatrick, Secretary of Education William J. Bennett, and Assistant Secretary of State for Human Rights Elliott Abrams. He also has served on the State Department Policy Planning Staff, as Senior Advisor to the Director of the U.S. Information Agency, as an aide to Senator Phil Gramm of Texas, and as Consulting Editor of *The American Spectator* magazine.

Mr. Shattan has published widely in leading journals of opinion, including *The American Spectator*, *Commentary*, *Policy Review*, *The New Republic*, and *The Washington Quarterly*. A former Bradley Fellow at The Heritage Foundation and a National Fellow at the Hoover Institution on War, Revolution and Peace, he holds a B.A. from Brooklyn College and an M.A., M.A.L.D., and Ph.D. from the Fletcher School of Law and Diplomacy. He is currently a Director of the White House Writers' Group, based in Washington, D.C.